Feeding China's Little Emperors

Feeding China's Little Emperors

Food, Children,

and Social Change

EDITED BY **Jun Jing**

Stanford University Press

Stanford, California 2000

Stanford University Press
Stanford, California
© 2000 by the Board of Trustees of the Leland
Stanford Junior University

Printed in the United States of America
CIP data appear at the end of the book

Acknowledgments

This book is the result of a larger research project entitled "Food, Consumption Patterns, and Dietary Change in Chinese Society," funded by the Henry Luce Foundation's US-China Cooperative Research Program (1993–97) and managed by the Fairbank Center for East Asian Research, Harvard University. Preliminary discussions also were held during the summer of 1994 at a workshop entitled "China's Changing Diet: Food, Consumption, and Culture," sponsored by the Chiang Ching-kuo Foundation and the Peabody Museum of Anthropology, Harvard University. In addition to the present volume, these two grants also supported research that led to the publication of *Golden Arches East: McDonald's in East Asia*, edited by James L. Watson and released by Stanford University Press in 1997. Preliminary papers on Chinese children's food were first presented at a workshop in 1997 sponsored by the Henry Luce Foundation and the Department of Anthropology, Chinese University of Hong Kong. The contributors to this book are grateful to these institutions for their generous support of our research. We wish to acknowledge, however, that our funders bear no responsibility for the views, opinions, and interpretations presented in this book.

J.J.

Contents

Figures and Tables

Figures

Tables

Contributors

Bernadine W. L. Chee holds an M.A. in Social Anthropology from the University of Hawaii at Manoa and is currently a Ph.D. candidate at the Department of Anthropology of Harvard University. Her research and fieldwork deal with issues of social identity, urbanization, and patterns of food consumption in Beijing.

Maris Boyd Gillette holds a Ph.D. in Social Anthropology from Harvard University and is now an assistant professor at the Department of Anthropology of Haverford College. Her research and fieldwork have concentrated on the social history and the culture of consumption among urban Chinese Muslims in the city of Xi'an, northwest China.

Suzanne K. Gottschang holds a Ph.D. in Medical Anthropology and Public Health from the University of California, Los Angeles. Her research and fieldwork have been concerned with maternal and child care in Beijing and social implications of medical science.

Georgia S. Guldan is an associate professor of Nutrition Science at the Chinese University of Hong Kong. Previously, she taught at Southwest China Medical School. She has published extensively on child development and participated in major cross-sectional surveys of children's health in Hong Kong and in Sichuan province of southwest China.

Guo Yuhua is an associate professor and senior research fellow at the Institute of Sociology under the Chinese Academy of Social Sciences. She holds an M.A. in Folklore Studies from Beijing Normal University and a Ph.D. in Sociology from the Chinese Academy of Social Sciences. Her publications have focused on aging, family relations, and Chinese food. She is currently working with her colleagues to research the social history and political transformations of a rural township in northwest China.

Jun Jing holds a Ph.D. in Social Anthropology from Harvard University and has been teaching at the Department of Anthropology, the City College of the City University of New York. He is author of *The Temple of Memories: Power, History, and Morality in a Chinese Village* and has written numerous articles on Chinese religion, environment and economic development, and rural politics, for both English and Chinese publications.

Eriberto P. Lozada, Jr., holds a Ph.D. in Social Anthropology from Harvard University.

He is now an assistant professor at the Department of Anthropology of Butler University. His field research and publications have been devoted to Catholicism in south China, issues of transnationalism, and relations of popular culture and mass media.

James L. Watson is Fairbank Professor of Chinese Society and Professor of Anthropology at Harvard University. He is author of *Emigration and the Chinese Lineage* and editor of several volumes, including *Golden Arches East: McDonald's in East Asia*, *Death Rituals in Late Imperial China*, and *Between Two Cultures: Migrants and Minorities in Britain*.

Zhao Yang is a junior research fellow at the Research Center of Economic Development under the State Council of the People's Republic of China. He has published numerous articles in China on the country's economic reforms. He is currently completing his Ph.D. in Sociology at the Hong Kong University of Science and Technology.

Feeding China's Little Emperors

Introduction

Food, Children, and Social Change in Contemporary China

Jun Jing

There are more than 300 million children under the age of sixteen in the People's Republic of China, representing one-fifth of the children in the world. Unlike earlier generations, these children have few siblings or none at all, born as they were under the Chinese government's stringent population control policy. Growing up in the post-Mao transition to a market economy, they have been surrounded by a new prosperity and an emerging culture of consumerism. By any measure of living standards, they are far better off than their parents were as children. But if we believe what has been said about them by the news media, we might get the impression that many of these children are a willful generation of "little emperors." They are often described as insufferably spoiled, showered with attention, toys, and treats by anxiously overindulgent adults, because their parents and grandparents have tried hard to focus their energies on catering to the whims of their one little link to the future.

In retrospect, the term "little emperors," or *xiao huangdi* in Chinese, became a popular reference point after a series of eye-catching articles appeared in Chinese newspapers in the early 1980s, when more and more urban couples were having only one child. It was at this point, as the anthropologist David Wu (1994:2–12) has shown, that child development experts in China began talking about the danger of "drowning children with love" (*ni ai*). In an article published in 1983, Ye Gongshao, an educator and specialist in child development, warned that a defining characteristic of families with "little emperors" is the "4-2-1 syndrome" (*si-er-yi zonghe-zheng*), meaning four grandparents and two parents pampering one child (Su Songxing 1994:13). Although Chinese scholars and journalists later invented the term *xiao huanghou*, or "little empresses," in reference to female single-children, the androcentric term "little emperors" has been more commonly used in China. It certainly remains a familiar term in Chinese mass media in referring to the country's only children as a whole.

The main title of this book — *Feeding China's Little Emperors* — is intended to reflect this term's popularity. Our book, however, is not an attempt to predict whether the Year of the Rat on the Chinese lunar calendar will be replaced by the Year of the Brat. Some children in China are indeed spoiled, notably in urban areas, where a couple is allowed only one child. As fertility declines and personal income rises, even the Chinese countryside has its share of spoiled children, particularly in an increasing number of prosperous villages and small towns where the government's one-child policy has been introduced.[1] But for the time being, studies of China's singletons are tentative and by no means conclusive. Widely differing, even contradictory, theories about their psychological characteristics are advanced year after year in bewildering succession. On this matter, there are no simple answers (see, e.g., Ding et al. 1994:50–53; Fan et al. 1994:70–74; cf. Baker 1994:45–47; Zhang Zhihua 1993:79–81).

The focus of this book is food, a matter that profoundly affects all children in China, including the singletons who now make up about 80 percent of the children enrolled at primary schools, daycare centers, and boarding nurseries in urban China. As elsewhere, the food children eat in China has a wide range of health consequences as well as cultural, political, and socioeconomic ramifications. These issues are discussed in detail by this book's nine contributors. In Chapter 1, Georgia S. Guldan offers a statistically grounded analysis of the changes in child feeding patterns and the impact of these changes upon children's growth and health.

In Chapter 2, Bernadine W. L. Chee provides an intimate portrait of a group of only children in Beijing by depicting the close relationships between food consumption, peer-group pressure, parental control, and school education. Chapter 3, by Maris Boyd Gillette, is an ethnographically rich discussion of the consumption of trendy foods among children in a Muslim community in the northwestern city of Xi'an and how some of the adults of this community perceive these foods in light of their ethnic identity and their sense of modernity. In Chapter 4, Guo Yuhua uses her research experience in Beijing and a rural village of Jiangsu province to make a provocative argument about generational differences in attitude and knowledge with regard to food consumption. Chapter 5, by Eriberto P. Lozada, Jr., is a vividly written case study of Kentucky Fried Chicken restaurants in Beijing, concentrating on the adjustment of global business practices to local settings. Chapter 6, my own contribution to this volume, deals with the issue of cultural authority as applied to child care and children's consumption of food in a rural community in the northwestern province of Gansu. In Chapter 7, Suzanne K. Gottschang uses her fieldwork experience at a Chinese hospital to provide an insight into the connections between the practice of breastfeeding, the Chinese government's public health policies, and the marketing of infant formula by international corporations. Chapter 8, by Zhao Yang, is about how the extraordinary success of the Wahaha Group of Hangzhou has been built upon the claim that its products are not only explicitly designed for the improvement of children's health but also rooted in traditional Chinese medicine. Chapter 9, by James L. Watson, is a veteran anthropologist's response to the chapters of this book and a summary of his observations of dietary changes and attitudes toward children in Hong Kong and mainland China.

In the following pages, I will try to provide the reader with a general account of five major issues discussed in the different chapters of this book. First, the average Chinese citizen's diet has undergone dramatic changes since the early 1980s,[2] and these changes have a direct bearing on the health of Chinese children. Second, a specialized food industry catering specifically to children as consumers has emerged in China — a new development, historically speaking. Third, state intervention in child development in general and in children's consumption of food in particular bolsters the government's attempt to legitimize its coercive population policy, helping it to cast itself as a modernistic and compassionate regime. Fourth, the integration of China's domestic economy with transnational economic forces has drawn the intimate relationship of childhood, parenting, and family life into a global consumption culture. And last, new eating habits forge new identities, which in turn reflect the emergence of new social values among the young. The connections among these five issues will be explained below; they are explored in greater detail and from different perspectives in the chapters that follow.

Dietary Reformation and Consumeristic Children

A transformation in the very concept of childhood is occurring in East Asia's metropolitan areas, one that we are only beginning to understand. As James L. Watson (1997:14–20) has noted, one aspect of this transformation is the emergence of new classes of affluent customers and families. Another is "the independent buying power of the young and their increasing influence over the spending habits of their parents" (Mintz 1997:199). These changes have reverberations in the food that adults and children eat.

In China, even in the early 1980s, the average citizen's diet consisted primarily of grains and other plants, and it was substantially different from that in the West (Chen Junshi et al. 1990:6–7). In cities, food was still rationed in the early 1980s, a sign of the stagnant agricultural sector. Agricultural reforms, initiated in the years after Mao Zedong's death in 1976, began changing, among other things, people's diets. In the brief period from 1981 to 1987, the consumption of grains and vegetables by urban residents leveled off or declined, but their consumption of cooking oil, meat, poultry, eggs, and seafood increased between 108 percent and 182 percent. In the same period, the consumption of cooking oil, meat, poultry, and eggs by rural residents also rose dramatically, increasing by more than 200 percent (State Statistics Bureau 1988, table 2, p. 718, and table 3, p. 755). This dietary transition has been followed by new health problems, which are increasingly being intensified by commercialism.[3]

The onslaught of commercialism is evident even at some of China's most venerated sites. At Badaling, a much-visited section of the Great Wall in the northwestern outskirts of Beijing, stands a figure recognized throughout the world. The statue depicts Colonel Sanders, impeccable in his white suit and goatee, holding a jumbo tub of Kentucky Fried Chicken. In Confucius' hometown, the small and usually sedate city of Qufu in Shandong province, a loud carnival to promote local beer and liquor is staged each fall to coincide with the nationally televised celebration of the ancient sage's birthday. The increasing commercialization of Chinese society has affected every age group, yet schoolchildren and preschoolers have become perhaps the most determined groups in absorbing the swift profusion of consumer goods, including factory-processed foods. Although they are still under a measure of parental control over what they can eat, children as young as three and four often try to control their own and their family's choice of staples, and snacks, and restaurants. This phenomenon is relatively new; until recently, Chinese children ate what they were fed and were not permitted to dictate their own diet. The scene today has changed radically. Children now have more money in their pockets than their parents did at their age, and they spend it on personal consumption. More often than not, their money goes to candy, cookies, chips, instant noodles, chocolate, nuts, soft drinks, and ice cream. A specialized service sector, which involves domestic companies, joint ventures, and foreign corporations, has emerged to provide for these highly discerning young consumers.

Catering to children can be very profitable. In 1995, the average couple in urban China spent as much as 40 to 50 percent of their combined income on their child. Also in that year, children in Chinese cities received an aggregated yearly income of US$5 billion in the form of weekly allowances and birthday and holiday gifts from their parents and grandparents — a sum roughly equivalent to Mongolia's gross domestic product (Crowell and Hsieh 1995:44–50). In describing the flow of money to children at their birthdays, a Chinese writer points out that China has acquired a huge population of "little gods of longevity" (*xiao shouxing*). These toddlers, preschoolers, and teenagers celebrate their birthdays as if they were entitled to all the special respect once normally reserved for "old gods of longevity" (*lao shouxing*), that is, the elderly:

> Birthday celebrations used to be simpler for children than for the elderly. Now the situation is reversed. One child after another has learned to act like a "little god of longevity." No longer satisfied with the traditional ways of celebrating birthdays, they turn to Western ways for help. They are determined to reinvent and celebrate extravagance with such things as birthday cakes, birthday parties, birthday flowers, birthday gifts, birthday cards, and birthday "red envelopes" (i.e., cash presents). Some concerned agencies conducted surveys to investigate this phenomenon; they found that the cost of a birthday party for these "little gods of longevity" is at least several hundred *yuan* and can exceed 1,000 *yuan*. (Cao Lianchen 1993:47)

We do not know which "concerned agencies" conducted the surveys cited in this passage. We have learned, however, that a large number of Chinese children may be enjoying much greater financial leverage over their parents than American children do. A 1995 survey of 1,496 Chinese households found that children in Beijing determined nearly 70 percent of the family's overall spending. American children, by comparison, had an overall influence rate of 40 percent. The scholars responsible for this survey, James McNeal and Wu Shushan, also found that in terms of food and beverage purchases, children in Beijing influenced their parents twice as much as children in American families (quoted by Crowell and Hsieh 1995:44–50). In short, we are witnessing the emergence of a child-specific culture of consumption in China. For this reason, we are also seeing the emergence of a specialized vocabulary for the category of children's food.

Defining Children's Food from a Historical Perspective

In this book, two key terms we employ are "children's diet" (*ertong yinshi*) and "children's food" (*ertong shipin*). The former stands for what children actually eat on a regular basis, while the latter represents what can be consumed by children and is often intended specifically for them as a special category of edibles. We want to emphasize that the term "children's food" is relatively new in China's popular culture. Until recent years, it rarely appeared in Chinese publications. Take for example the 1979 edition of *Cihai* (*The Sea of Words*), a Chinese dictionary similar to *The Oxford English Dictionary*. In this encyclopedic dictionary of more than 9,000 entries based on quotations from ancient and modern texts, we cannot find a single entry for "children's food." Although there is a short entry for "infant supplementary food" (*ying er fuzhu shipin*), it says nothing about solid foods. One may speculate that the dictionary's compilers simply assumed that children's diet after weaning resembled that of adults. The following discussion bears out this assumption.

To borrow a phrase from the anthropologist Jack Goody (1982), China's "high cuisine," which came into being no later than at the end of the Han dynasty (206 B.C.–A.D. 220), is embodied in a rich variety of delicacies. An even richer food vocabulary seduces the human appetite all the more through the vivid, entrancing representations of delicacies and gourmetship in literature, popular dramas, paintings, and folklore. This high cuisine, however, was confined to the nobility during the Han dynasty, and it was enjoyed in later dynasties by expanding but still very small segments of society. The majority of the population had to satisfy themselves with a "low cuisine," typified by a few delicacies such as meat dishes during festivals and grain for the rest of the year. Beginning in the late Ming dynasty (1368–1644), the introduction of such New World crops as corn, potatoes, and sweet potatoes brought about a revolutionary change. Partly due to the proliferation of these new foods, China's population exploded, increasing from 265 million people in 1775 to 430 million in 1850 (Taeuber 1964:20; He 1988:54–55). And yet the massive poor still had few dietary choices when they entered the twentieth century; food shortages continued to be a constant threat to the majority of the population (see, e.g., Gamble and Burgess 1921; Buck 1930; Li Jinghan 1933:297–324; Fei 1939:119–28; Yao-Hua Lin 1947:55–96).

Thus, it is not surprising that an analysis of food vendors' account books of the late Qing (Meng and Gamble 1926) found little variety in the diet of Beijing's working-class families. This situation remained unchanged by 1926–27, when the sociologist Tao Menghe conducted a detailed study of 48 Beijing households headed by handicraft workers. Tao found that 80 percent of these households' food expenditures went to grains, 9.1 percent to vegetables, 6.7 percent to condiments, 3.2 percent to meats, and only 1 percent to miscellaneous snacks (Tao 1928; see also Yang Yashan 1987:98). A more sophisticated survey of 260 Shanghai working-class households, conducted in the late 1920s, found greater variety: 53.2 percent of their income went to grains, 18.5 percent to vegetables, 7 percent to meat, 4.4 percent to seafood, and 1.9 percent to fruit (Yang Ximeng and Tao Menghe 1930; quoted by Spence 1992:175). But with so much of their income devoted to food, these Shanghai working-class households had little left for other expenses. As for Chinese farmers in the 1920s, a pilot study for a comprehensive survey of 800 farm households in the rural county of Dingxian, north China (Li Jinghan 1933:297–324), found that 80 percent of an average rural household's food expenditures went to millet, sweet potatoes, and sorghum. Meat was consumed almost exclusively at festival times (see also Gamble 1954:100–123).

Although children's diet was not singled out in these surveys, many fond memories of food from childhood can be found in biographical accounts by Chinese writers who grew up in well-to-do families. Lu Xun (1881–1936), arguably China's most famous modern writer, composed a nostalgic essay in 1927 in which he described the vegetables and fruits he ate as a child and how much he missed his old home in later years whenever he tasted water chestnuts, broad beans, wild rice shoots, and muskmelons (Lu Xun 1969: vol. 16, p. 6). A much richer account of food and childhood can be found in a collection of newspaper articles that H. Y. Lowe (Wu Hsing-yuan) wrote in 1939–40 about an almost idyllic way of life in Beijing (Lowe 1984). Lowe fondly recalled eighteen kinds of foods and beverages that he had enjoyed as a child.[4] His descriptions of these foods, accompanied by vivid depictions of toys, games, and temple festivals, suggest that they were children's favorites. But it should be noted immediately that only the "dried cake powder" and "old rice powder" that Lowe mentions in his engaging account were eaten exclusively by children. They were made at milling establishments and were intended to supplement mother's milk. These commercial products were cooked at home into a thick paste and smeared in fingerfuls into the baby's mouth.

The Sino-Japanese War and the civil war of the 1930s and 1940s were catastrophes, not least for food production and supply. Mao's post-1949 campaigns to transform China into a socialist society did little to enrich the variety of foods that had had a special appeal to children like Lowe. Throughout our research for this book, we were reminded by older informants that children's diet in the period from the early 1950s to the late 1970s was extremely simple and similar to that of adults. Urban babies, at least by the mid-1950s, had the alternative of bottled milk and milk powder. They were weaned earlier than rural babies, and many began eating solid and adult-like foods by their first birthday. In rural areas, while babies were still being breastfed they received mouthfuls of food that their mothers or other caretakers chewed for them in advance. After weaning, they received most of their nourishment from the family table. On such matters as infant feeding, weaning, and solid foods, an American delegation of child development experts had this to say about urban and rural China in the mid-1970s:

> Supplementary feeding was said to begin at around six months, rarely before that, and to consist initially of cereal-based porridge. Over the following months pureed vegetables, fruits, bean curd, and eggs are added. The exact sequence and ages reported varied from place to place and from informant to informant. Rice, noodles, and finally chopped meat — mainly chicken, pork, and fish — are added in the second year. Weaning is usually from breast to cup or small bowl. Children begin to feed themselves with a spoon in the second year; chopsticks are mastered at three or a bit later (Kessen, ed., 1975:205–6).

This further indicates that, before the post-Mao economic reforms, Chinese children's diet after weaning quickly began to resemble that of adults. I should add that as late as the early 1980s, China's centrally planned economy was characterized by a lack of incentives in the agricultural sector, which in turn necessitated the strict rationing of food supplies to the urban population (see, e.g., Sidel 1972; Croll 1983; Whyte and Parish 1984:55–109; Potter and Potter 1990:225–50). In both the countryside and cities, the majority of children had neither the luxury nor the freedom to choose what they ate.

This pattern of food consumption has undergone a major transformation since the early 1980s, when the Maoist communal farming system was replaced by a household responsibility system with the family as the basic productive unit. Reforms in the agricultural sector gave farmers incentives to work harder, a major factor behind the bumper harvests in successive years. Also in the first half of the 1980s, per capita income in urban areas began to rise, setting the stage for various commercial products under the general category of children's food to appear and soon flood the Chinese market.

As a linguistic marker of social change, the term children's food has become a part of China's popular culture. This generic term includes, in literal translation: (1) "children's nutritional supplements" (*ertong yingyangpin*); (2) "children's health food and beverages" (*ertong jiankang shipin yinliao*); (3) "children's medicinal food" (*ertong yaoshan*); and (4) "infant and baby food" (*ying you er shipin*), also known as "small children's supplementary food" (*xiao er fushi*). Judging by their commercial claims, these foodstuffs are supposed to benefit children's health. More specifically, "children's nutritional supplements" and "children's health food and beverages" are said to have the general function of "improving" (*jian*) a child's normal physical condition; "children's medicinal food" allegedly achieves the specific goal of "invigorating" (*pu*) a child's weak or diseased condition; and "infant and baby food" is intended to "add" (*tian*) solid or semi-solid nourishment to an infant's otherwise milk-based diet.

The consensus of the Chinese medical community is that many of the commercial products under the general category of "children's food" are not necessarily health-enhancing and that they complicate an already worrisome dietary trend in which traditional staples have increasingly given way to high-cholesterol foods such as eggs and red meat. Desperate for more effective official intervention to reverse this trend, a leading Chinese research institute in charge of monitoring public health made the rare decision in 1996 to grant an interview with an influential American newspaper, to publicize the institute's concerns over the growing rate of obesity among elementary school children in urban China (Tempest 1996).

State, Family, and Children

The Chinese government has a special interest in children's food consumption. Among other things, intervention in what children eat is an extension of the government's population policy. A growing body of literature on this subject has given us insights into the effects of the coercive and intrusive power of the Chinese state bureaucracy; however, this literature has failed to shed much light on how the state has managed to convince people to see the world in a certain way and accept certain ideas as their own. The Chinese government is not merely satisfied with controlling the pace or extent of declining fertility. In a parallel but more subtle form of social engineering, the Chinese government has tried to educate the public to heed the officially identified need to improve the country's "population quality" (*renkou suzhi*). This concept covers not only physical and mental fitness but also officially desired occupational skills and educational achievement in the country's labor force. To publicize its vision of a desirable "population quality," the government has repeatedly urged Chinese citizens to be aware of their country's "population crisis" (*renkou weiji*) — that is, its inadequate intellectual capital in the race to catch up with the world's wealthy and technologically advanced countries.[5]

To improve the quality of China's population, the government has emphasized what it considers to be "scientific" knowledge of childbearing and child rearing. One of the major campaigns in the government's attempt to publicize scientific ways of bearing and raising children ran from April 1988 to October 1989 and was aimed at the countryside. The core of this particular campaign was an essay competition addressing topics ranging from pregnancy, hereditary diseases, and disease prevention to marriage customs, breastfeeding, and children's diet. Over 10,000 letters and 2,000 essays were sent to the Chinese Medical Association, whose Popular Science Society evaluated the essays. Mostly written by medical professionals and birth-control officials, the prize-winning essays and noteworthy letters were broadcast on television and radio; they were also printed in two magazines and a newspaper specializing in issues of public health.

In urban areas, one effort of the Chinese government to educate the public is the promotion of "baby-friendly" hospitals, in conformity with an initiative adopted by the World Health Organization (WHO) and the United Nations Children's Fund (UNICEF). Since 1992, China has certified more than 5,000 baby-friendly hospitals; a chief function of these hospitals is to offer introductory courses to pregnant women on the importance of breastfeeding. This baby-friendly effort was begun by the Chinese government as a response to an alarming decline of breastfed babies in the late 1980s. In Beijing and Shanghai, for example, only 10 percent of new mothers breastfed their babies in the late 1980s. Nationwide, the breastfeeding rate was 30 percent in 1990; it climbed to 64 percent in 1994. This increase was, the Chinese government quickly claimed, a result of its dissemination of scientific information about child care.

These public education measures suggest that the government's attempt to manage motherhood by controlling women's fertility and their feeding practices has to do, simultaneously, with the correct management of childhood. In trying to educate the public about the dietary, medical, economic, and educational issues of childbearing and child development, the state is in a position to continue its influence over the family even after the couple has satisfied official requirements for birth control.

In this regard, the Chinese government has behaved in a strikingly similar fashion to Michel Foucault's descriptions of eighteenth-century Europe, where the "family-children complex," especially in France and Britain, became the "eye of power" in a movement of state expansion and medical acculturation. "The long campaign of inoculation and vaccination [in Europe] has its place in this movement to organize around the child a system of medical care for which the family is to bear the moral responsibility and part of the economic cost" (Foucault 1980:174). The result was the creation of child-care clauses in family laws, thereby bringing children into a multilevel discourse about public health that involved state authorities, philanthropic societies, welfare institutions, and medical professionals. "The family is no longer to be just a system of relations inscribed in a social status, a kinship system, a mechanism for the transmission of property. It is to become a dense, saturated, permanent, continuous physical environment which envelops, maintains and develops the child's body" (1980:172–73). In China, the reach of the state's power literally extends into the woman's womb, because the government's population policy entails coercive methods, including forced abortion, tubectomy, and the compulsory use of intrauterine devices.

But if the Chinese government has acquired the image of an Orwellian "big brother" because of its often harsh population policy, the regime is equally determined to cast itself in the image of a "caring master" by demonstrating a keen interest in improving child care and maternal health. Remaking the state's image in this manner is important for political legitimization. An apt example is the launching of publicity campaigns to promote new, "scientific" ways of childbearing and child rearing.

In the vast literature of these educational campaigns, children's food consumption occupies a conspicuous place amid lengthy discussions of the importance of following the government's population policy. Here is a passage about food, taken from a typical manual that urges the public to acquire scientific child-rearing knowledge as a second step in their acceptance of the government's childbearing policy:

> Some kindergartens make children eat cornmeal porridge, cornmeal buns, and millet porridge. They do so out of concern for children's health and their moral character. But when certain parents see their children eating these coarse grains, they become incredibly upset. They have no idea that the nutritional value of coarse grains is not necessarily less than in refined rice or wheat flour. In fact, the amount of protein, calories, calcium, and iron is greater in millet than in refined rice and white wheat flour. . . . Similarly, there is a higher content of calcium and calories in corn than in rice or wheat. Because different foods have different nutrients, eating a mixture of two different kinds of whole grains or a combination of the coarse cereals mentioned above is an important measure in fostering children's physical growth. Moreover, eating coarse grains will help prevent children from acquiring picky, unhealthy eating habits. (Hu 1993:239)

The author of the above passage is a military doctor and founder of a fertility research center; he writes in the preface of his book that he hopes the publication of his work will serve as "a small droplet of water on the meticulously conceived and cultivated flower buds (i.e., children) of thousands and thousands of families." To provide a further note of personal concern about the growth of these "flower buds," he says that his medical practice has exposed him to heartbreaking encounters with babies who became crippled because their parents did not know the scientific ways to conceive and raise them.

Considering that these instructions for parents usually appear to be objective, scientific, sympathetic, and, most of all, apolitical, it stands to reason that the official discourse on childbearing and child rearing embodies a secret of what Louis Althusser calls "ideological state apparatuses" (1971:143–47). These are institutions chiefly known for their educational roles rather than their coercive and administrative functions. In China, Althusser's "ideological state apparatuses" are represented by the mass media, schools, baby-friendly hospitals, publications of popular science, officially sanctioned charity institutions, and agencies of health education. These organizations are more numerous, disparate, and functionally polymorphous, in contrast to the naked use of repression through the threat of physical attack, economic punishment, or political persecution. As the official discourse on how to bring up a healthy child spills into the newspapers people read, the television programs they watch, the public billboards they see in streets, and the conversations they have among themselves, the public may overlook the infiltration of the Chinese state into a crucial sphere of family life precisely because it is subtle and non-coercive. It is in this sense that the government's childbearing policy is interlocked with its public campaigns regarding child rearing.

Economic Reform and Transnationalism

Economic reforms began in the vast Chinese countryside earlier than in the cities, and the ideas for rural reforms came mainly from within China itself. After the launching of urban reforms in the mid-1980s, the post-Mao regime was attracted by various overseas development models, but particularly South Korea, Taiwan, Hong Kong, and Singapore. That these countries and regions became known in China as *si xiao long*, or "Four Little Dragons," has deeper cultural connotations than the mere catchphrase suggests. "Dragon" evokes China. The populations of Taiwan, Hong Kong, and Singapore are predominantly Han Chinese; South Korea, although not Han, clearly falls within the China-centered, originally Confucian culture of East Asia. "Dragon" further implies not only China but an illustrious China, a spiritually worthy China, and a militarily powerful China. Since China proper was once the principal dragon of East Asia, Chinese intellectuals and politicians have tried to uncover the secret of what they regarded as the "successful modernization process" in the four little dragons.

A few prominent overseas Chinese helped explain this secret to the post-Mao leadership. Singapore's former prime minister, Lee Kwan-yew, energetically justified his authoritarian methods of governance as practicing Confucianism and as a key to Singapore's social order. A relentless advocate that China incorporate Confucianism into its economic reforms, Lee took time off in 1985 to visit Qufu, Confucius' birth and burial place; thereafter Lee took into his own hands the task of finding scholars from overseas for a conference on Confucianism in 1987 in Qufu. Also around this time, the very popular lectures on Confucianism and East Asian traditions by the Harvard-based Taiwan philosopher Tu Wei-ming were attracting huge audiences of students and young scholars at Chinese universities.

With the central government's endorsement of Confucius as a salvaged symbol of Chinese culture, domestic and foreign investment poured into Qufu. A city of no more than 60,000 people, it has become one of China's hottest tourist sites. Every year, Qufu receives more than a million domestic tourists and about 15,000 visitors from overseas. Meanwhile, a small local liquor industry boomed into a national center for breweries and beverage factories, the premium products of which all bear trademarks referring to the ancient sage, including the widely advertised "Family Liquor of Confucius Mansion." Confucius also has become an important icon of China's new nationalism. But a cornerstone of this nationalism is something that the Maoist variety vehemently rejected: commercialism. Zhang Xiaogang, a Chinese intellectual known for his critical views of government policies, said in a 1997 interview in New York, "Without managed commercialism, official nationalism will fall on its head." He added:[6]

> Nationalism and commercialism can be twin brothers. This is so for the simple reason that one of the Chinese Communist Party's strongest means of enhancing its legitimacy is its constant claim of how much it has achieved for the people and the fatherland. They always demanded the gratitude of the one-hundred-old-names (i.e., common people) for having defeated the Nationalist regime, driven foreign imperialists out of the mainland, and all that. Now the Party wants everybody to acknowledge that it has also accomplished economic reforms, allowed private businesses to operate, and brought foreign investors back into China without having to endure the kind of disasters that the former Soviet Union suffered in the meantime.

What, precisely, are the connections between food, children, and the post-Mao commercialism? One link, it can be argued, is the presence of multinational corporations. Historically speaking, the influence of foreign companies in China is not a new phenomenon, as those familiar with the British East India Company's role in opening up the Canton trade in the eighteenth century will know. What is unique about the present converging of multinational giants on China is their ability to become "glocal." By this we mean the ways in which modern multinational corporations adjust to local conditions. Becoming "glocal" entails the integration of markets, trade, finance, information, and corporate ownership with worldwide networks of economic activity, and the tailoring of globally marketed products to fit local tastes.

The ability of transnational corporations to become glocal hinges on their active participation in local affairs, including sponsorship of school events to align their products to the local context of childhood. This business strategy reflects an understanding that profits can be made when an international product sheds its foreign characteristics and merges with the local culture of consumption. It is important to point out here that a significant number of the transnational corporations in China make their headquarters in overseas Chinese societies of the Pacific Rim. But regardless of whether they are directed by people of Chinese ancestry, transnational corporations are engaged in a cultural transformation of mainland China in the sense that their products are marketed not merely as commodities but as cultural goods. This is certainly the case in the production and marketing of food for children.

About 28 million babies are born in China each year, four times the number born annually in the United States. To take advantage of this market potential, H. J. Heinz Co., the American food giant, produces a rice cereal for Chinese babies at a plant in the southern city of Guangzhou. This joint venture, Heinz-UFE (United Food Enterprise of Guangdong) Ltd., was established with an initial investment of $10 million in 1984 on the recommendation of the former secretary of state, Henry Kissinger (Liu Zhuoye 1990:36–38). In its first few years, Heinz-UFE was mainly engaged in market research, testing reactions at hospitals, and quality control. By the late 1980s it had gone into full-scale production, becoming in 1990 a profitable company in a country where many foreign investors do not expect to turn profitable during their first decade. Its $15 million China sales constituted a mere fraction of Heinz's $6 billion in revenues, but Heinz was making the same 15 percent margins it did in the United States, where it had 15 percent share of the $925 million baby-food market (Duggan 1990:84). Also in 1990, Heinz had to deal with its arch-competitor; Nestle, an old hand at selling baby food worldwide, invested $6 million in a plant near the northeastern city of Harbin, to produce ice cream and other dairy products (*Wall Street Journal* 1995, B:1).

The marketing strategy of Heinz's Guangzhou plant offers an informative glimpse into the commercialization of children's appetites in China. In an attempt to associate its product with the aura of children's high achievement, Heinz's entry route into the Chinese market was university towns and high-tech districts in large cities. The intention was obvious: If the best and brightest Chinese embraced Heinz's rice cereal, there would be a ripple effect of emulation. China's enclaves of higher education and scientific progress were not the only focus for Heinz's marketing. Since the prime-time advertising on Chinese television was considered a bargain (see *Forbes* 1993:12, *Wall Street Journal* 1995, B:1; *Newsweek* 1994:39), Heinz has done most of its advertising there. With televisions in more than 95 percent of urban Chinese households, Heinz clearly wants to take advantage of the well-known 4-2-1 factor in urban China: four grandparents and two parents coddling one child.

Not surprisingly, Heinz's commercials show plump, smiling babies and offer a quick message on vitamins and minerals in scientific-sounding jargon to assure viewers of their products' high nutrition. It is also worth mentioning that Heinz displays its brand name in English, accompanied by a line in Chinese characters on its cereal packages stating that its product is made of "high-protein, nutritional rice powder" (*gaodanbai yingyang mifen*). The combination of the foreign version of Heinz's brand name with the scientific-looking label in Chinese seems intended to convince consumers that this Western food is better than comparable Chinese products. Projecting the product's Western and scientific aura promotes the association of vitamin-enriched rice cereal with a "modern" way of life. Selling the Heinz rice product along with a dose of science and modernity has a special appeal in a society where the urban family's priority in spending its disposable income is its single child.

Then there is a more crucial aspect of product promotion, namely the nutrition education program that Heinz has launched to influence Chinese bureaucrats and child-care professionals. The Heinz Institute of Nutrition Science holds a symposium in a Chinese city each year, bringing in nutritionists from North America to give lectures and to make diet proposals. Deftly promoted by Heinz's Chinese partner, some of the institute's proposals were incorporated into the Chinese National Nutrition Development Plan (Liu Zhuoye 1990:38), the basis of China's third national nutrition survey in 1993–95 (Cui Lili 1995:31). In the meantime, the Heinz-UFE rice cereal became a "recommended food for Chinese babies" after winning two top prizes at food competitions jointly sponsored by the Chinese government and food industry.

The Heinz-UFE case reminds us that Chinese children now live in a global consumption culture. In a worldwide trend since the waning of the Cold War — dramatized by the collapse of the former Soviet Union in 1991 and by China's move to a market economy — giant multinational corporations have achieved "a degree of global integration never before achieved by any world empire or nation-state" (Barnet and Cavanagh 1994:15). As money, commodities, ideas, and people unendingly chase each other around the world, the march of commerce through national boundaries depends on a worldwide system of image-saturated information technologies to attract customers, including children.

Corn, Chocolate, and Generational Identity

In social anthropology, the consumption of food is commonly analyzed as a symbolic system that reflects the variations of economic status, group identity, political power, religious belief, educational achievement, and aesthetic values (see, e.g., Bourdieu 1984:177–99; Campbell 1987; Friedman 1989:117–30; Goody 1982; Mintz 1996). A similar understanding abounds in anthropological literature on China (Anderson 1988; Chang 1977; J. Watson 1987). Hence much has been said about how food is used in China to transmit such social values as hard work and frugality. On the transmission of social values through food, the anthropologist Fei Xiaotong made this observation based on his fieldwork in a southern Chinese village in the 1930s:

> Culture provides means to procure materials for satisfying human needs but at the same time defines and delimits human wants. It recognizes a range of wants as proper and necessary and those lying outside the range as extravagant and luxurious. A standard is thus set up to control the amount of consumption. . . . A child making preferences in food or clothes will be scorned and beaten. On the table, he should not refuse what his elders put in his bowl. If a mother lets her child develop special tastes in food, she will be criticized as indulging her child. . . . Thrift is encouraged. Throwing away anything which has not been properly used will offend heaven, whose representative is the kitchen god. (Fei 1939:119)

The above observation characterizes the childhood experiences of an infinite number of Chinese citizens both before and after the Communists came to power. During Mao's rule, from 1949 to 1976, frugality remained not only a habitualized necessity but also a matter of survival.[7] Steel output was rising, nuclear weapons were tested, the Great Leap Forward (1958–60) was launched to accelerate productivity, and the Cultural Revolution (1966–76) was undertaken to prevent China from taking a capitalist road. None of these developments did anything to sweeten the thin breakfast gruel. In particular, we must mention the nationwide famine in the later phase of the Great Leap Forward. Most people with any sense of twentieth-century history will know of the great horrors in which millions have perished — the Holocaust in Europe, the Gulag in the former Soviet Union, and the Killing Fields in Cambodia. But the catastrophic Chinese famine from 1959 to 1961 does not even have a commonly recognized name. In China's official propaganda, the famine is still labeled "the three years of natural disaster," although bad weather had little to do with it. The famine was a policy-generated disaster (see, e.g., Becker 1996; Jowett 1989:16–19; Kane 1988; Dali Yang 1996).

Depending on how the statistics are interpreted by different demographers, the famine is believed to have cost 30 million to 45 million lives. Under famine conditions, the very young are at particular risk and women's fertility declines drastically. In 1960, at the peak of the famine, half of the deaths in China were of children under ten years old. The country's total number of births dropped from 27 million in 1957 to 15 million in 1961 (Jowett 1989:17). Periods of famine-induced demographic declines are often followed by a baby boom, and in China this was certainly the case. In the aftermath of the famine, some 35 million babies were born in 1963, and over the next three years China registered 90 million births. Many of the parents of China's current generation of grade-school children were among the post-famine babies, whose later childhood experience was disrupted by the chaotic decade of the Cultural Revolution (see Chan 1985; Chin 1988; Gao Yuan 1987; Lupher 1995:321–44; Wen Chihua 1995).

Even at times when famine was not lurking, the opportunity to eat just a little bit of what were considered to be delicacies could be remembered for a lifetime. A Beijing woman had this to say about the food she ate as a child during a visit to her father's "cadre school," one of the thousands of "reform-through-labor" farms set up for government officials who were brought down in the Cultural Revolution:

> The lunch my father returned with [from the farm's public
> canteen] was almost inedible. . . . Looking at the bowl of soup
> on the table, I could see my father's clouded face reflected
> there, floating with a few vegetables. "What? Is this soup or an
> edible mirror?" I murmured, trying to release my anger and
> lighten up the mood in the room. No one responded, but I
> could sense my father's eyes inspecting me for being so
> picky. . . . My chopsticks unexpectedly struck something soft
> at the bottom of the bowl. "It must be sausage," I thought.

The smell of sausage rushed into my nose, the taste of sausage into my mouth. . . . I dug up the soft thing from the bottom of my bowl. What caught my eye was no sausage but a preserved egg. (Wen Chihua 1995:81–82)

At least this Cultural Revolution child could imagine the smell of sausage and actually had a preserved egg for the reunion lunch with her father; there were far less fortunate adults and children throughout China. When Mao died in 1976, the average per capita dietary intake was only marginally higher than in the years immediately before the start of the Sino-Japanese War in 1937 (Smil 1985:248). After many years of radical political campaigns, ringing exhortations, and ambitious goals, the future was anything but promising and fundamental change was needed.

Such a change first took place in the late 1970s, when an earlier experiment with the now well-known "household responsibility system" was resumed to terminate the communal farming system. This quickly made available unprecedented supplies of food to a larger share of the Chinese population than at any time since 1949. To be specific, the unleashed entrepreneurial energies in the countryside were followed by an immediately encouraging result: Per capita annual availability of processed grain at the end of 1982 was close to 230 kilograms, surpassing the highest level of the the 1950–81 period. Per capita annual availability of vegetable oil, sugar, meat, and fish in 1982 also achieved record highs of 4.1, 5.3, 12.6, and 4.8 kilograms respectively (Piazza 1986:94–95).

Reflecting the rapid diversification of agriculture, especially the increase in non-grain crops and animal products, the contribution of grains (rice, corn, millet, and wheat) to the average Chinese diet fell to its lowest level of the 1950–81 period. Containing 2,728 calories of energy, nearly 70 grams of protein and 40 grams of fat per day, the Chinese daily intake of calories in 1982 exceeded the 1979–82 averages of the world's developing countries. Record crop production in 1983 and 1984 was followed by further agricultural diversification in the second half of the 1980s, giving rise to a growing consensus among scholars that the "food problem" in China was no longer how to provide adequate supplies for all, but how to increase consumption by the unfortunate few (Smil 1995:801–13).

The shift away from production of traditional staple crops to more profitable pursuits, both agricultural and non-agricultural, was reinforced by the enormous demand for a richer variety of food products in cities and in the countryside. The launching of urban reforms in 1985, including the eventual abolition of food rations and the boom in factory-manufactured foodstuffs, depended on the headway made in the agricultural sector of the national economy. This historical moment would set the stage for the rise of the so-called *xiao kang* families.

In Confucian ideology, *xiao kang*, or "small prosperity," means a state of society in which people live and work happily with a sufficient supply of goods to meet basic needs. Back in 1979, Deng Xiaoping set the target of *xiao kang* livelihood for the whole country to be achieved by the year 2000. To translate Deng's wish into a concrete figure, the central government planners put the target at $800 per capita GDP in 1980 dollar values. Although the target has yet to be reached nationwide, the per capita GDP in certain areas has surpassed that goal. This reflects a pattern of economic development in post-Mao China of "points-line-surface progression," meaning that the coastal cities and special economic zones (i.e., the points) are developed first, gradually bringing about prosperity to the whole coastal area (the line). From there, prosperity is expected to spread inland, thereby realizing Deng's wish to extend *xiao kang* status over the entire country. Per capita GDP was $694 in 1996, but it is interesting to note that the urban average is three times higher than the average for villages and rural market towns. The average of coastal cities is double that of the average, and the average of special economic zones is again double that of the coastal cities. The GDP differential is as high as twelve times when we compare the special economic zones with the average village or rural market town. All this means that a considerable number of urban families and a smaller number of rural families are already at the *xiao kang* level.

Who are these families? The main categories are: managers who work in the roughly 100,000 joint ventures and wholly owned foreign companies; owners of the 20 million private enterprise and self-employed businesses, a large number of managers of the 21 million industrial enterprises in small towns, and a large number of managers in foreign trade corporations, banks, insurance companies and stock brokerage firms; and managers in well-run and profitable state enterprises. The total number of *xiao kang* families, or "middle-income households," to be more precise, is probably in the region of 30 million for the whole country or around 20 million in the cities. The latter constitutes close to 20 percent of the urban population.

It is in the *xiao kang* households that tensions between parents and children over food have become most acute. In a lighthearted essay on diets and culinary arts, the comedian-turned-playwright Huang Zongjiang offers the following Beijing family scene: A father brings out for breakfast a plateful of steamed cornmeal buns, known in north China as *wotou*. He is upset by his daughter's scornful look at the yellowish buns. "You must not forget your class origin," the father says accusingly and then tries to tell his daughter how lucky he felt as a child in an impoverished coal-mining community to have a cornmeal bun or any food to eat at breakfast. His lecturing is curtly interrupted. "*Your* class origin is cornmeal buns," the daughter says. "*Mine* is chocolate" (Chen Shujun, ed., 1989:296).

This depiction of intergenerational conflict is, of course, intended for humorous effect, playing upon the somewhat exaggerated equation of corn with the poverty of the past and chocolate with the affluence of the present. Chinese citizens over the age of 40 would probably agree, as the playwright suggests at the end of his essay, that this kind of generation gap is increasingly hard to reconcile when youngsters have less and less idea what their own parents and grandparents used to eat. The essential point of such complaints is not youth-bashing, or the question of how little children know about the childhood experience of their elders; it is about the escalating challenges of cross-generational understanding and communication in a rapidly changing society. Food talks, but it may speak in very different languages as a society changes.

1

Paradoxes of Plenty: China's Infant- and Child-Feeding Transition

Georgia S. Guldan

This chapter examines trends in diet, growth, and health among children in the People's Republic of China. It also explores two paradoxes that emerge from these trends: first, urban children, despite eating and growing better than their rural counterparts, are experiencing a rise in obesity and other chronic ailments and their risk factors; and second, although rural children are breastfed longer than their urban counterparts, their growth is poorer. What aspects of these children's diets help explain these paradoxes? What are the growth and health consequences of these diets? How has the Chinese government dealt with the nutritional problems associated with child-feeding practices?

I will address these questions on the basis of my experience as a nutritionist in China and Hong Kong since 1988. The first five-and-a-half years were spent at the West China University of Medical Sciences in Chengdu, the capital of Sichuan province. There I first looked at local urban and rural eating habits. Then I focused on the feeding of infants, particularly in rural areas, where I both studied and tried to improve feeding practices and growth. Later, I moved my research base to Hong Kong, where I added preschool and school-age children to my work, both in Beijing and Hong Kong. When I combine my findings with those from other studies, various diet and health transitions can be detected.

The Chinese children I have studied are undoubtedly better nourished, grow faster and bigger, and are generally healthier than their counterparts fifty years ago. However, new problems have emerged, particularly in urban areas, due to overnutrition — the excessive consumption of energy and nutrients that can contribute to obesity, diabetes, and other ailments. In the following pages, the chief focus is on the nutritional well-being of children on the Chinese mainland, with Hong Kong data introduced for comparison. But before addressing the questions raised above, I will provide a brief introduction to the Chinese food system.

After the political, social, and economic upheavals of the Great Leap Forward (1958–60) and the Cultural Revolution (1966–76), economic and agricultural reforms were launched in the late 1970s, transforming China's food supply. In the countryside, agricultural production was diversified and food processing and marketing expanded, thanks to the new "household contract responsibility system," which allowed rural households to produce whatever they wanted and to sell it on the open market in urban areas. The resulting changes in the food supply altered the diets of both rural people, particularly those who lived near the markets and could best take advantage of the reforms, and urban residents, who gained access to more varied foods. The Chinese population as a whole, therefore, enjoyed more and better food with more variety than ever before. Although these developments have included rapid growth in the livestock sector, enabling greater consumption of animal protein and fat, the current food system provides China's billion-plus population with a generally health-promoting grain- and vegetable-based diet.

The Chinese household's participation in this food system follows two general patterns, depending on whether the household is a member of the smaller but more affluent urban minority or the 70 percent of the population that lives in the countryside. These two groups enjoy very different living standards and degrees of modernization; their education levels, means of earning a livelihood, and access to health and other social services differ greatly. In few areas are these differences more evident than in their diets.

For most Chinese, rural and urban alike, grains and cereals

remain the most important component of the diet. However, the rural population in many areas still produces much of its own food. By contrast, urban dwellers normally purchase food from shops and markets. For both groups, grains and cereals are supplemented by varying amounts of fresh and salted vegetables, oil, meat, poultry, fish, eggs, and fruit. Some rural residents now buy a higher proportion of non-staple foodstuffs with the cash income they earn from sales of farm products or from family members' non-farm employment. After cereals and grains, vegetables are the most important non-staple food item.

In two 1989 surveys in which I participated in Sichuan province to study dietary patterns — in Chengdu, a city of 4 million residents, and in a rural village — we found clear urban/rural differentials (Guldan et al. 1991). From the food frequency data gathered in households in those two sites, we found that the urban households surveyed were consuming rice, vegetable oil, green vegetables, "lean" meat (mostly pork), and wheat on a daily basis, and other vegetables, pickles, fruit, eggs, soy products, and meat fat at least weekly. Their rural village counterparts, however, had a more monotonous daily diet of rice, oil, and vegetables; they consumed other foods at least monthly but not weekly.

Infants' and Children's Dietary Patterns

The urban/rural differences in infants' and children's diets begin with breastfeeding rates and duration, and are especially noteworthy. The nutritional, immunological, psychological, and economic benefits of breastfeeding are now well established. Despite these benefits, a decline in breastfeeding has been observed worldwide, beginning in the nineteenth century in Europe and the United States with industrialization, the manufacture of processed milks, and the medicalization of infant feeding that accompanied the institutionalization of health care (Apple 1994). The breastfeeding decline continued into the second half of the twentieth century, when it embraced China as well. Studies in China show clear

Table 1. Urban and Rural Infant Feeding Patterns in China (1983–85), n (%)

Feeding pattern	Urban		Rural	
Breastfeeding	27,424	(49)	25,087	(75)
Mixed feeding	20,352	(36)	7,729	(23)
Bottle feeding	8,403	(15)	594	(2)
Total	56,189	(100)	33,410	(100)

Source: Adapted from P. Y. Yang et al. 1989.

urban/rural disparities in breastfeeding rates. Table 1 is based on a twenty-province breastfeeding survey of 95,578 infants up to the age of six months; the survey was conducted from 1983 to 1985.

Traditionally, breastfeeding was the norm in China, but modernization has brought with it more artificial feeding, particularly in the urban areas. The higher rates of breastfeeding in rural than in urban areas can be seen clearly in Table 1.

Reflecting the same contrasting trends, Figure 1 shows a comparison of breastfeeding rates in four-to-twelve-month-old infants in urban Sichuan in 1992 and in rural Sichuan in 1993. Additionally, a cross-sectional nutritional surveillance study in 1990 in rural Hubei found that 16.2 percent of infants were breastfed for 24 months (Taren and Chan 1993). Consistent with the lower breastfeeding rates found in urban China, a 1993 infant-feeding survey of 3,717 healthy infants in Hong Kong revealed that only 18 percent were breastfed immediately after birth; by age one month the rate dropped to 11 percent, with most infants fed from formula (Lui et al. 1997).

Although there is no standard definition of the term "weaning" (*duan nai*), it is used here to refer to the period during which the child's diet gradually changes from a liquid, milk-based diet to a semi-solid and then solid diet based on staple foods of the adult diet (Draper 1994). I have developed Figure 2 to diagram the weaning process. The World Health Organization, United Nations Children's Fund (UNICEF), and other health agencies and specialists usually recommend exclusive breastfeeding for the first four

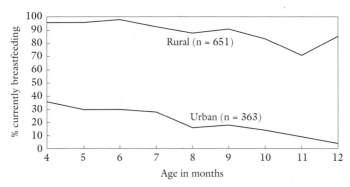

Figure 1. Rural (1992) and Urban (1993) Rates for Currently Breastfeeding Infants from Four to Twelve Months Old in Sichuan

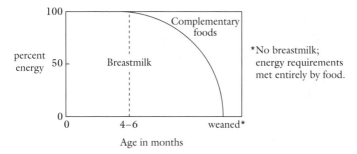

Figure 2. The Weaning Process

to six months, but in practice, complementary weaning foods are often given earlier, without clear benefit, along with the mother's milk. The age at which termination of breastfeeding is recommended can vary from around six months to more than two years.

The weaning period is a precarious time for children in developing areas such as rural China. After four to six months, breastmilk alone can hardly meet the nutritional needs of the rapidly growing and more active infant. The child must be given hygienic and calorie- and nutrient-dense foods to complement the breastmilk. Unfortunately, in rural China, the traditional complementary food has been watery rice and other grain porridge, a low-calorie food, with little else, except perhaps vegetables. This thin gruel cannot satisfy the infant's nutritional needs because the infant's small stomach cannot process large enough quantities. Since rice porridge has less than half the calorie density of breastmilk, infants fed this watery food tend to grow slowly. The result of this extended overdependence on breastfeeding and scanty complementary feeding before the age of one year is higher malnutrition and retarded growth among rural children than among urban children.

As promoted by UNICEF in cooperation with medical institutions in China (see Chapter 7 by Suzanne Gottschang in this volume), exclusive breastfeeding is recommended for the first four to six months, followed by the gradual addition of appropriate complementary feeding until the child is weaned. Rural mothers are encouraged to continue breastfeeding their children for at least one year if possible, because breastmilk is especially important to a child's health if complementary feeding is inadequate.

In our surveys of both urban and rural infant feeding patterns, we found "insufficient milk" to be the most common reason cited either for not breastfeeding at all or for early cessation. Unfortunately, this perceived insufficiency, common all over the world where breastfeeding rates have declined, is usually due to infant behavior cues such as crying and restlessness leading to maternal insecurity and anxiety, which may in turn adversely affect the reflex that releases milk from the breast. In focus-group discussions in Chengdu, mothers of infants told us they were afraid their infants might "starve" (Guldan et al. 1995). The anxious mother, with modern milk formulas readily available, often responds by supplementing her "inadequate" breast milk with bottle feeds. Supplementing compounds the problem by providing less stimulus for further milk production.

In our surveys of rural infants in Sichuan, rice porridge was one of the most commonly used complementary foods, and it was often given by itself or with vegetables at ages up to one year. Simple ways to add calories to rice porridge are to use less water and add mashed egg yolk, oil, or ground meat or tofu if available. However, such additions are not customary, and some are not available on a daily basis in some rural households. The additions to the rice porridge of these calorie- and nutrient-dense foods must be actively taught to those mothers who do not realize that their infants are growing slowly because watery rice porridge is inadequate as a complementary food during weaning.

In our infant-feeding promotional work, this educational suggestion was largely ignored unless we continuously reinforced it. Barriers to providing better complementary foods include not only a lack of time among women employed in agriculture, and sometimes industry, but also attitudes regarding what food is suitable for young children. Our attempts to improve complementary feeding practices by promoting "scientific infant feeding" (*kexue weiyang*) met with resistance from many mothers, even though we emphasized adding only locally produced or otherwise easily available foods. Although the mothers could learn and cite the better weaning practices, they did not always follow them.

However, in our rural Sichuan project, higher breastfeeding rates were maintained throughout the child's first year, anemia rates declined, and feeding practices in the group receiving nutritional education were better than in a control group. Also, the twelve-month-old children in our education group showed better growth than their counterparts in the control group (Guldan et al. 1993).

Besides the overdependence on breastfeeding and rice porridge in the countryside, other differences were found in the quality of complementary foods between urban and rural Sichuan. The feeding differences we found in our surveys are shown in Table 2. Note that the rural infants received almost no nutrient-dense foods or animal protein, whereas such foods were common in the diets of the urban infants.

These infant-feeding practices, particularly in the countryside, have their roots in traditional practices, in which extended breastfeeding — into the child's second or third year or even longer — and overdependence on breastfeeding after the first six months were

Table 2. Number and Percentage of Rural (1992) and Urban (1993) Sichuan Infants Aged Four to Twelve Months Given Complementary Foods on a Daily Basis

Food	4–6 months		7–9 months		10–12 months	
	urban	rural	urban	rural	urban	rural
Cow's milk*	90 (68)	28 (11)	91 (76)	24 (11)	88 (80)	21 (12)
Powdered milk	47 (35)		33 (28)		21 (19)	
Wheat products	21 (16)	39 (15)	75 (63)	45 (20)	74 (67)	54 (31)
Vegetables	35 (26)	34 (13)	98 (82)	90 (40)	101 (92)	95 (45)
Meat	7 (5)	6 (2)	56 (47)	9 (4)	69 (63)	13 (8)
Fruit	32 (24)	12 (5)	67 (56)	38 (17)	76 (69)	34 (20)
Rice porridge	26 (20)	86 (34)	81 (68)	136 (61)	90 (82)	116 (67)

* *Note*: Cow's milk figure in rural area included fresh or powdered milk.

common. After reviewing medical texts and family records of imperial China, Hsiung Ping-chen (1995) found that breastfeeding was the predominant method of feeding infants, extending well into the second and third year of life, and sometimes even into the fourth or fifth. Although the medical texts provided rational, technical guidance in some ways, Hsiung also found while the child was being breastfed, little other food was being provided. Complementary feeding was recommended in only very small amounts starting at three or seven days after birth.

The guidelines also emphasized soft and delicate foods, and avoiding overfeeding. These recommendations stemmed from a concern less to promote the infant's growth and nutrition than to promote the development of the infant's digestion and absorption capability, prevent illness, and minimize "crying and uncooperativeness."[1]

Some of these beliefs persist, more in rural than in urban Sichuan; when mothers were asked what foods are beneficial to their infants between four and twelve months, their replies stressed steamed rice, eggs or egg yolks, powdered milk, cooked meat, breastmilk, mashed vegetables, rice porridge, fruit, fish, and a local tonic (Guldan et al. 1993). By contrast, when asked what should not be fed to their infants, they replied "cold," "raw," and "hard" foods. Also cited were cookies and cakes, soy products, soup, peanuts, and again fruit and fish. My survey did not include any Sichuan children older than twelve months. However, in 1991, I surveyed 9,603 rural children up to three years old in Hubei, Anhui, and Henan provinces. Of the 1,237 infants between 31 and 35 months old, 13 percent were still being breastfed (UNICEF Beijing 1992).

These infant urban/rural feeding differences persist into adolescence, as can be seen from results of the Chinese government's third national nutrition survey, conducted in 1992 (Ge et al. 1996). Dietary data for the six- to twelve-year-olds and thirteen- to seventeen-year-olds can be seen in Table 3. Male/female differences are minor, but large urban/rural differences can be observed, particularly in the percentages of calories from fat, grain, and animal protein. The diet of the rural children contains about the same calories as that of urban children, but a significantly smaller proportion of it comes from fat and from animal protein. For comparative purposes, we can look at Hong Kong, where twelve-year-olds in a survey ate more protein and fat but fewer total calories and carbohydrates than urban Chinese children (Lee et al. 1994).

Growth and Health Consequences

As diet and feeding methods differ, so do children's growth and health. Growth differences are indeed evident between urban and rural infants and children in China; they can be sensitively yet easily measured by anthropometric measurement of weight and height (or length for infants). The rate of growth and body size are influenced by dietary intake, energy expenditure, and general health, and slowing or cessation of growth is an early response to nutritional inadequacy. Growth measurements, used in the West since the early 1800s, but now used worldwide, can also predict performance, health, and survival. From large-scale surveys of children in different populations, growth curves can be generated and used as reference norms by which to evaluate, monitor, or screen the nutritional status of children in the corresponding population.[2]

Table 3. Dietary Intake of Nutrients and Foods by Age, Gender, and Urban/Rural Residence Among School-Aged Children in China and Hong Kong

	Energy (kcal)	Protein (g)	Fat (g)	Percent energy from: fat	protein	carbo-hydrate	cereals	animal food
CHINA								
6–12 yr olds (n = 11,630)								
urban (n = 2,808)								
M	2,037	71.5	63.8	27.4	13.9	58.7	56.4	17.9
F	1,881	65.2	58.2	26.8	13.8	59.4	56.8	16.8
rural (n = 8,822)								
M	1,920	58.0	39.5	18.5	12.1	69.4	70.4	7.2
F	1,806	54.0	36.2	17.9	12.0	70.1	71.2	6.7
average	1,891	59.3	44.0	20.5	12.5	67.0	67.1	9.6
13–17 yr olds (n = 14,608)								
urban (n = 4,687)								
M	2,651	83.6	72.9	24.4	12.7	62.9	63.3	12.7
F	2,225	69.3	62.7	25.0	12.5	62.5	61.9	12.1
rural (n = 9,921)								
M	2,582	83.9	49.6	15.7	11.8	72.5	75.4	4.3
F	2,440	71.2	43.9	16.0	11.7	72.3	74.8	4.0
average	2,586	77.2	52.4	18.8	12.0	69.4	71.7	6.5
HONG KONG								
12-yr olds (n = 179)								
M	2,466	123	82	28.9	19.8	51.2	—	—
F	1,845	90	60	28.7	19.6	51.6	—	—
average	2,164	107	71	28.3	19.7	51.4	—	—

Adapted from Ge et al. 1996 (China) and Lee et al. 1994 (Hong Kong).

Traditionally, there has been a concern for slow growth and undernutrition in children, particularly in developing countries, but now there is the additional concern for the emerging problem of overnutrition. In China and Hong Kong, we see both of these problems.

Using anthropometric measurements to assess the growth and nutritional status of children is also a test of health and food policies, because children's nutritional status depends on household foods and other available resources and how these are distributed within the household. The evidence for this relationship comes from "secular trend" data, which show that in industrialized countries over the last hundred years, children have matured earlier and become taller than previously, apparently a result of the improved diet following the Industrial Revolution. Environmental factors affecting the growth of the child, including maternal education and hygiene conditions, interact with diet and contribute to this development trend. Additionally, evidence within populations shows that children's height is often associated with socioeconomic status.

In most developing countries, differences in child growth are observed, with the majority of children shorter than the better nourished and more privileged children in their own society and children in developed countries. In China, too, rural children, who represent most of the country's 300 million children, grow at significantly slower rates than urban children. Very few surveys link diet to anthropometric status in Chinese children, but this difference in growth is established during the weaning period, when growth should be at its most rapid, and is believed due at least in part to the differing feeding practices of infants in the two groups. This results in a substantial amount of mild to moderate malnutrition in the rural areas, beginning during the weaning period before the first birthday. Our Sichuan data, showing the growth differences in the urban and rural infants between the ages of four and twelve months, clearly demonstrate this differential (Fig. 3).

The resulting differences in stature between urban and rural populations are in themselves not a major cause for concern, but there is ample evidence that stunted growth puts the child at an increased risk of delayed motor and mental development, and puts the adult at an increased risk of disease and premature death. The consequences of growth delay are well recognized. After analyzing data from 3,000 children in Beijing and in urban and rural Gansu and Jiangsu provinces, D. T. Jamison found that rural students were consistently further behind in growth and in school than

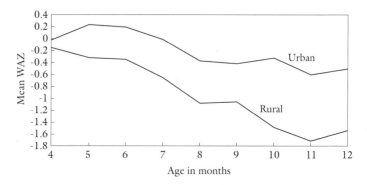

Figure 3. Mean Weight-for-Age Z-Scores (WAZ) in Urban (n = 363) and Rural (n = 651) Infants from Four to Twelve Months Old (NCHS References)

those in the urban centers of those provinces and in Beijing. Children with low height-for-age were consistently behind, and height-for-age predicted grade level in school (Jamison 1986).

Evidence from China and Hong Kong demonstrate clear urban/ rural differences as well as secular increases in child anthropometric data over time. In developed regions of the West, where socioeconomic status is fairly uniform, heights of children are not increasing, and differences between groups do not exist; it is believed that the children's growth has reached its genetic potential. However, in Asian populations, it appears that the end point has not yet been reached (Ulijaszek 1994). Therefore, socioeconomic and feeding differences are contributing to differences in children's growth in China over time and also between urban and rural areas, as well as between China and Hong Kong.

Since the 1970s, surveys in China have found growth disparities between rural and urban areas as well as differing rates of malnutrition (ACC Sub-Committee on Nutrition 1997). In addition, changes are evident in Chinese children's growth data over time. A similar trend is seen in Hong Kong children's growth data as well, with children measured in 1993 significantly taller, heavier, and earlier-maturing than those measured in 1963 (Leung 1994).

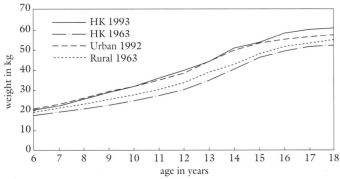

Figure 4. Growth in Weight of Males in Urban and Rural China (1992) and Hong Kong (1963 and 1993)

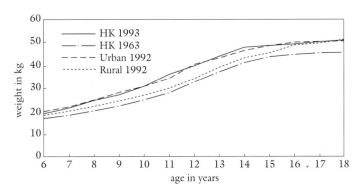

Figure 5. Growth in Weight of Females in Urban and Rural China (1992) and Hong Kong (1963 and 1993)

Figures 4 through 7 depict some of these stature differences in China's urban and rural areas, and in Hong Kong in 1963 and 1993.

The urban/rural gap in children's growth is widening among children aged two to five, however, according to one group of researchers (Shen et al. 1996). Although height increased in both urban and rural areas between 1987 and 1992, the net increase for rural children (0.5 cm) was only one-fifth that for urban children (2.5 cm). The researchers concluded that these increased disparities

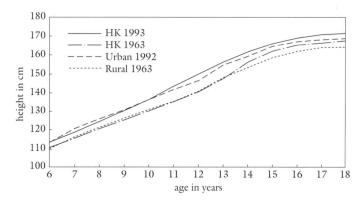

Figure 6. Growth in Height of Males in Urban and Rural China (1992) and Hong Kong (1963 and 1993)

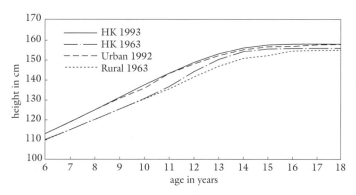

Figure 7. Growth in Height of Females in Urban and Rural China (1992) and Hong Kong (1963 and 1993)

were probably due to an uneven distribution of resources to and within rural areas during the economic reforms of the past two decades, and that compensatory measures are needed to mitigate further negative effects on nutrition in the countryside. A much smaller study of 109 infants in a rural village of Shandong province did not find evidence of growth problems (Huang Shu-min et al.

1996:355–81). However, this study, conducted in 1991, was flawed in that it analyzed the infants against 1985 rural growth data and did not compare them with more rapidly growing urban infants of the same period.

Among those taller, heavier children that are now appearing in the cities especially, however, are some children who are overweight or even obese, and who suffer the health problems associated with obesity, such as high blood pressure, hyperlipidemia, and impaired glucose tolerance, a possible precursor of diabetes. Surveys from various cities reveal these problems linked to overnutrition (Sun Xun 1991; Ma Liqing and Wang Xiaofeng 1993; Lu Huiling et al. 1993) in urban children, along with persistently high levels of poor growth and iron deficiency anemia in other children in the same populations.

This information should be able to give us a clearer picture of the consequences of dietary differences in urban and rural children. A small survey in Beijing in 1995 put the prevalence of obesity among children from eight to seventeen years old at 13.2 percent; in some age subgroups of males the rate exceeded 20 percent (Ye and Feng 1997). A 1991 anthropometric survey of 45,188 students in 45 secondary schools in Chengdu found that while obesity had increased from 3 percent in 1988 to 7 percent in 1991, another 32 percent of the students were found to be mildly undernourished (Su Yingxiong et al. 1991).

In Hong Kong, obesity was clearly evident in the 1993 anthropometric survey of 24,709 infants and children up to eighteen years of age, with obesity peaking at 21 percent among eleven-year-old boys (Leung 1994 and 1996). When the serum cholesterol levels of Hong Kong and Guangdong seven-year-olds were compared, the Hong Kong group had significantly higher levels, even higher than those found in Australia, even though Australian children consumed more fat (Leung et al. 1994). Additionally, in Taiwan, a 1991 survey of 1,168 Taipei seventh graders found obesity prevalence rates of 15 to 17.3 percent for males and 14.6 to 15.6 percent for females (Yen et al. 1994). A later study found the clustering of hypertension, diabetes mellitus, and dyslipidemia among obese Taipei schoolchildren (Chu et al. 1998).

Although obese children may be active and generally "in good health," the detrimental health effects of obesity usually do not strike until adulthood. However, an ecological survey in 65 Chinese counties of adult dietary and lifestyle factors, analyzed together with secondary data on disease-specific mortality rates, suggested that diseases such as cancer and coronary heart disease may share a common nutritional etiology based on the enrichment of diets with animal products (Campbell et al. 1992). That same study also found that the physical stature of adults, both height and weight, was greater in areas in which the chronic "diseases of affluence" were more common.

The dietary changes from 1978 to the present, along with the disparities between rural and urban China and between China and Hong Kong, all represent part of a phenomenon known as the "nutrition transition." In this transition, lifestyles and nutrient proportions in diets undergo changes as living standards rise, and these together produce health changes. The dietary change is in the direction of a more Western diet. By Western diet, I do not mean Western food items so much as Western dietary proportions, particularly a higher proportion of fat and lower proportion of carbohydrates. In the case of infants, this transition also means lower rates and shorter durations of breastfeeding.

The dietary changes of this transition also affect health and growth, and ultimately disease and death rates. In China, health policy immediately after 1949 was quite broad-based and equitable, emphasizing both rural peasants and urban workers. It was at this time that China led the way with its rural "barefoot doctor" system, a pioneering effort that influenced the development of preventive and primary health care worldwide. Thanks to these policies, as well as to relative peace after decades of war and civil conflict, infant mortality declined and life expectancy increased. Since 1978, however, the market-oriented economic reforms have led to a commoditization of health services, in which they are purchased rather than provided by the state. One unintended effect has been a widening of urban/rural inequities in these services.

For women and children, particularly in rural areas, the commoditization of health services has meant fewer resources for such preventive efforts as child health care, nutritional services for young parents, and infant weighing to encourage healthy growth and diagnose malnutrition. From 1985 to 1989, the urban health care system was basically intact and improving somewhat; the rural system, however, was disintegrating, with fewer per capita health professionals, hospitals, and hospital beds, despite greater health care needs in the rural areas, as indicated by higher infant mortality rates and lower life expectancies (Shi 1993). The rural maternal and child health network was perhaps most severely affected, since infant mortality stopped declining in the rural areas after 1978. Lawson and Lin (1994) examined the 1978 to 1990 mortality statistics in China and found, in addition to urban/rural mortality differentials among adults, that the infant death rates from respiratory infections, diarrhea, and accidents had risen up to ten times higher in poor rural communities than in large city populations. A survey of 180 villages by seven Chinese medical schools in conjunction with Harvard University's School of Public Health found that 30 percent had no village doctor, 28 percent of the people did not seek health care when they were ill because they could not afford it, and 51 percent of those who were advised to enter a hospital refused to go because of the cost (Hsiao and Liu 1996). It would appear that policies are needed now to overcome the disparities between rural and urban areas in nutrition, health, growth, and in access to health care.

Public Policies and Government Actions

Until the early 1980s, there was little official interest in intervening in child nutrition (Croll 1986). With growing impetus from the single child policy, however, the Chinese government began organizing studies of children's nutritional status and called for the establishment of advisory and practical services to reduce the incidence of low birth weight and to enhance children's life expectancy and growth. Although growth data on urban children extend back to 1915, data on rural children were not collected until 1979 (Shen and Habicht 1991). Since then, frequent urban and rural anthropometric surveys have been conducted to monitor child development and emerging health problems as a guide to public policy.

The Institute of Nutrition and Food Hygiene of the Chinese Academy of Preventive Medicine in Beijing is in charge of nationwide surveys. Led by this research institute, a third national nutrition survey was conducted in 1992, and it included a dietary survey (n = 240,000), anthropometric survey (n = 50,000), and biochemical examination (n = 17,000) in 30 provinces, municipalities, and autonomous regions. Results from this survey have been used to monitor developments in diet, growth, and morbidity patterns in various regions (Ge 1996:43). Additionally, the Chinese Academy of Preventive Medicine and the State Statistical Bureau have collaborated in various urban and rural household surveys by using a food and nutrition surveillance system established in 1988 (Chen Chunming 1997). The purpose of collecting these data is to provide a basis for socioeconomic development planning and nutrition policy-making. The information gathered has been used to set priorities in strengthening nutrition education, focusing on nutrition for children, particularly those in the weaning-age group, from two to eighteen months, and targeting poorer areas.

Based on nationwide and regional surveys, China's first dietary guidelines were promulgated in 1988 (Chinese Nutrition Society 1990). The guidelines, similar to those in Western nations, are not intended specifically for children, but for the entire population. Nonetheless, they do serve as a common focus for promoting good nutrition and health in the country. In 1997 they were updated (Chinese Nutrition Society 1997), and include the following points of emphasis: (1) eat a variety of foods; (2) eat plenty of vegetables, fruits, and starchy roots; (3) eat dairy and soy products daily; (4) regularly eat fish, eggs, poultry, and meat, but less fatty meat and animal fat; (5) balance food intake with physical activity; (6) eat fewer salty and oily foods; (7) drink alcohol in moderation; and (8) pay attention to food hygiene.

China's leading outreach organization for the improvement of children's nutritional status is the All-China Association for Better Nutrition Among Students, which was established in 1989 to strengthen student nutrition in primary and secondary schools and also universities. The association is charged with disseminating information and promoting healthy school meals and snacks. In 1990, it designated May 20 as an annual Chinese Student Nutrition Day to be marked with ceremonies, speeches, and distribution of pamphlets to promote student nutrition and healthy school meals (Cui Lili 1994). In addition, in 1994 a School Nutrition Unit was created at the Institute of Nutrition and Food Hygiene under the Chinese Academy for Preventive Medicine to conduct nutrition education research among school children. Each year it joins with the All-China Association for Better Nutrition Among Students to promote Student Nutrition Day activities. International Children's Day — June 1 — is another occasion often commemorated with healthy child contests and health education for parents. In some of the health contests, participating children are judged by their height and weight, and for children under six months, breastfeeding is a requirement.[3]

Government policies and measures to improve children's nutrition are also reflected in an important decision in 1992 aimed at increasing the breastfeeding rates and halving the infant mortality and malnutrition rates by the year 2000 (Information Office of the State Council 1996). In addition to health and nutrition, this document stresses increasing school enrollment, including preschool education and education for disabled children, and child immunizations. Breastfeeding is supported on a national level with the involvement of the Ministry of Health as part of China's efforts to respond to UNICEF's worldwide Baby-Friendly Hospital Initiative program. More about breastfeeding promotion can be read in Chapter 7 of this volume.

Another important policy decision resulted in "The Outline of Chinese Food Structural Reform and Development in the 1990s" (Wang Xiangrong 1993). This decision was promulgated in June 1993 by the State Council with the collaboration of the State Planning Commission, and the Ministries of Finance, Agriculture, Water Resources, and Internal Trade. This policy recognizes urban/rural and regional disparities and the need for promotion and education. It is one of the few nutritional policies in any developing country to be coordinated with agricultural policy, and to incorporate a preventive approach to disease.

In response to the 1992 International Conference on Nutrition in Rome, the "National Plan of Action on Improving the Nutritional Status of the Chinese Population in the 1990s" was drawn up. Among the major goals for the year 2000 set by the Chinese government in the plan are several for the protection of preschool children. They include: (1) reducing severe malnutrition by 50 percent; (2) eradicating vitamin A deficiency, (3) reducing by one-third the prevalence of iron deficiency anemia, and (4) eliminating iodine deficiencies. The plan calls for increasing the rate of exclusive breastfeeding in four- to six-month-old infants to 40 percent and the overall rate of breastfeeding combined with other feeding methods to 80 percent (Chen Junshi 1996).

Conclusion: China at a Crossroads

The spread of obesity in the world and its attendant serious health consequences raise difficult health policy questions for many countries. For developing countries such as China, with a large under-nutrition problem, energy intake for the rural infants should be raised while energy and fat intake for some members of the smaller overnourished urban group should be kept low or perhaps lowered. China must therefore formulate policies to tackle its immensely challenging "double burden" of both over- and under-nutrition among its children in such a way that messages intended for one group do not increase risk for the other. What will the roles of the private and public sectors be in promoting the healthy development of the country's "little emperors"? To what degree will the new policies and institutions help control obesity among mostly urban children and simultaneously narrow the urban/rural growth gap? It is too soon to tell. National policies in China, as in other countries, are often driven by political and economic factors, not simply health goals. Future child growth surveys will provide a test of the effectiveness of current food and health policies.

My experience in China as a nutritionist and researcher has convinced me that at this stage in the country's development, widespread community-based public health nutritional measures could be crucial, not only in coping with the unintended and recently recognized health effects of dietary changes that have accompanied the country's new affluence but also in overcoming the older nutrition problems linked to its residual poverty. Well-planned and executed measures would help blunt the emerging diseases of affluence in the cities. In addition, if parents, teachers, journalists, school authorities, caterers, health officials, and the food industry worked together, much could also be done to solve the problems of undernutrition in the countryside, as well as of overnutrition in both rural and urban areas. China holds many surprises for its watchers, and I have learned not to try to predict new developments. Nevertheless, broad-based improvements in the nutrition of China's vast numbers of children would be welcomed and ultimately contribute much toward healthy human development.

2

Eating Snacks, Biting Pressure:

Only Children in Beijing

Bernadine W. L. Chee

> *It is true that these days a single child [in China] enjoys bet-*
> *ter food and clothing. . . . However, the popular notion of the*
> *4-2-1 [grandparents, parents, and only child] syndrome pro-*
> *vides only a one-sided view of overindulgence in affection and*
> *care. What we saw in the single-child family is another un-*
> *reported aspect. . . . We saw parents constantly attempting to*
> *control, monitor, and correct their child's behavior.*
>
> — *David Wu 1996:16*

In recent years, scholars have brought attention to the pressures and strains in the lives of children born under the one-child policy of the People's Republic of China (PRC). The image portrayed is that of children leading highly regimented lives under the rigid, controlling influence of parents. This presents an opposing picture to earlier reports in the PRC and foreign media of Chinese parents' indulgence of happy, carefree single children (see, e.g., R. Baker 1987). These two views appear contrary, showing both marked pleasure and pressure in the world of China's only children. How can such opposing views be reconciled? How can this paradox be explained?

Whereas single children may be very common in other nations, such as Estonia, the drastic fertility decline (see Kristof 1993) under the one-child policy has led many only children in China to occupying a central and special position in family life (Xue 1995). In urban areas of China, where they form a majority among children, single children experience extraordinary peer relations when compared with only children of other places and times.

The impact of China's one-child policy has been the subject of important previous research (e.g., Kaufman 1983; Greenhalgh 1990). The finding that single children and multiple-sibling children actually have not demonstrated significant psychological differences in China, for example, dispels previous assumptions about the country's only children (Falbo et al. 1996:270, 280). David Wu and others have demonstrated instead that statistically significant psychological and behavioral differences correlate with rural/urban residence, preschool attendance, and parental backgrounds of children born after 1979 in China (D. Wu 1996:5–12; Falbo et al. 1996). A 1991 survey of 500 parents of Shanghai preschoolers demonstrates that even though single children were "centers" of families in the home, they received no special treatment at school (Xue 1995:8).

Taking an alternative approach to these and other studies of China's children born under the one-child policy, I undertook an interview project in 1995, in collaboration with Guo Yuhua of the Chinese Academy of Social Sciences, to utilize the subject of food as a primary investigatory tool to understand childhood experiences and family relations in urban Beijing. Our decision to conduct interviews centered on food topics was informed by anthropological studies demonstrating that commodities such as food are "a nonverbal medium for the human creative faculty" (Douglas and Isherwood 1979:62). Food consumption[1] in particular has been shown to serve as a symbol or a code (Mennell et al. 1992), describing certain human relationships, such as inclusion and exclusion (Powdermaker 1932:236; Simoons 1961:121; Ohnuki-Tierney 1993), high and low (Goody 1982; J. Watson 1987), and intimacy and distance (Douglas 1975:249–75). Eating may also tell us about ourselves, for, as Sidney Mintz has observed, eating is "a rutted habituation" that is "so close to the core of our memories, to the formation of our character and the launching of our conscious experience, that its substances may be said to become a part of us" (1993:262).

In our 1995 study, we assumed that the process of deciding which foods to eat, who will eat them, and how much to eat would also become a rutted habituation along with the fact of eating.[2] Analyzing these negotiations about food consumption would, we anticipated, provide a vital perspective on the pleasures and pressures of children born under the one-child policy.[3] After the interview project, my study of Chinese children's food consumption continued at a Beijing restaurant, which served as one of the sites of my long-term field research in the Chinese capital. Observations at this restaurant and conversations with clients and restaurant workers helped me better understand the material I had collected through the interview project.

Description of Interview Project and Basic Findings

To test our assumptions, we interviewed children from two Beijing primary schools and their parents in June and July of 1995. In the Haidian district of northwest Beijing, we selected ten children from the second through fifth grades (eight to eleven years old) and their parents, many of whom were intellectuals — not unusual in a district in which universities and research institutions are concentrated. In the Chongwen district of southeast Beijing, we contacted ten second-grade children (eight years old) and ten fifth-grade children (eleven years old), as well as their parents, who worked in factories, offices, and other workplaces. At the Chongwen district school, we specifically asked teachers to help us select interview candidates who achieved a variety of academic grades and who came from high-, middle-, and low-income families.[4]

In our household interviews, lasting from one and one-half to two hours, we asked students and parents about what they usually ate for breakfast, lunch, dinner, and at other times.[5] This inquiry was aimed at understanding their "food cycles" (J. Thomas 1994). We also invited discussion of topics not anticipated by our questionnaire, treating the subject of food and eating as a conversation stencil that the interviewees could cut as they saw fit.

Since the material and experiential pleasures enjoyed by some only children have already been well documented and are confirmed here by children's descriptions of the types and variety of foods they consume, I shall focus in this chapter on the pressures in children's lives both in and outside of school. In an attempt to explain the paradox of pleasure and pressure, and, in particular, the high degree of pressure felt by the children we interviewed, my analysis will concentrate on four girls and six boys from the class of fifth-graders at the Chongwen district school. These eleven-year-olds were more articulate than their eight-year-old schoolmates. In addition, they were from the same class under the same teacher, unlike the children we interviewed from the Haidian district school.

The data we collected from the school in the Haidian district support the essence of my analysis.[6] Moreover, this discussion draws on my own fieldwork at a Beijing restaurant in 1996–97, when I had ample opportunities to observe how adults and children decided on what dishes and drinks to order.

Our findings indicate that inter-single-child relations deserve further investigation. Many studies have looked at single children in China *vis-à-vis* parents, teachers, non-single children in China, and in relation to single children in other parts of the world. Few, if any, investigations have considered China's only children in comparison and in conjunction with each other. This perspective revealed substantial social pressure among some of the only children we interviewed. Perhaps because our study focuses so closely on the content of the interviews themselves rather than on general statistical analysis, we were particularly able to comprehend and analyze the personal factors behind the social pressures experienced in the daily lives of these children.

My analysis reveals that interlocking forces of kinship and history play a vital role in shaping the dynamics between parents and only children, contributing to stress among the children we interviewed in Beijing. Another approach to our interview material from Beijing is offered by Guo Yuhua in Chapter 4 of this volume. Her chapter combines our interviews of the 30 children in Beijing with fieldwork findings from a rural community in Jiangsu province, focusing on sociological issues of learning and knowledge production.

Although my chapter addresses urban children, I am also mindful of their rural counterparts. While the one-child policy makes exceptions for ethnic minorities and for urban couples who are themselves single children, for example (Feeny 1989), its most striking characteristic is that in rural areas, where the majority of China's population resides, couples are allowed a second child in instances when having only one child (in many cases, a girl) would cause economic hardship. We can assume that during periods when the policy was less well enforced, higher percentages of second births and even higher-order births in rural areas would have resulted (Huang Shu-min et al. 1996). A rural-urban disparity further indicating the limits of my analysis here is that mortality rates and incidence of severe malnutrition are far higher in rural areas, whereas in urban areas of China, rapidly rising rates of obesity in children concern nutritionists (G. Baker 1998; Turner 1996). Therefore my chapter should be read in the context of disparate rural-urban life chances in the PRC.

Severe Peer Pressure Up Close

The ten Beijing schoolchildren whose personal narratives are examined here cannot be neatly classified as "spoiled children," nor can their parents be simply considered to be "overindulgent adults." For example, although Sun Xuan (Lofty)[7] refused to eat most vegetables, neither did he pester his parents with requests for expensive food products as some of his classmates did. Zhao Zhigang (Resolute) sometimes purchased popsicles "on the sly," yet he followed his parents' relatively conservative habit of eating few snacks at home. Meanwhile, the mother of Shen Li (Lee), who expressed consternation at her son's refusal to eat vegetables, showed little concern about either the quantity or the quality of the snack foods he ate.

Given the subtle variations in children's attitudes toward food consumption, there were striking similarities in accounts by four children of heavy pressure from classmates to consume certain foods. In particular, we observed that harsh peer pressure strongly influenced children's consumption of *xiaochi*, or "snacks."

To describe comparative and evaluative behaviors that play a large role in peer pressure, people in China commonly use the term *panbi*. Its first part, *pan*, means "to climb," as of a person climbing up a rope or a wall (Wu Guanghua, ed., 1993:1879). However, *pan* also describes climbing in a social sense. For example, *gao pan*, or "to climb high," means to "make friends or claim ties of kinship with someone of a higher social position" (1993:1879). The second part of this interesting term, *bi*, has the double meaning of "competition" and "comparison." In brief, *panbi* means "climbing and comparing." This term is well understood by students at the higher levels of primary schools to refer to advancing oneself by competing and comparing with other people.

In our interviews, *panbi* was manifested in children's choosing to eat trendy foods as a symbol of prestige, material wealth, and personal happiness. Moreover, participating in faddish, commercialized snack consumption often had a decisive influence on social positioning. An articulate girl, Zhang Yue (Moon), told us:

> Once a classmate brought a package of New Continent ice cream to school. I said, "I have not seen this kind before." She said that the [commercial] market had been selling them for a long time; New Continent was the most famous — how could I not know? After school I went and bought one. It was winter, and although it tasted good, I was so cold that my teeth were sore.

Zhang Yue was clearly motivated by a cutting comment from her classmate to purchase a particular food product. She explained,

"Whenever there is a new product that I have not tried before, I buy it immediately. I have to try new things. Otherwise, when classmates are chatting, if everyone has tried something and you have not tried it, then you have nothing to say." Thus for Zhang Yue, purchasing and consuming trendy foods had a decisive impact on social inclusion and exclusion. Her classmates shared the same kind of sentiment, revealing the severity of the *panbi* problem. Take Gao Tianjun (Handsome), for example. His parents earned less than 1,000 yuan (less than US$120) per month, and so, they said, their money was exhausted monthly. Nevertheless, they placed a strong emphasis on education and spent 320 yuan (US$38) annually on his calligraphy lessons. They explained that Gao Tianjun was not picky about eating. Whenever they asked him what he wanted to eat for dinner, he would usually respond, "I'll eat whatever there is" (*you shenme, chi shenme*). However, even this child felt pressure from his classmates to consume trendy foods. His father told a story to illustrate, prefaced by a request that the interviewers should not laugh at them.

One day while on an outing, Gao Tianjun asked his father for Wall's ice cream.[8] His father said to the interviewers: "I thought, if the child wants it, then I will buy it for him. [But] as soon as I saw how expensive it was for one, 3.50 yuan (US$.42), I said, "You sure know how to choose [*ni zhen hui tiao*]." Unexpectedly, the child really wanted it. "So, I bought it for him." At that time, continued the father, his son explained that once when he was at school, his classmates had asked him, "Gao Tianjun, have you tried Wall's?" He had told the classmates that he had tried it. The classmates then asked him, "How did it taste?" He had replied that it tasted very good.

Gao Tianjun's father remarked: "Actually, the child had never tried it before. He gave a response that was not in accord with his heart (*jiangle weixin hua*), afraid that others would laugh at him. In light of this, I had to buy it for the child to taste." The father disclosed that this event had made him feel uneasy. As the father told this story, the interviewers observed that Gao Tianjun's eyes brimmed with tears.

Why did a child like Gao Tianjun or Zhang Yue find the questions from classmates about trendy snack consumption to be so unpalatable, responding to inquiries as if they were latent threats? A discussion by Wu Qiang (Strong) provided us with a likely explanation. When we asked him about sharing food during field trips, he observed that "classmates share when they eat together. [But] there are some who eat on their own. There is one classmate who others say is from the countryside. [We] often hit him (*lao da ta*)." Thus, the social stigma attached to rural origins pushed one of the students beyond the margins of social acceptability. Classmates punctuated his exclusion with violence. Gao Tianjun's "not speaking in accord with his heart" no doubt stemmed from a desire to avoid this and other penalties for the ostracized.

Like Gao Tianjun, classmate Shen Li (Lee) achieved inclusion through conspicuous consumption and food distribution despite the fact that his father was in prison. In addition to owning many toys and having a large allowance, Shen Li often bought different things to eat. His classmates would ask him if he wanted what he had bought. He would taste it, and if he did not like it, he would give it to his classmates. "Because I often give them something to eat," Shen Li explained, "they will also give something to me when they have it." Thus, as a center of networks of exchanges in food, Shen Li earned a secure place among classmates, effectively negating the social impact of his family background.

Discussion

Examining children's interactions close up revealed the *severity* of the peer pressure they felt to act or to say certain things. However, was it purely the threats of violence and derision by classmates that caused these children to so desperately seek approval?

To answer this question, I suggest the following ideas. First, nine of the ten children examined here are only children: Zhang Yue has a younger brother who returned home from preschool just once a week. For those children without sisters and brothers, the possibility for developing a network of prescribed sibling relations would at once be removed. Unless cousins lived nearby, a single child could only choose from her or his classmates to be close companions, protectors, and sources of pooling resources.

While the lack of siblings can be a problem for single children elsewhere in the world, I suggest that its impact may be greater in the urban areas of China, where the majority of children are only children. That is, if a child in a class with a majority of single children seeks friends from within that class, she or he would encounter much competition to secure companionship.

At another level, the benefit of peer social relations to help assuage the loneliness of only children also explains why children prize inclusion. For example, the mother of Wang Yanru (Like a Swallow) mentioned to us that her daughter had been looking forward to our interview, just because it would give the girl some companionship for a Saturday during summer vacation. Her mother, a government researcher, commented that the childhood experience of her daughter's generation was far lonelier than that of her own, when children had fewer homework demands and more siblings to play together.

The competition for peer ties would be further intensified if children knew — or if parents told them — the importance of personal relationships in China. Mayfair Yang (1994) has demonstrated that *guanxi*, or "personal relationships," are important to social mobility in urban Beijing. Skill at developing *guanxi* may be encouraged at a young age. For example, the father of a fourth-grader with whom I was familiar in Beijing in 1997 remarked with a knowing look that although his son did not have high marks at school, the boy "had very many friends."

Another explanation of why these students engaged so heatedly in comparisons with classmates is that doing so serves the process of self-understanding. As psychologists have observed, "The peer group helps the child develop a concept of himself. The ways in which peers react to the child and the bases upon which he is accepted or rejected give him a clearer, and perhaps more realistic, picture of his assets and liabilities" (Mussen et al. 1974:515; see also Birch 1980:489–96). Without siblings at home, single children probably rely more heavily on responses from classmates in order to gain insight into themselves.

In areas such as Beijing where single children compose the majority of children born since 1979, such a motivation explains in part the high frequency of the question "have you tried (name brand) snack?" among children whom we interviewed. In addition, it helps to explain why *panbi* is so prevalent in the single child generation. The intense competition between this sizable proportion of single children no doubt influences non-single children, too, as is suggested by the testimony of Zhang Yue.

Compromise and Acquiescence by Parents and Grandparents

The parents of the ten students I describe in this chapter took different approaches to negotiating their children's diets. One approach followed by the parents of seven of the ten children was to ask the child what she or he wanted to eat; some parents considered their child's eating preferences to be the most important factor in arranging dinner.

Gao Tianjun's parents in particular saw the food their son ate as a reflection of the family's improved financial situation and as a special way of showing him their love. His father observed that in the past, Hebei province, from which he and his wife originated, was poor. He and his wife grew up eating simply prepared foods without using much cooking oil, such as is required when stir-frying or deep-frying. "Now life is much better," said Gao Tianjun's father. His wife added, "Now for the child we are much more particular; we also stir-fry."

Other parents also catered to their children, thinking it would improve their diet or appetite. For example, Wang Yanru's mother remarked that she herself was raised with the lighter taste of Cantonese cuisine and did not care for the heavily flavored food that her daughter liked. The mother explained, "But then I think that she is younger. If she does not like this thing, then she will just not eat it or will eat less of it." Wang Yanru's mother and her father consequently "yielded" (*qianjiu*) to their child's tastes.

Some parents, however, met with obstacles in negotiating with their children over meals. For example, Sun Xuan's parents had been unable to convince their son to eat vegetables with the exception of string beans since early childhood. Shen Li refused the pleas of his mother to eat vegetables, except for tomatoes stir-fried with eggs. Most revealing of the modes through which children overcame parental disapproval, however, were descriptions of how children like Zhang Yue obtained pocket money for snacks.

Zhang Yue was largely able to deflect her mother's control over her eating of instant noodles, a snack (*xiaochi*) in China, through the pocket money provided by her father. Her father worked in a bank, while her mother was a nurse. Her parents did not go to restaurants often because the very good ones were "too expensive." Zhang Yue's mother wanted to moderate her daughter's high consumption of instant noodles. However, she said her husband would "indulge" his daughter, giving her four or five yuan (US$.48–$.60) in spending money. The girl's mother remarked, "I do not approve of her eating those things. But she will buy them when she is out, and there is nothing I can do about it." Zhang Yue's parents thus disagreed between themselves, and the parent favoring consumption managed to overcome the protests of the other parent.

The story of her classmate Wu Qiang's strategy of manipulating guardians is also revealing. His mother and father, employed at an inn and a wholesale store, respectively, went out to eat at least once a month — more often than most of the other families in this class whom we interviewed. His mother attempted to guide her child's eating. Wu Qiang explained, "In the vicinity of the school, there are some stalls at which classmates buy things. Mother said that people's hands were really dirty; [and] she would not let me buy unclean things."

Undaunted, Wu Qiang campaigned for pocket money. He told

his mother, "All of my classmates have pocket money. Some class-mates have 10 *kuai* [10 yuan] a week." Our interviews showed that six of the ten fifth-graders mentioned receiving pocket money from their parents, and four of them received it regularly. The amount ranged from two yuan (US$.24) a week to two to five yuan (US$.24 to $.60) a day, which the children used to purchase snacks, breakfasts, toys, or books.

Wu Qiang's mother said she did not give him spending money at first. However, she observed that his classmates "all had money to spend, and he would not ask us; he asked his paternal grand-mother. [His] grandmother then told this to us. I only give him two *kuai* a day."

The tacit pressure on Wu Qiang's mother by her mother-in-law resulted in the boy's buying the very snacks that his mother told him he should not purchase: "I usually do not allow him to buy things from the stalls," his mother said, "but sometimes he buys them secretly. If you are not around them, there is no way you can control them." Thus, the experience of Wu Qiang and Zhang Yue shows that children turned to their parents and grandparents to relieve the pressure from classmates to consume snacks; eventually, a parent acquiesced and permitted the child's consumption of the desired food.

Food, Parents, and Children

Reflecting on the kinship identification of parents, and, in some cases, grandparents, we can see why they would comply with chil-dren's requests. Elders' identities as parents and grandparents are much more intense with respect to an only child than with multiple children and grandchildren, a common situation in recent memory. Consider, for example, two grandparents. Under Confucian tradi-tion and China's pro-procreation policies of the 1950s, they might have had three children and nine grandchildren. These grandpar-ents would have divided their attention and resources among nine grandchildren.

Now imagine a second scenario in which the grandparents had three children, but, because of the one-child policy implemented in the 1980s, they wound up with only three grandchildren. That is, instead of the nine grandchildren they might have imagined having for most of their lives, they had only three grandchildren to provide them the identity of "grandparents." The grandparents might have been more inclined to yield to these three grandchildren than to the nine grandchildren in the earlier scenario.

A parent's bond with his or her child may be even more intense. In the earlier scenario, they might have had three children. Under the population controls in effect since the 1980s, however, they would have been restricted to one child who would offer them their only opportunity to realize the kinship identity of "parent." This child's success and happiness would have been the sole gauge of their parenting responsibilities, hopes, and efforts.

Such potent elder/child bonds, when viewed from the perspective of older generations accustomed to multiple children, imply that single children in China wield surprising power. With this understanding of the interface of kinship identity and history, we would expect that an only child can persuade one of six parents and grandparents to grant the child's wish to consume. Moreover, we can see that the dynamics of "4-2-1" grandparent-parent-child ratios mentioned in the PRC press are even more in the child's favor than the numbers alone can indicate.

We also need to view these parental compromises from the perspective of the historical experiences of single children's parents. Having grown up during the Cultural Revolution (1966–76), these parents react to what James McNeal, professor of marketing at Texas A&M University, calls "compensation syndrome," meaning that they are determined to provide their children with the material wealth they lacked when they were growing up under Mao (Crowell and Hsieh 1995:47; see also McNeal and Yeh 1997:45–57). Since the "Socialist Market" economic reforms were put in place in the 1980s, parents have more disposable income to spend on their children than did most parents of the recent past in China (Crowell and Hsieh 1995). Aggravating this situation, observes marketing researcher James Chadwick, is that many children in this generation can be "cleverer" than their parents, who grew up during the chaotic Cultural Revolution, and, consequently, can manipulate them (Chadwick 1996).[9]

Although this discussion largely concerns parents in relation to only children, the crucial issue may not be the fact of having only one child, but rather of having fewer children due to the one-child policy than one wanted and of having more resources under the Socialist Market Economy to bestow on them. Thus, the explanations above may also apply to families having two children, a common situation in smaller cities with fewer mechanisms of control and in rural areas, where the government allows for a second child to avert economic hardship (Greenhalgh 1990; Huang Shu-min et al. 1996:367).

An Alternative Approach: Unified Parental Control

The discussion above highlights the social forces and individual motivations informing child requests and parental acquiescence regarding food consumption in seven of the ten families. In this section, I will examine the three families in which parents were unified in restricting their children's food consumption. This analysis reveals how and why parents succeeded in encouraging their children to comply with their guidelines in a social climate permeated with *panbi* peer pressure.

In the first of the three families, the mother of Chen Ji (Beauty) was an accountant, and her father worked at the Great Hall of the People, where important Communist Party conferences are held and foreign dignitaries entertained. Both of Chen Ji's parents had a high school education. Her mother paid close attention to her daughter's diet, taking pains to provide a variety of fish in addition to northern "home-style" dishes. Particularly worthy of note was that on Sundays, Chen Ji's parents would take her to the store and occasionally buy a small portion of new food products for Chen Ji to sample. Nevertheless, she did not especially care for snacks, and she was not picky.

In the second family, the parents of Lu Tianhua (Flower) both worked at secondary schools. Her mother was very attentive to nutrition, and she kept tight reins on her daughter's eating. Both parents restricted her consumption of chocolate because they said it could lead to excessive internal heat (a traditional Chinese medicinal concept) and obesity, and could affect her appetite.[10] As for ice cream, her mother noted that they had "restrained her since she was small." Her parents also remarked that they did not permit her to ask her paternal grandparents for money.

The third family lived in a single room with a black-and-white television set, exceptional in Beijing where color television sets had been the norm for nearly a decade. When we asked the son, Zhou Rong (Glorious), about his ice cream consumption, he said that he did not even want to try Wall's ice cream. His parents praised his behavior, saying that he really "understood things" (*dongshi*) and could forgive his parents' economic difficulties.

Academic Performance and Dietary Discipline

Interestingly, the parents in each of these families expressed a marked and, one might even say, fervent concern for their child's education and future prospects. Chen Ji's mother remarked that she had tried her best to meet her daughter's educational needs. If her child required something for study, even if it were expensive, she would buy it. Lu Tianhua's parents echoed Chen Ji's mother, adding that if something was not necessary for their daughter's education, they would not purchase it, even if it was inexpensive. Meanwhile, Zhou Rong's parents said that their own level of education was not high since they had not attended college, and they "especially wanted" their child to go to a university. Although some of the parents in the other seven families also placed a strong emphasis on their children's education, they did not express these sentiments so articulately.

More important, perhaps, in each of these families with strong parental control over their children's eating, the parents were unified in their approach. They treated food as a special means of education in issues of health and discipline. In Chen Ji's case, her mother took an active role in determining her daughter's diet, choosing not only to control her eating habits but to augment her daughter's culinary and nutritional knowledge. This effort served as a defense mechanism against competition from classmates on questions of food consumption, such as those faced by Zhang Yue and Gao Tianjun. In the second family described above, Lu Tianhua's parents kept a firm grasp over their child's diet in ways that most of the other parents had not, such as by controlling her popsicle consumption since early childhood, and by forbidding her to ask her grandparents for money — an act that reinforced her parents' authority. Finally, Zhou Rong's parents demonstrated the importance of thrift through their actions in everyday life, and they made a special point of praising their son's maturity in not being attracted to luxury food items.

These parents treated eating as a matter of education. Some of the factors contributing to leniency toward children's food consumption in the seven families discussed earlier were thus obviated in these three examples of parents who approached eating more as a matter of training than of gratification. Facing resolute and unified elders, these three children neither voiced protest nor put up resistance; instead, they "understood things" and subordinated themselves to their parents.

Behind the Pleasure-Pressure Paradox

In this section, I shall demonstrate that kinship identity and the impact of major policy changes by the PRC government not only influenced parental acquiescence in the area of food consumption but also parental pressure on children to produce academically. That is, the very elements contributing to material pleasure for these single children, for instance in snack consumption, caused these children to suffer pressure in school. I assume in this discussion that from the children's perspectives, homework and educational demands were equivalent to work (as opposed to recreation), and that their school performance and promotion to better schools would ultimately bear upon their employment prospects.

David Wu has documented the heavy intellectual demands placed by some parents on young children of only four, five, and six years of age (1996:16–19). Older children, however, can face even greater challenges. One thirteen-year-old Beijing girl who passed the entrance exam in 1995 for a middle school attached to the People's University in Beijing remarked afterward, "I was really tired last year and fully resigned to go off to the Balkans to die" (Crowell and Hsieh 1995:50). Her mother, on the other hand, was ecstatic, exclaiming, "The kid did good." Another girl, aged twelve, declared, "My friends and I all feel that our parents don't care enough about us. They are only concerned about how well we do in school" (1995:47). Wu attributes the demands placed on these single children to an intense form of child socialization, or *guan*, the traditional Chinese concept of "governing, monitoring, interfering, and controlling" (D. Wu 1996:13).

An example of this heavy academic pressure was provided by a child and her mother we interviewed. They felt especially free to communicate with us because, coincidentally, we had a mutual acquaintance. We asked them to describe the girl's typical school day, and they responded by discussing at length the difficult workload faced by children at the fifth-grade level. The mother explained that her daughter, though tired at times, was better off than some of her classmates, who on occasion stayed up until eleven or twelve at night to finish homework. She observed, "Parents know that competition is fierce now. Sometimes if [a child] misses one point — just half a point, then the difference is tremendous: some will go to better schools, and some will not be able to attend good schools." What lay behind this statement was, of course, that children who attended good secondary schools would have better opportunities to attend the university and ultimately to secure desirable jobs, since in China a high premium is placed on educational achievement as a qualification for jobs.

I would like to suggest that if most of the parents of the children in the class we interviewed had only one child and concentrated their financial and personal resources on that one child's education, then a class of such children would face tremendous competition in academic testing, even greater than there would have been if the class had been dominated by multiple-sibling children. Consider from the perspective of kinship identity that instead of three possibilities of having a well-educated child in the family, parents had only one. Rather than diffusing their emphasis on education over three children, they would concentrate on just one. A study conducted in Shanghai shows that single children do indeed experience greater pressure from parents than multiple-sibling children do (Xue 1995:7).

From the perspective of political history, if the compensation syndrome for parents who experienced the Cultural Revolution resulted in their being materially generous to their children, it might also cause them to be demanding toward their children, who are enjoying better schooling conditions than they knew in their youth. For example, an accountant, with whom I was well acquainted in Beijing during 1997 and who had been a Red Guard during the Cultural Revolution, encouraged her daughter one afternoon to study harder by saying, "If I had had the educational opportunity when I was young that you have now, where do you think I would be today?" Although many parents around the world could make the same statement, it carries special weight in China, where the turmoil in the educational system during the late 1960s and 1970s is said to have contributed to a "lost generation."

Furthermore, as I shall discuss in greater detail below, just as businesses focused on child-parent relations to improve sales, so too did this fifth-grade class's teacher apply pressure to child-parent ties in order to encourage children to produce during the Socialist Market Economy era. Although surely the motivations of most teachers are selfless with regard to urging students to achieve, one mother suspected ulterior motives in some of the teachers she knew. She expressed her opinion that teacher salary increases were based on student test scores. Consequently, teachers placed high demands on children to excel and parents to help. At parent-teacher meetings, some teachers would give extra homework exceeding the guidelines set by the Ministry of Education[11] and tell the parents, "I am doing this for the sake of your children." Parents, wanting their children to advance academically, accepted the obligation to supervise homework assignments and did not protest against what they actually perceived to be heavy burdens for young children.

Thus, parents sought to provide their children both with material satisfaction in the present and educational advancement for secure futures. The conditions informing these parents' dual goals could be found in their kinship identity and politico-historical experiences of growing up during the Cultural Revolution (1966–76), becoming parents under the one-child policy from 1979 to the present, and earning more disposable income under the Socialist Market Economy policies during the 1980s and 1990s. As a consequence, single children sometimes found themselves in head-to-head competition with each other, facing high stakes both in teacher-administered academic tests and in peer *panbi* contests. In this way, material pleasures for these children were often paradoxically linked to social and academic pressures.

Conclusion: The Vulnerability of Single Children

Underlying the intense competition for prestige among the ten Beijing classmates in matters of snack consumption and also academic production were the combined influences of history and kinship that children and their parents experienced. Furthermore, the high degree of pressure felt by some of the children we interviewed supports the idea that pitting an only child against other only children places her or him into an unusually uncomfortable position. Indeed, the personal cost for an only child to improve her or his standing *vis-à-vis* the others rises every time a new, faddish snack is purchased and a higher test score achieved, thereby increasing the stakes for consumption and the sacrifices for production.

In our interviews with the ten fifth-graders, we saw clear evidence of advertising's strong influence on children's snack purchases. Advertising methods included colorful packaging, television commercials, collect-and-win promotions, and games. During the summers of 1994 and 1995, the streets of Beijing and other major cities were cluttered with brightly colored mobile stands of Wall's, New Continent, Meadow Gold, and a plenitude of other brands of ice cream appealing particularly to children. KFC, McDonald's, Shanghai Ronghua Chicken, and many other fast-food restaurants displayed large banners that celebrated the end of the children's academic year with the offer of gifts (for a minimum purchase).

From the perspective of marketers, children are more than just a single market (Stipp 1988; McNeal 1992). McNeal and Chyon-Hwa Yeh, senior statistician at the Procter and Gamble Company, have observed that children around the world constitute an enormous market potential, not just as one market but as three: as a current market spending its own money, as an influence market determining parental spending, and as a future market that will eventually become "a firm's total customers" (1997:45). Such an approach toward children is common in today's multinational corporations. McDonald's, for example, which already has 38 restaurants in Beijing alone (Advertiser News Services 1997:A2), was recently found in the High Court of the United Kingdom to have designed advertisements that were "in large part directed at children with a view to them pressuring or pestering their parents to take them to McDonald's" (Hobson 1997). Such marketing practices aim to cultivate a desire in children to consume a product which they can obtain only through the financial assistance of their parents.[12]

On the basis of our study in Beijing, it can be argued that targeting children as consumers creates and sustains disjunctures in the parent-child bond whose repair lies in consumption. Given the birth limits the PRC government has imposed on urban couples, encouraging children to become active and competitive consumers holds great promise for the sale of consumer goods in China. A study of 1,496 children in kindergarten through the fifth grade of Beijing and Tianjin, for example, confirms that China's urban children's "average influence on family purchases substantially exceeds that of US children and probably exceeds that of children anywhere in the world" (McNeal and Yeh 1997:56).

The unusual influence of only children over family purchases and the sheer numbers, with over 65 million single-child families in China, explain the determined convergence of transnational corporations on the Chinese market. James Chadwick, the director of strategic development for the advertising firm Grey Hong Kong and Grey China, for example, conducted a five-month survey of Chinese children in 1996. Why did he conduct such an extensive study? He explained: "Obviously everybody's interested in Chinese kids at the moment. Western marketers are particularly interested in them because they have a whole range of global brands which have worked in other parts of the world, and they are interested to bring [these] to China" (Chadwick 1996). The business community's view of Chinese children as a huge market for global brands has already affected and will continue to affect the fierce competition between children by providing ever more novel items designed to attract them.

The intense pressure felt by children in consumption and achievement discussed in this chapter brings to mind Emile Durkheim's assertion that rising prosperity may cause mental suffering of greater severity than that occurring during times of poverty. Durkheim sought to account for the rise in suicides during periods of rapid economic expansion in Prussia and Italy during the mid- and late nineteenth century. He reasoned that poverty serves as a restraint on aspirations because "actual possessions are part of the criterion aspired to" (1951:254). On the other hand, during periods of economic expansion, the "limits are unknown between the possible and the impossible. . . . Consequently, there is no restraint upon aspirations" (1951:253). Among the children with whom we spoke in Beijing, aspirations to realize material happiness and to gain social inclusion were strongly encouraged by the climate of competition between companies that aimed to sell trendy snack foods and other goods to children. As a result, children feel anxiety and tension in relations with both peers and parents. When the children studied here become young adults, pressures on them to consume will likely become even greater as business groups continue to whet the appetites of people in China.

My last point concerns the physical health of children in China, the subject of Georgia Guldan's Chapter 1 of this volume, which I have examined here in relation to snacking behavior. Inattention to snacking behavior may put a generation of China's children at risk, as exemplified by the condition of children raised in Hong Kong under British rule. A 1996 report revealed that Hong Kong children had the world's second-highest cholesterol rates, after Finland (Mathewson 1996). Such a finding is not surprising, since another poll of 2,760 Hong Kong students revealed that potato chips, sweets, ice cream, French fries, and other deep-fried foods topped the list of their favorite foods (*Xinhua*, Feb. 19, 1997).

Studies in the PRC have already cited rising obesity as a problem among children. For example, a report sponsored by the Ministry of Public Health and other PRC government organs found that up to 12.03 percent of the male student population in urban areas were obese during a 1995 survey (Ye and Feng 1996). Nutritionists in the United States emphasize that in tackling the problem of obesity, "snacking behaviors are a key area of concern" (Kennedy and Goldberg 1995:122). Since overweight children are significantly more likely to have medical problems in adulthood, such as heart disease and diabetes (see Turner 1996; Kennedy and Goldberg 1995:122), the impact of snack consumption deserves further study.

The current lack of nutritional education in China's schools poses a serious threat when we consider the impact of marketing strategies for snacks and foods that are specifically aimed at the country's most vulnerable people, its children. In supplementary interviews I conducted in Beijing, for example, neighborhood shopkeepers uniformly volunteered the notion that snacks "are harmless to children." Meanwhile, children and parents told us that they did not receive instruction in nutrition through the schools, and two parents who worked as teachers at a primary school even asked us for basic guidelines in child nutrition.[13] Rising obesity and other health problems of children in China indicate that we should be gravely concerned about the social motivations behind their eating behaviors.

3

Children's Food and Islamic Dietary
Restrictions in Xi'an

Maris Boyd Gillette

One warm spring afternoon in 1995, I rode my
bicycle over to Aifeng's house, as I did several times a week during
the eighteen months I stayed in Xi'an.[1] Aifeng had plans to visit a
wholesale market, and asked me to accompany her. With an extra
hand to carry packages, she would be able to buy more of the items
her family needed. I had gone shopping with Aifeng many times,
but in the past we had stayed in the Muslim district, where Aifeng
lived. Just behind her house was a small street market where ten to
twelve farmers from the nearby countryside gathered daily to sell
fruit and vegetables. This time, however, we rode our bicycles for
ten minutes outside of the Muslim district until we reached a busy
wholesale market just east of the Xi'an city wall.

The market was a large, concrete-paved lot studded with several
roofed, wall-less edifices and encircled by small shops. In the stores,
under the covered areas, and out in the open, several dozen vendors
displayed boxes and bags of packaged food, soap, paper products,
and other factory-produced goods. Aifeng had clearly visited the
market many times before; she knew exactly where to buy the
cheapest bulk toilet paper and laundry detergent. I helped her load
the household goods she bought onto our bicycles and then followed her toward the food vendors.

Although the offerings were plentiful, Aifeng bought only two
types of food. She meticulously checked through the many brands
of factory-produced, individually packaged instant noodles (*fang-*

bian mian) for sale until she finally found a large box labeled *qingzhen*, or "pure and true." The term *qingzhen* possesses many meanings in China, but it most frequently refers to food that meets Islamic standards for dietary purity.[2] Like the vast majority of the Muslim district's residents, Aifeng kept a *qingzhen* diet. Aifeng also purchased some packaged snacks for her granddaughter, a one-and-a-half-year-old girl who, along with her father (Aifeng's son) and mother, lived in the upper two floors of Aifeng's house. A vast array of mass-produced, packaged snacks, including candied nuts, puffed rice, chocolates, crisps, biscuits, and hard candies, were for sale at the market. Aifeng purchased enough of these foods to fill two large bags. Later, when we returned to her house, she immediately gave some to her granddaughter, and offered others to her school-age nieces who had stopped to visit.

It was not until months later that I realized the significance of our trip to the wholesale market. At the time I simply noted what goods Aifeng had bought; only afterward did I realize that, unlike the instant noodles she had purchased, the snacks she had bought for her grandchild were not marketed as *qingzhen*. Furthermore, while Aifeng had spent a great deal of time studying the labels of the instant noodle packages, she had paid very little attention to the labels of the snacks she bought for her granddaughter. Based on everything I had seen and been told about the Muslim district and its residents, Aifeng had violated the local standards for Islamic dietary observance by purchasing food for her granddaughter that was not *qingzhen*.

Such an act was difficult to reconcile with what I knew of Aifeng and her family. Aifeng sold *qingzhen* stuffed breads (*baozi*) in a small restaurant she operated with her family on Barley Market Street (*Damaishi jie*) in the Muslim district. She was intimately familiar with which foods were *qingzhen* and which were not, and was careful to adhere to the Islamic dietary proscriptions. In fact, Aifeng was a devout Muslim whose religious observance went far beyond the minimum level of eating *qingzhen*. Although her business and family obligations prevented her from worshiping five times a day (as stipulated in the Qur'an), she nevertheless donated money, food, and other goods regularly to the mosque, upheld Islamic precepts of dress, fasted during Ramadan, and worshiped at the mosque whenever she could. Given the importance she placed on being a Muslim, why did she buy snacks for her granddaughter that were not *qingzhen*?

Children's Food in China

As Jun Jing describes in the Introduction, foodways in the People's Republic of China (PRC) have undergone significant transformations in the wake of Deng Xiaoping's economic reforms. One obvious effect of the reform policies has been the appearance of a variety of new foods on the market, including the mass-produced, packaged snack foods discussed here. These foods have had a profound impact on the nutritional intake of PRC citizens, particularly that of children. The consumer practices surrounding these new foods also indicate that important changes have occurred in the character and quality of family relations: the balance of power between older and younger generations appears to be shifting (see Bernadine Chee's Chapter 2 and Guo Yuhua's Chapter 4 in this volume).

Both of these phenomena have affected the Xi'an Muslim district. During June 1997, I asked Peng, an eleven-year-old resident, to record his total dietary intake for seven days (see Appendix). Peng's food diary revealed that he ate mass-produced snacks similar to those Aifeng purchased for her granddaughter on a daily basis. Peng's high-school-age brother was the only other member of his immediate (nuclear) family who ever ate these foods, but he and his parents agreed that Peng's consumption far outstripped his brother's, at that time and in the past. This pattern matched the eating practices of other children I observed during eighteen months of field research in the Xi'an Muslim district in 1994 and 1995.

Peng was able to eat these snacks because his parents were providing him with "occasional" spending money that amounted to three yuan a day, a fact they had not fully appreciated until we examined his food diary together. They and Peng's brother assured me that Peng was the first member of their family ever to receive what was, in effect, an allowance. The qualitative (and quantitative) shift in parent-child relationships suggested by Peng's intake of the mass-produced foods was replicated in families throughout the Muslim district.

The consumption of mass-produced snack foods described here differs from the other studies in this book in its religious and ethnic implications. In the Xi'an Muslim district, the new snacks mark an ideological and empirical transformation in local Islamic observance and ethnic practice. They represent a significant modification of the centerpiece of Chinese Muslims' collective identity, namely food preparation and eating habits.

Chinese Muslims or Hui

The Xi'an Muslim district is a small ethno-religious enclave containing approximately 30,000 Chinese Muslims. The vast majority of the district's residents are members of the "Hui nationality" (*Huizu*), one of the PRC's 55 officially recognized minority groups (*shaoshu minzu*). Altogether China's minorities make up 8.04 percent of the total population. The Hui are the third largest minority nationality, and the largest of the eleven minorities officially designated as Muslim (Gladney 1991:26–27).

China's minority nationalities have received considerable scholarly attention in recent years, both inside and outside China. Of concern to many American social scientists have been the ways in which "nationality" (*minzu*) designation relates to ethnic affiliation (see, e.g., Gladney 1998, 1991, 1990; Lipman 1997; Harrell, ed., 1995; Harrell 1990; McKhann 1995). According to the government, China's nationalities conform to the Stalinist criteria for "nationality" status, possessing common territorial, linguistic, economic, and psychological traits (Jin 1984; see also Gladney 1998), but the widely dispersed and linguistically and occupationally diverse group known as the Hui fails to meet a single one of the official criteria. Their status as a nationality rests entirely on a historical perception of difference stemming from their Muslim heritage and Islamic observance (Lipman 1997, 1987; Gladney 1991).

Observance of the Islamic dietary restrictions, or eating *qingzhen*, forms a core element of Hui collective identity. The best understood and most familiar aspect of *qingzhen* food consumption is the Hui abstinence from pork. This marker of difference is fundamental and basic: Chinese of all ages, classes, and "nationality" affiliations referred to it when they learned that I studied the Hui. Invariably any mention of Chinese Muslims evoked the remark, "Hui do not eat pork."

A variety of scholarly works have discussed the importance of the pork taboo and *qingzhen* food consumption to maintaining ethnic boundaries between the Hui and China's majority nationality, the Han. One foundational study of this divide is Barbara Pillsbury's article "Pig and Policy" (1975), which is based on ethnographic research conducted on Taiwan. The most important study of *qingzhen* in the PRC is Dru Gladney's *Muslim Chinese* (1991), which explores the concept of *qingzhen* in four distinct Muslim communities. Gladney's work reveals the centrality of *qingzhen* to Hui identity, as well as the critical role that official policies have played in causing a meaningful ethnic identity to coalesce around the "Hui nationality" label.

Qingzhen

While Gladney's study demonstrates that the concept of *qingzhen* is not limited to dietary practices, when I asked residents of the Xi'an Muslim district to explain what *qingzhen* meant, most people responded by talking about food. Many Hui stated the most important characteristic of *qingzhen* food was that it was "particularly clean" (*tebie ganjing*), or sometimes "clean and sanitary" (*ganjing weisheng*). Food can be clean in several respects, and one of the most fundamental is in its content. As Jishu, imam of one of the local mosques, put it, *qingzhen* means "Hui must eat clean things." He said that the foods proscribed in the Qur'an, namely pork, alcohol, blood, and animals that have not been slaughtered in the Islamic fashion, were "dirty" and Hui could not eat them.

Residents of the Muslim district stressed that pork was especially dirty. They believed that the pig was a disease-carrying animal with filthy habits, living in dirt and eating trash. Jiqing, a gatekeeper at a local mosque, exemplified the dirtiness of pigs by the speed at which pork rots. According to him, if a person took a piece of pork and a piece of lamb and left them out for a week, when she or he returned to examine the two meats the pork would be maggoty and disgusting, but the lamb would still be "good," that is, dry and edible. This explanation of pork's dirtiness also appears in a pamphlet for sale in one of the district's Muslim products stores (Ma Tianfang 1971).

Xi'an Hui were extremely concerned with keeping pork away from food, cooking utensils, and the house. Many residents talked about how important it was for Hui not to eat anything that had touched pork or come into contact with lard. Chen, who worked in the public showers owned by one of the mosques, spoke at length about Hui fears that pork products would "pollute" (*ran*) their food. The contaminating power of pork made it impossible for Hui to use cooking or eating utensils that had ever contained it. For this reason, she said, "We are not willing to eat one mouthful of your food, nor drink one mouthful of your tea."

As Chen's remarks suggest, fears about coming into contact with pork products, or even utensils or dishes that had once contained pork, caused the Muslim district's residents to avoid any food that was not prepared by Muslims. Doing so meant refraining from patronizing non-Hui restaurants or food stalls and refusing to eat or drink at the homes of non-Hui. In this way, the pork taboo negatively affected Han food businesses. More deeply felt, however, were its effects on social situations that involved Hui and

Han. If Hui visited a Han home, they did not accept any food or drink from their host. This refusal to consume was a striking violation of hospitality in the Chinese setting, where visiting should include both the offer and the receipt of at least a small quantity of food or beverage. Even a cup of hot tea, the most common form of hospitality offered to guests in China, was unacceptable to a Chinese Muslim guest in a Han house. The very cup in which the tea was served, if it belonged to a Han, would cause most Xi'an Hui to refuse it, for they believed that simple washing could not cleanse Han dishes of the residue of pork.[3]

In addition to food content, food preparation techniques also played an important part in determining which foods were *qingzhen* and which were not. Yan, who worked in her family's restaurant, stressed the care that Hui took with food preparation when explaining *qingzhen*. She pointed out that Hui washed vegetables, dishes, and hands in separate basins, and kept different types of food segregated and "in order" (*fenjie*). Other Hui, both men and women, explained *qingzhen* by indicating that Hui washed frequently, and paid close attention when they cooked. One man noted that the character for *qing* has the ideographic representation of water in it, which, he said, shows that Hui "rely on water" (*yi shui wei zhu*).

To a large extent, *qingzhen* was equated with being Muslim. To make *qingzhen* food, one woman told me, you must have "washed a major ablution" (*xi guo da jing*), that is, washed yourself according to the proper Islamic procedure. As Jiqing explained, the *qingzhen* signs food entrepreneurs hung over their establishments showed that the cook was a "believer" (*mumin*). To produce *qingzhen* foods, one had to be Muslim, and in Xi'an, being Muslim meant being Hui—as evidenced by the local habit of using the terms "Muslim" (*Musilin*) and "Hui" (*Huimin*) interchangeably. *Qingzhen* encapsulated the essence of being Muslim in the Chinese context. It was central to local conceptions of identity: as Yan put it, "*Qingzhen* means Hui."

The foods that Aifeng bought for her granddaughter and that Peng consumed were diverse in flavor and ingredients. Most were new arrivals to the area; residents said that the vast majority of such mass-produced snacks had been available in the area for only ten years. One exception to this was soda. Mingxin, a butcher, remembered seeing Chinese-made sodas for sale in the late 1970s. At that time a soda cost eleven *fen* per bottle, a price no ordinary person could afford; only the children of cadres and important people drank it.[4] Nevertheless, although soda had been present for a longer period, Mingxin placed it in the same category as chocolate, biscuits, and hard candies: all were "foreign" foods, produced in "foreign" factories or made by "foreign" machines. He pointed out that even though many Chinese factories produced such foods, they "had learned about them from the West." Mingxin was not alone in perceiving a great variety of new foods on the market as products of "the West" — meaning Europe and the United States — even though many of them were manufactured in Asia. This perception was widespread in the Muslim district, especially with regard to snacks wrapped in machine-made packages.

In Xi'an the number of foods actually imported from the West was limited, and their high prices tended to prevent most Hui from buying them. The majority of mass-produced snacks that locals ate were made in China. Many foreign-brand foods available in Xi'an were produced in Chinese factories, some of which were located in Shaanxi province. By 1997, even such well-known "Western" products as Coca-Cola were made and bottled in Shaanxi.

Residents of the Xi'an Muslim district identified certain foods as Western based primarily on what they learned from the media and large department stores and supermarkets. Hui regarded some foods as Western because they saw them being served and consumed in media representations of the United States, Canada, and Europe. Television programs, both those made in the United States and those made in China about the West, played an important role in educating locals about Western foods and foodways. In addition, movies, news programs, and newspaper articles all made "the West" a meaningful category in the imaginations of my informants, none of whom had ever traveled to the United States or Europe.

Xi'an's Chinese Muslims also learned about Western foods from the products available in department stores, wholesale markets, convenience stores, and a few supermarkets. Supermarkets (*chaoji shichang*) were a new phenomenon in Xi'an when I arrived in January 1994. A Hong Kong firm called the Seastar Overseas Company (*Haixing haiwai gongsi*) had recently opened two supermarkets near the city center when I arrived; by the time I left in August 1995, at least two more stores had opened in Xi'an. One of these supermarkets was quite close to the Muslim district, and attracted some of its residents. This supermarket, the many department stores that lined the main streets surrounding the district, the small convenience stores scattered throughout the area, and the nearby wholesale markets sold a variety of packaged, mass-produced foods.

Between 1994 and 1997 the available products included such beverages as Coca-Cola, Sprite, Tang fruit drink, Nestle powdered milk, and Nestle instant coffee, and such foods as Snickers, M&M's, McVitie's Digestive Biscuits, and several kinds of Keebler cookies and crackers, many of which, such as mango-flavored sandwich cookies, I had never seen before. These foods were originally developed in Europe and the United States, and had spawned a variety of Japanese and Hong Kong imitations. The Hong Kong brands, especially Khong Guan and Garden biscuits and crackers, were particularly popular in Xi'an. Many PRC companies also sold Western food spinoffs in Xi'an, such as carbonated drinks, crackers, crisps, cookies, ice cream bars, and candy.

In addition to brand-name promotions, media representations also contributed to the development of stereotypes about Western foods and their ingredients. Butter and milk in particular were regarded as typical of Western food. Even in snacks produced locally, the presence of dairy ingredients lent them an aura of foreign-ness and luxury. For Hui in their thirties and older, dairy products symbolized a high standard of living. Mingxin remembered craving milk as a child, when little was available and his family was too poor to buy it. He commented that low levels of milk production were partially to blame in the past, but since the reform period began in 1978, China's cows had been "science modernized" (*kexue xiandaihua*) and so dairy products were both readily available and affordable.

A number of Xi'an enterprises sold foods such as fresh yeast bread and cakes containing ingredients that caused Hui to regard them as "Western." Unlike the packaged, preserved factory food, local restaurants and bakeries made these foods daily and sold them fresh. However, Chinese Muslims generally refused to consume them; most would only eat the locally made "Western" foods that other Hui produced. No one I knew ate food from the American fast-food chain Kentucky Fried Chicken, the Han Chinese fast-food chains that sold hamburgers, hot dogs, pizza, fried chicken, and the like, or the many bakeries outside the Muslim district that produced yeast bread and oven-baked cakes. Hui also abstained from carbonated beverages that came from soda fountains rather than cans or bottles. They justified their abstinence on the grounds that these locally produced Western foods were not *qingzhen* since they were not made by Hui.

As the preceding discussion makes clear, a number of foods identified as "Western" did not fall into the category of foods Hui were willing to eat. When foods were made in local restaurants and food stalls, residents of the Muslim district would eat only those foods made by Muslims. This was because, "Western" or not, foods made by Hui were by definition *qingzhen*. What was more perplexing was that Hui also ate foods that were produced in factories and thus not made by Hui. Three factors made these foods acceptable: they were not made with pork, they were perceived to be Western, and they were the product of industrial production techniques that did not involve the extensive use of the hands.

An event from Aifeng's and my shopping trip shows the importance of the first two criteria. After Aifeng had purchased her food, I began sorting through the piles to buy some for myself. As I looked at the offerings, I was drawn to a different sort of food than Aifeng was. What was to me more exotic and novel were the factory-produced versions of traditional Chinese food like mung bean cakes (*lüdougao*) and peanut cakes (*huashengsu*).[5] Seeing me rummaging through the boxes and sacks, Aifeng came over to examine what I planned to buy. When she saw the factory-made mung bean cakes, she shook her head. "We can't eat those," she said. "They aren't *qingzhen*."

Clearly Aifeng placed mass-produced mung bean cakes in a different category from the packaged snacks she had bought for her daughter. What caused her to perceive the cakes and the instant noodles with which she took such care to purchase a *qingzhen* brand as requiring attention to *qingzhen*? The answer lies in their familiarity. The mung bean cakes and noodles were the result of industrial food production techniques, but they were recognizably Chinese. They were foods that Hui knew how to make, and ones that were commonly prepared and consumed throughout China. Aifeng knew that when non-Muslims prepared mung bean cakes or noodles they made them with lard; only Hui made such foods with vegetable oil. Her experience and upbringing told Aifeng that she could only consume traditional Chinese foods if they were made by Hui. Even factory-produced "traditional" foods were associated with pork, unless they were certified *qingzhen*. Aifeng and her neighbors recognized factory-produced foods such as mung bean cakes and noodles as part of a local universe in which foods were either Hui and edible or Han and inedible. Western mass-produced foods, however, stood outside of this realm.

Young Consumers

Many residents of the Muslim district bought Western industrial foods, but although many Hui adults purchased them, few actually consumed them. Most of these foods were eaten by children. By and large, Hui adults limited their intake of mass-produced foods to carbonated beverages, coffee, and juice-based drinks. None of these beverages were popular with adults over thirty, and they did not form a part of most adults' daily food intake. Generally, such beverages were used to host visitors and guests. Soda, for example, was an indispensable part of any formal banquet at a restaurant, and was also served with the meals that Hui provided for guests at circumcisions, engagements, and weddings. When the Barley Market Street Anti-Alcohol Association, a grassroots organization dedicated to keeping alcohol out of the Muslim district, hosted a public rally, it provided soda to everyone who attended. Most families I knew kept bottles of soda or boxes of juice drink on hand in the refrigerator for guests, especially during the summer, when temperatures in Xi'an soared well over 100 degrees Fahrenheit.

The other mass-produced Western food that occasionally formed part of the adult Hui diet was candy. Like the Western beverages, mass-produced candies were not eaten daily by the Hui adults I knew but rather were offered to guests. Packaged candies were placed out on trays for guests to eat casually during the lengthy celebrations of life-cycle rituals or brought out for important visitors. Candy also constituted an item of exchange during marriage transactions. Families whose children became engaged or married participated in formal rites of gift-giving (similar to those described in Yan 1996:176–209). In the Muslim district, these exchanges frequently involved food. For example, at one stage during the marriage process, the bride's family presented the groom's family with gifts of nuts, dates, and other fancy snack foods (*gaodian*). A wide variety of traditional pastries were used on this occasion, but packaged hard candy also frequently constituted one of the items exchanged.

Despite these gift exchange and hosting practices, most Hui adults found "Western" foods unpalatable. A frequent comment Hui adults made was that they "could not get accustomed" (*bu xiguan*) to the taste of candy, soda, or other Western foods. In general, locals complained that Western foods were "too sweet" and "not filling" (*chi bu bao*). Hui used these foods for gift exchanges and hospitality because they were novel, expensive, and associated with the West and what the West represented, not because they thought the foods tasted good.

Hui children, on the other hand, ate factory-made Western food in large quantities. Parents and grandparents regularly purchased packaged Western snacks for children to eat between meals. Many families I knew kept supplies of these foods at home. Aifeng frequently fed this type of mass-produced snack to her granddaughter when the little girl cried or if she started playing with something Aifeng did not wish her to play with — in short, when Aifeng wanted to distract her. Peng's father bought large cases of soda for his sons; he explained that offering this treat was one way he rewarded his children and encouraged them to work hard in school.

Most parents enabled their children to eat snack foods by giving them spare change. I frequently saw children run up to their parents and ask for a few *mao*.[6] The parents' usual response was to hand over a little money and send the children away. Children spent this money at the small, family-run convenience stores in the area, quite a few of which were near primary and middle schools. Among school-age children, trips to the convenience store occasioned comparisons about who had tried which snacks, queries about which snacks contained toys, and judicious expressions of preferences. Children frequently ate these foods in or around school property, and the schoolyard formed an important venue for the dissemination of knowledge about new snacks.

Some Chinese Muslims questioned the propriety of consuming Western foods. Jishu, an elderly imam, refused to drink carbonated beverages or eat any foods associated with the West because he believed they were not *qingzhen*. Although he did not criticize others for eating these foods, he said that he hoped his abstinence would inspire other Hui to emulate him. Most ordinary Hui avoided offering Western food to imams and members of the community considered to be particularly devout. For example, at the weddings, funerals, and engagements I attended, imams and other "men of religion" were not served Western soft drinks, though lay guests were. Nor did the banquets provided by the mosques for collective religious rituals (such as the annual summertime mourning ritual for the Hui massacred in Shaanxi during the late nineteenth century or the wintertime celebration of the Prophet's Birthday) include any foods associated with the West: no factory-produced snacks, canned or bottled beverages, or local Hui-produced yeast breads or cakes.[7]

"Neutral" Foods

For most Chinese Muslims, mass-produced Western foods were neither *qingzhen* nor taboo. Instead, they fell into an amorphous category of their own. The apparent neutrality of mass-produced Western foods derived in part from the absence of pork or lard in such products. For example, on one occasion I asked Peng's father if Hui could eat chocolate. He responded with a puzzled look. "Of course," he replied. "Chocolate? There is nothing in that (*mei sha*)." "Nothing" meant no pork; neither chocolate nor the other foods Hui considered Western were made with pork or lard.

On another occasion I spoke with Aifeng's daughter Xue, a young woman in her twenties who worked in a department store, about Western foods. Xue had traveled to Beijing with her co-workers on a trip sponsored by her work unit; when she described her visit, she complained about how difficult it was for her to find food that she could eat while she and her co-workers, who were all Han, were sightseeing. Because her Han colleagues ate in places that were not *qingzhen*, she often went hungry. Indeed, she chose to sit outside during meals, so concerned was she to avoid violating *qingzhen*. After listening to her remarks, I asked her whether she could eat in Western restaurants like Kentucky Fried Chicken: did the *qingzhen* food taboo apply to such places? Xue replied that she could not enter or eat in fast-food restaurants because they were not *qingzhen*. And what about the ice cream bars they sold on the street,

I asked, could she eat those? What about when she was thirsty? "About some foods it is hard to say (*shuo bu qing*)," she responded. "I could eat an ice cream bar, or drink a soft drink, or even eat packaged biscuits (*binggan*) if they didn't have lard in them."

Intrigued by the neutrality of mass-produced Western foods, I visited Zenglie, a retired professor of Hui history whose family lived in the district. Zenglie characterized these snacks as one stage in a historical development whereby Hui came to eat foods that were once avoided. It used to be, Zenglie said, that Hui would not drink water that did not come from wells owned by Hui; now everyone drank the water that came through the pipes the government installed. Sweets (*tianshi*) and non-alcoholic beverages (*yinliao*) were also foods that had once been prohibited. However, Zenglie noted, in the past such foods were all made by hand. Now they were made in factories, so Hui could eat them.

The Food Industry and Food Production

Industrial production clearly played an important role in rendering the new foods acceptable to Hui. Such foods differed from the vast majority of edibles sold and consumed in the area: most foods available in Xi'an during the mid-1990s were hand-made. "Handmade" in this context signified more than just the degree of personalization this phrase denotes in the contemporary United States. Rather, it refers to the absence of almost every kind of foodprocessing machine or tool, and to the extensive and intensive use of hands in all forms of food preparation.

As described above, cleanliness figures highly in the Hui concept of "pure and true." Hui criticized Han for being dirty, not just because they consumed pork, but also because they regarded Han as less than sanitary. Several Hui commented to me that Han did not wash their hands after using the toilet, and that Han washed their hands in water Hui considered stagnant. Given the nature of local food-preparation techniques, these sanitation practices assumed a high degree of importance.

Noodles were one of the most popular foods for sale on the streets of Xi'an, both inside and outside the Muslim district. They were sold in establishments that ranged from fancy hotel restaurants to tiny street stalls seating fewer than ten customers. In most restaurants and stalls, noodles were made to order; the urbanites I knew criticized and avoided establishments that sold pre-prepared dried noodles. In the Muslim district, as on many of Xi'an's smaller streets and alleys, fresh noodles were almost always made in the customer's presence. Though noodles could be pulled, rolled, or cut in an assortment of shapes and sizes, all involved significant use of the hands.

Typically, noodle preparation began with making the dough. The cook poured flour and water into a large basin, and then stirred the mixture with chopsticks. As the dough thickened, the cook abandoned the chopsticks in favor of hands. Once the right proportions of flour and water were achieved, the dough was removed from the basin and kneaded by hand. Kneading took anywhere from ten to twenty minutes. Then, if the cook were preparing cut noodles — the simplest sort to prepare — he or she flattened the dough with a rolling pin, using his or her hands to stretch the flattened dough. Once the dough had reached the desired thinness, the cook cut it with a knife. He or she would stop after cutting the right amount of dough for a single bowl, pick it up, and put it to the side in a pile. This process would continue until all the dough was cut.

Once cut, the noodles were ready for boiling. When a customer appeared, the cook would grab one of the piles of noodles with his or her hands and throw them into a big wok filled with water that was heated by a large, round coal-burning stove that was probably made from an oil drum. After a few minutes, the noodles were removed with chopsticks, placed in a bowl, and seasoned to the customer's taste. If the customer wanted them with meat, the cook would cut a few slices of pre-cooked meat, pick them up by hand, and place them in the customer's bowl. Then green bean threads, cilantro, and onions would be added, also by hand. Finally, the cook would ladle broth into the bowl, and serve it to the customer.

Noodles were by no means the only sort of food made by Xi'an restaurateurs that involved the use of hands, nor did noodle preparation involve the most intensive use of the hand. Steamed stuffed buns (*baozi*), dumplings (*jiaozi*), stovetop-baked flatbread (*tuo tuo mo*), and most other foods sold on the streets of Xi'an all required hands-on preparation. Only a couple of the hundreds of food stalls in the Muslim district possessed machines for food preparation; most enterprises hired multiple laborers to hasten and increase food production.

The contrast is clear: foods that Hui made were produced by hand, on site, while the customer watched; packaged foods, on the other hand, were made by machine, in distant locations, and away from the consumer's gaze. The physical distance between where mass-produced foods were made and where they were consumed, the invisibility of the production process, and the use of machines all contributed to the Hui tendency to regard these foods as neutral.

Industrial processing also defamiliarized food by rendering its products significantly different in appearance from the foods that Chinese made by hand (see Hendry 1993 for a discussion of the transformative effects of wrapping in Japan). The mass-produced foods were sealed in plastic, glass, or aluminum. Their wrappers were air-tight and leak-proof; they were packaged with expensive materials that could not be produced in the Muslim district. Local packaging was much more casual. Hand-made foods were wrapped in paper and tied with string, or put into flimsy plastic bags tied by their handles. Often consumers would bring their own dishes or bowls to transport their purchases home. Indeed, much of the hand-made food produced in Xi'an was consumed on the spot rather than taken home.

Ingredients and food type also contributed to the strangeness of "Western" factory-made foods. They were standardized in color and shape. Many were dyed. Some were dried and coated; as a category they tended to be crisp. By contrast, hand-made Hui foods were irregularly shaped and varied in size. They were made without artificial colorings, and they tended to be soft.

Children's Food and Islamic Dietary Restrictions   87

Mass-produced Western food was alien: encased in sealed containers, made by unfamiliar and unseen production techniques, containing ingredients that were rarely used in local cuisine. Unlike the mass-produced mung bean cakes, they were not "Chinese" but visually, texturally, and orally exotic and foreign. Their "Western" quality was an important reason why Hui consumed them. In the eyes of many Chinese Muslims, the West represented wealth, advanced technology, science, and modernity. By eating the Western factory foods, Hui linked themselves to progress, scientific knowledge, and prosperity.

Largely because of the images and stories of the West transmitted since the economic reforms, Xi'an Hui regarded the West as modern, advanced, liberal, and wealthy. Purchasing and eating food that was Western allowed Hui to assume something of these qualities. Local residents used Western food to make a statement about their cosmopolitanism and familiarity with things foreign. While most adult Hui did not like the taste of ice cream, soda, chocolate, or potato chips, many liked to think of themselves, and liked to be thought of, as modern, progressive, and aware of the world outside China. One way of creating this image was to purchase Western foods, give them as gifts, keep them around the house, feed them to children, and serve them to honored guests. Since only two Hui families made Western-style foods, very little hand-made Western food was available in the Muslim district. Furthermore, the yeast bread and cake these families produced were highly perishable and limited in variety. Hui who wanted to use the contents of their pantry to create a modern, affluent image had little choice but to buy factory-made products, even though they did not meet some of the criteria for *qingzhen*.

Factory-made Western food had the added attraction of being intimately tied to industry, and through this to science and modernity. Things scientific had an immense power in the Muslim district. Residents referred to the Qur'an as "extremely scientific" when justifying their belief in Islam, and "scientific" methods of Islamic education, which involved the use of language cassettes, were privileged over the "old" methods of rote memorization. Hui associated science with development, improved sanitation, and high standards of living. The "advanced technology," as one resident termed it, through which factory-made foods were produced, enhanced their attractiveness.

The modern, scientific aspect of Western factory-made food was particularly important for children. Adult Hui wanted their children to succeed in contemporary society. They wanted their children to have wider experiences than they had had, and to ascend higher on the social ladder. This desire was most obviously manifest through the stress parents placed on their children's education. Parents willingly paid extra money to send their children to better schools, enroll them in extra tutorials, or hire private tutors. Providing their children with Western mass-produced food was another means parents used to prepare their children for the modern world. Through these foods parents hoped to introduce their children to things foreign and equip them to live in an industrialized, technologically advanced, cosmopolitan world.

The French sociologist Pierre Bourdieu writes that "taste classifies, and it classifies the classifier" (1984:6). Xi'an Hui wanted to be classified as modern. Their pursuit of secular education, their enthusiasm for living in high-rise apartments, their preference for religious education that used the technologies of modern life such as language cassettes and videotapes, their desire to make the pilgrimage to Mecca and enjoy the experiences of foreign travel such as riding in airplanes — all demonstrate that residents of the Muslim district approved of and wanted to participate in modernization (see Gillette 2000 for further discussion). Consumption of packaged, mass-produced Western foods was yet another arena in which they pursued modernity. In this case, what was occurring in Xi'an was not the "logical conformity" of taste to social position that Bourdieu describes (1984:471; see also 1990) whereby people prefer goods and services that express their existing social position.

Rather, Hui consumption of Western mass-produced foods is an instance of people developing a taste, or instilling a taste in their children, for what they wanted to be: advanced, cosmopolitan, modern.

The Government and Mass Production

Consumption of mass-produced foods was also part of an ongoing reconfiguration of the relationship between the Shaanxi provincial government and Chinese Muslims, both with the Muslim district and with the wider community of Hui residents elsewhere in Xi'an and Shaanxi. During the summer of 1996, one high-level provincial official told me that the government's Religion and Nationalities Bureau was debating a policy that would certify factories as *qingzhen*. Four criteria had been decided upon: in factories officially designated as *qingzhen*, the "cook" must be Hui (he did not elaborate upon who, in the factory production process, would be considered the cook); the ingredients must not contain pork or pork products; leaders of the factory must be Hui; and at least 25 percent of the factory workers must be Hui. This last point was revised during the week I was visiting; a few days after our initial conversation this official told me that the percentage of factory workers who must be Hui had been increased to 45 percent. He explained that if this policy went into effect, it would apply to many enterprises, including those that did business with Islamic countries. Fears that Muslims from outside China would disapprove of the criteria had caused the provincial government to raise the required percentage of Hui employees. By June 1997, this policy to regulate *qingzhen* had passed through all the necessary administrative channels, but no actions to implement the policy had yet occurred.

The provincial government's debates about certifying factories as *qingzhen* took place in the context of a more general effort to define the meaning of *qingzhen* in secular terms. A few years prior to these debates, the city government's Religious and Nationalities Department created criteria for certifying hand-made Hui foods as *qingzhen* (see Gillette 1997:108–37). Although residents of the Muslim district linked *qingzhen* closely to religion, the government sought to use nationality-based criteria to redefine *qingzhen* as a category based on nationality affiliation. In both the city and the provincial government's eyes, membership in one of the officially created Muslim nationalities determined which foods and which food producers were *qingzhen*.

The Shaanxi provincial government's proposed policy raised questions about the significance of contemporary *qingzhen* labeling, at least for me. Did the instant noodles Aifeng selected, which were advertised as *qingzhen*, adhere to the standards for "pure and true" that had been set by local Chinese Muslims, or did they more closely resemble the secular definitions propounded by the government? Such labeling had enormous potential to mask food preparation practices that diverged widely from those considered clean in the district. By allowing factories to market their industrial products as *qingzhen*, the government added another level of complexity to the Hui evaluation and use of mass-produced foods: did *qingzhen* mean Islamically pure, made by a member of the Hui nationality, or made in a factory whose employees were mostly non-Muslim? The government's actions also foregrounded the puzzling question: to what extent can a machine be considered *qingzhen*?

Hui and Han Eat Together

Local standards of *qingzhen* have shifted in the Xi'an Muslim district. The availability of mass-produced Western foods was transforming what *qingzhen* meant, particularly with regard to children's food consumption. Hui attitudes toward mass-produced foods suggest that *qingzhen* was still defined in opposition to Han, but not in opposition to the West or what the West represented, namely, science and modernization.

This phenomenon reaffirms Bourdieu's insight about social identity, that "difference is asserted against what is closest, which represents the greatest threat" (1984:479). To Xi'an Hui, the food of their next-door neighbors, the Han, was quintessentially polluted. However, they did not feel the same way about factory-produced Western food, even if it was made by machines operated by Han. In part, their attitude reflected that the Hui, like nearly everyone else in China, wanted to modernize. Eating Western mass-produced food was one means of achieving a progressive and scientifically advanced image. Most Chinese Muslims elevated the goal of modernization over strict adherence to *qingzhen* guidelines. To reach this goal, *qingzhen* was being reinterpreted solely as that which was not Han, rather than that which was Muslim.

The need for such redefinition was a relatively recent development. Throughout most of the Muslim district's thousand-year history, residents had limited contact with the West. Beginning in the 1980s, however, opportunities to encounter the West through the media and through interactions with foreign visitors to Xi'an increased dramatically. In addition, many more Western products became available than ever before. Xi'an Hui associated such products with "the good life" they saw in media representations and in the material lifestyles of foreign tourists. They embraced this image of wealth and modernity by consuming food they perceived as "Western." Western foods were carefully categorized as distinct from Han food, even when both were made through mechanized factory production.

The consumption of mass-produced Western foods connected Hui with consumers of similar products in the United States, Europe, Japan, and elsewhere. As Jack Goody writes, "processed food is more or less the same in Ealing as in Edinburgh" (1982:189). However, eating this food has not led to cultural homogeneity (see also J. Watson, ed., 1997). While the Hui treatment of candy and crisps may resemble that found in the United States, for example as a snack for children, in other ways it differed markedly. Residents' use of candy and yeast breads as part of the formal engagement presents given by the groom's family to the bride's family, for example, was a practice not found in mainstream American society. More important, Western food in the Muslim district possessed a significance it did not have outside China. One difference was that Western food was not regarded as suitable for regular meals, even in forms that most Americans consider to be substantial, such as yeast bread. Instead, it was closely linked to children and to childish practices such as snacking. Another difference was its special value and quality. Coca-Cola in the United States is quite ordinary and inexpensive, but in Xi'an it was a prestige food, served to honored guests in homes and at banquets.

Despite the sharp distinction Hui made between themselves and Han, and the care they took to avoid mass-produced foods that were considered "traditional Chinese," the consumption of Western mass-produced foods made it easier for Hui to interact with Han. For although Hui adults differentiated between Han foods and Western mass-produced foods, the snacks they allowed their children to eat, and the soft drinks they drank, were also found in the homes and mouths of Han. These foods provided a common ground for Hui and Han to eat together. Hui visitors at Han households could accept Han hospitality if offered a can of soda rather than a cup of tea. If food was the most important factor that kept Hui separate from Han, then the consumption of Western, mass-produced foods diminished the differences between Hui and Han, particularly for children. One wonders where and how the boundary between Hui and Han will be drawn when the children of the 1990s have grown up.

Food and Family Relations:

The Generation Gap at the Table

Guo Yuhua

The consumption of food is at once the most ordinary of human activities and one fraught with significance. It not only satisfies our bodily needs but also is associated with our concepts of self, group, and even nationality. Perhaps for this reason, it has been suggested that "one of the best ways of getting to a culture's heart would be through its stomach" (Chang 1977:4). This is certainly the case in China, where one's knowledge of what food to consume and how has been widely seen as a yardstick of one's personal maturity and as a crucial matter of aesthetics (Chen Shujun, ed., 1988; Wang Renxiang 1994). There is little doubt that many social variables — gender, ethnicity, profession, social status, and educational attainment — influence one's knowledge of food (see, e.g., Anderson 1988; Lin Naisang 1989; Wang Mingde and Wang Zihui 1988). In contemporary China, we must consider yet another variable: when an individual came of age. In the past two decades, China's transition to a market economy has been accompanied by greater integration with a global culture of consumption. Within the sphere of personal consumption, the availability of new foods has altered the tastes of an entire generation of young people born since Mao's death in 1976. Their attitudes toward food, a reflection of childhood experiences quite different from those of their elders, have contributed to a generation gap in terms of social values and personal aspirations.

The goal of this chapter is to explore Chinese children's dietetic knowledge and to compare it with that of their parents and grandparents. "Dietetic knowledge" in this discussion refers to the basic ideas that shape people's dietary desires and their explanations for their eating habits. It implies learning to construe the meaning of food as a biological necessity and as a cultural symbol. Phrased differently, a particular body of dietetic knowledge is a special combination of conceptual models, practical information, and social values that can profoundly affect a people's foodways, health, and interpersonal relationships.

But why, precisely, do we need to examine dietetic knowledge through the prism of generational differences? This question will be addressed throughout the pages that follow. In brief outline, childcare in China involves the joint effort of two senior generations of family members: parents and grandparents. It can be said that the dietetic knowledge of Chinese grandparents in their fifties and above — in other words, people born before the founding of the People's Republic in 1949 — is characterized by an emphasis on dietary balance, a notion derived from popularized principles of traditional Chinese medicine. Although many of these ideas have persisted into the next generation, namely, those born during the Maoist era, who are the parents of today's children, this younger group has been strongly influenced by nutritional concepts acquired from modern science and Western medicine. By contrast, the rudimentary dietary ideas of school-age children can be said to arise from "the need to consume" rather than "the need to use" (Hang Zhi 1991:140). Especially when it comes to snacks, soft drinks, and fast food, Chinese youngsters appear concerned less with balance or nutrition than with the social values and cultural symbols of China's emerging consumer culture (Huang Ping 1995; Yan 1995:47–63).

These generational differences raise interesting questions about the transmission of culture. Until recently, family and school were centers of a Chinese child's education in the practical, social, and symbolic values of food (see, e.g., Croll 1983; Sidel 1972). This pattern of learning, however, has changed in urban centers and many prosperous rural areas, thanks to the commercialization of Chinese society and the proliferation of television sets at home. In the economic reform era, particularly since urban reforms were begun in the mid-1980s, business enterprises, Chinese and foreign, have employed aggressive marketing strategies in the hope of inculcating in young people as early as possible eating habits that will last for a lifetime. Television is one of the most powerful media to promote new food products. Typical television commercials often involve the deliberate use of children's cartoon characters to blur the distinction between eating for nourishment and eating for fun. In short, the process by which children learn about food has been taken over by the commercialization of Chinese society and the country's integration into the global economy. Before the implications of this trend are explored in greater detail, a few remarks should be made about the two research projects that produced the data for this discussion.

The first project was collaborative, based on structured interviews conducted in the summer of 1995 with 30 Beijing schoolchildren ages eight to eleven, and their teachers and family members. Bernadine Chee of Harvard University, a researcher at Beijing Normal University, and I worked with three graduate students from Beijing University to design and set up the interviews. The second project, also based on school and household interviews, was conducted by myself in 1994 in a village in Jiangsu province. In the following pages, the Beijing study will be emphasized while data from Jiangsu will be cited by way of comparison. The 30 children we interviewed were from two elementary schools. Ten of them were asked to keep a daily record of what they ate. The interviews in Jiangsu were with twenty eleven-year-old children, all in the fifth grade of a village school. Each research project also included visits to the children's homes to observe and document food consumption.

A central conclusion of these studies is that we need to rethink the relationship of food and childhood in China. It has been long assumed that Chinese children's notions of food, no matter how rudimentary they might be, should not deviate too much from those of their elders (see, esp., Stafford 1995). After all, Chinese children, once they are able to eat solid food at the family table, are taught by their parents or grandparents to recognize various categories of food, the importance of proper choices, and the distinction between everyday food and festival food. In the process of passing on knowledge from adults to children, parents exercise their authority. And it has often been taken for granted that a basic step in Chinese children's passage to adulthood is gradually coming to share with their parents and grandparents a common body of dietetic knowledge. This assumption is evident in most of earlier anthropological discussions of the relationship of childhood and food in Chinese society (see, esp., Diamond 1969:30–50; Fei 1939:119–28; Y. Lin 1947:55–96; M. Wolf 1972:53–79). And it has been reemphasized in a score of relatively recent works based on research in China, Taiwan, and Hong Kong (see, esp., Croll 1983; Stafford 1995; Tobin et al. 1989; Sidel 1972).

However, on the basis of my own research in Beijing and Jiangsu, I suggest that the assumption of a cross-generational commonality of dietetic knowledge may need to be modified, not because the assumption was wrong or unsupported by empirical data, but because the situation of Chinese school-age children has changed since those earlier studies. To support this argument, I shall examine the food-related attitudes that we recorded in our interviews with elderly grandparents, younger parents, and schoolchildren. For narrative clarity, I characterize the three generationally marked categories of dietetic knowledge that emerged as "traditionalist," "modernist," and "consumerist." These terms will be explained with references to traditional Chinese medicine, nutritional science, and post-Mao economic reforms.

The Traditionalist Knowledge of Food

The traditionalist dietetic knowledge is first and foremost associated with the pre-1949 generation, today's schoolchildren's grandparents. In our interviews, these people repeatedly cited traditionalist dietetic concepts regarding dietary balance. These are modeled after the culturally perceived correlation of the two basic forces that regulate the natural order: *yin* and *yang*. These forces are understood in Chinese culture as the primordial twin potencies of cold and heat, night and day, female and male, negative and positive, preserver and stimulator. Considered to be of equal value and as a symbiosis, *yin* and *yang* manipulate heaven and earth in the waxing and waning of seasons, exerting their power on human beings too. According to traditional Chinese medicine, the human body itself is of a *yin* and *yang* duality. The liver, lungs, and kidneys are predominantly *yin*; the gall bladder, stomach, and intestines are primarily *yang*. *Yin* stores the vital energy of life; *yang* protects the body from invasion. Both must be maintained in stalwart condition.

One way to prevent the imbalance of *yin* and *yang* is to maintain a balanced diet of hot and cold foods, a mixture of refined and crude cereals, and a fixed portion and category of foodstuffs for consumption at three different times of the day. These dietary concepts have been embedded in traditional Chinese medicine for centuries (see, e.g., Anderson 1980:237–68; Huang Shau-yen 1994: 435–77; Liy 1994:481–93), and are the basic elements of what I have termed traditionalist dietetic knowledge. As an integral component of the Chinese belief system and medical tradition, these dietary concepts continue to be reflected in everyday conversation about food, medicine, and health as well as in the unceasing popularity of traditional food prescriptions for pregnant women and for sick or frail children (see, e.g., Wu Ruixian et al. 1990; Wang Lin, ed., 1993).

To contextualize the ideas of a balanced diet, the distinction between "hot" and "cold" foods should be explained first. Briefly, meat, eggs, and any greasy foods are considered heat-producing in the body while seafood, green vegetables, and fruit are thought to produce cold. Many of the relatively new foods that have entered the Chinese children's diet can also be categorized as "hot" or "cold." Some of the grandparents interviewed in Beijing and Jiangsu made a special point about chocolate being a new food and classifying it as "hot." Chocolate is not bad, they said, but it has the quality of a hot and stimulating food. When too much is eaten, they said, it can cause nosebleeds, particularly in boys. So children's consumption of chocolate, they said, must be moderate.

Another noteworthy expression of the traditionalist knowledge of food is the value placed on a diversified diet and natural food. The first step in bringing up a healthy child, according to the older members of the households we visited, is to encourage the child to eat a wide range of foods. Meanwhile, they criticized what they considered to be "unnatural" food: nutritional supplements such as vitamin pills and medicinal tonics. One of the senior informants characterized the difference between "natural" and "unnatural" foods by saying: "It is pretty hard to know what is really inside the nutritional supplements. The natural kind of food that one can actually see is more reliable. Take shrimp and fish. They are good to eat, mouthful by mouthful. No matter how wonderful cod-liver oil or fish-brain derivatives can be, it is always better simply to eat more fish." This attitude was shared by many of the older people we interviewed in Beijing and rural Jiangsu. They were aware that a wide variety of commercial nutritional supplements were available on the Chinese market and that these were often marketed as "health-enhancing" and "life-prolonging." Speaking of his generation's attitude to such products, one grandfather said: "We know very little about scientific feeding methods. But whatever adults can eat, children can eat it too." Other grandparents articulated this view in different ways, but the basic point they made was identical — a weaned child can be fed as if he were a little adult. This is not to say, of course, that these older Chinese saw no differences between children and adults. They knew that children are very particular about the taste of food and that they have a special need for healthy food.

Our question of what is "healthy" food for children received quite different answers. We were told by one Beijing grandmother that spring is the most important time for a child's growth. Accordingly, she took upon herself the end-of-winter routine of fattening up her grandchild with a special treat: a braised pork dish that she cooked slowly over a simmering fire. Other elderly interviewees insisted that children and adults alike should eat a great quantity of vegetables and not too much meat. In general, the elderly people regarded meat, fish, and eggs to be indispensable to health, but consistently expressed the opinion that animal protein should be supplemented by grain, vegetables, and, if affordable, fresh fruit.

The Modernist Knowledge of Food

In addressing what today's young people should eat, the parents and grandparents in Beijing and Jiangsu shared many beliefs. Nonetheless, there were noteworthy differences in their dietary knowledge. For one thing, the parents we studied were far better educated than the grandparents, especially the grandmothers. No grandmother we interviewed in Beijing had a college degree. But both the mother and father of twelve of the thirty Beijing students we interviewed had attended college. In the Jiangsu village, most of the parents interviewed had completed junior high school, whereas most of the grandparents were illiterate.

Schooling and a familiarity with modern science have clearly informed the parents' ideas about diet, health, and child care. These ideas are "modernist" in the sense that they are based in Western medicine and modern nutrition science. Take for example "vitamins," a word we frequently heard in the interviews. The Chinese name for vitamins is *weisheng su*, or "life-supporting substances." As a manifestation of their understanding of the relationship among vitamins, food, and health, many of the parents said that they considered providing a vitamin-rich diet to be a special duty of enlightened parenthood. This was particularly the case among the parents we interviewed in Beijing. Most of the Beijing parents said that they encouraged their children to eat more vegetables, and some even forced their uncooperative offspring to eat raw vegetables to avoid the loss of vitamins during cooking. To overcome the problem of vitamin deficiencies, a few parents said that pork bones and pork or chicken blood should be consumed from time to time to add calcium and iron to children's diet. To deal with children who dislike the taste of foods their parents think are good for them, such as raw carrots, some parents told us that they dip the vegetable into hot water to change its flavor. As for milk, finicky children were persuaded to drink it flavored with sugar and malt. When children refused to eat boiled eggs, the eggs would be sliced into tiny pieces and seasoned to stimulate the youngsters' appetites. As one parent put it, "All kinds of methods have been invented to make children eat well." But once a child left home for school during the day, parental control diminished, for schoolchildren usually had pocket money to purchase snacks and soft drinks. Deeply concerned with safety and hygiene, the Beijing parents repeatedly said that they were against buying snacks from street vendors and small neighborhood stores, fearing that the snacks might contain too much artificial sweetening and coloring, or harmful hormone-treated ingredients. They were equally afraid that their children might eat the snacks with dirty hands and even accidentally eat the enclosed preservative packets.

The parents' fixation on healthy meals, food safety, and a vitamin-rich diet was occasionally accompanied by critical comments to the effect that their children's grandparents could not be trusted with the supervision of the children's diet, largely because they did not know enough about scientific nutrition. The older generation, a young mother complained, would never consider the nutritional content of food as an important part of "scientific child care," an attitude that she believed the grandparents acquired when they themselves were young parents who had few choices and had to make do with whatever food was available. Today's parents, she said, are blessed by "the suitable conditions for scientific child care." These include a higher disposable family income and exposure to scientific nutritional information.

The media from which they acquired this information included books, magazines, radio, and television; parents also had discussions at work with colleagues about cooking, the health benefits of certain foods, and ways to help children overcome eating disorders. Of course, applying "scientific" knowledge may not always be as efficacious as expected. A college-educated couple reported in disturbed tones that they tried to combine the nutrition concepts from Western medicine with those of traditional Chinese medicine to develop a healthy diet for their only child but the child still suffered from poor health. The child's mother worked for a publishing house specializing in medical books and health magazines. Her husband was a self-taught student of traditional Chinese medicine. They were both deeply puzzled that they had failed to make their child healthy despite their painstaking efforts to come up with a scientific diet. Although other parents we interviewed in Beijing had not conducted as much dietary research as this couple did, most had read books and articles in magazines, and newspapers on food, health, and child rearing.

In the Jiangsu village, scientific methods of feeding children were understood strictly as giving them vitamin pills. The vitamin supplements were given mostly in the children's first year. Since the vitamins usually were recommended by village or township doctors, they were regarded locally as medicine, something to protect infants from illness until they had passed their most vulnerable stage and began to eat solid foods. A similar attitude — viewing vitamin pills as medicine — was found by Jun Jing in a Gansu province village (see Chapter 6 of this volume) and by three other scholars in a village in north China (Huang Shu-min et al. 1996:355–381).

The Consumerist Knowledge of Food

The introduction of new foods and ideas about food is bound to modify lifestyles and dietary patterns in any society (see, e.g., Mintz 1986; Levenstein 1993; Johnston 1987; Laderman 1983; McElroy and Townsend 1989:165–239). With China's move to a market economy and greater trade with the outside world, children's appetites have become increasingly influenced by new, imported, and luxury foods, especially snacks and soft drinks introduced by foreign and joint-venture companies.

The dietetic knowledge acquired within the environment of China's budding consumer culture is defined here as "consumerist." People of all ages are affected, but perhaps it is most closely associated with those children who were born during the post-Mao economic reforms and population controls. These children are more familiar with the ethos of the market-oriented economy than the central planning system under which their parents grew up.

Regular meals, we learned from our home visits, remained under the control of parents and grandparents, although children's negotiations with their seniors at home over the choice of food at meals were neither uncommon nor unsuccessful. Where children definitely were evading parental control was in the consumption of snacks and soft drinks; in the little more than a decade since the launching of urban reforms, thousands of new brands of factory-manufactured snacks and soft drinks have appeared in supermarkets and neighborhood stores. Children in grade schools and kindergarten were the fastest learners in consuming new foods; they quickly became familiar with a long list of brand names, including the names of Western-style fast-food outlets and menus. By contrast, their parents, not to mention their grandparents, were far less knowledgeable about the names, tastes, appearances, or prices of new foods and drinks. It was not uncommon to hear in our interviews with parents and grandparents that it was their own youngsters who informed them about new food products. As children become full-scale consumers, they are assuming the role of culinary instructors by offering specific information to influence their elders' purchasing and dining decisions.[1]

Within the confines of the consumerist dietetic knowledge, the taste of food could become totally irrelevant. In an insightful observation, the father of a Beijing schoolgirl said: "Today's kids select their favorite candies according to the fanciness of the wrappers and packages. Sometimes they won't even bother to eat the candies. They are interested only in the appearance of the packaging and the small toys inside the packages." It should be explained here that the combination of food and play is not a recent invention in China. As early as the 1960s, biscuits were made in China in the shapes of cats, dogs, bears, zebras, and other animals. The difference is that the contemporary integration of food and play has the effect of effacing the dietary dimensions of food. Take for example a brand of instant noodles that became a hit among children when it was first marketed. Inside the package was a colored picture. If eight pictures of different colors were saved, they could be traded for an eye-catching T-shirt. This marketing technique caused children to compete with one another to become what one adult informant sarcastically called the factory's "mobile advertising." To win the T-shirt, which bore the factory's logo, the children would have to eat the factory's product regularly in order to collect the right pictures. Once the package is opened, it was often the parents who ended up eating the noodles. The diminished relevance of taste also can be seen in some Beijing children's obsession with fast-food chains such as McDonald's, Kentucky Fried Chicken, and Pizza Hut. They like these fast-food franchises not entirely because of how the food tastes but because of what "fun" (*hao wan*) and "nice ambiance" (*qi fen hao*) they say they find there. A Beijing mother said that at home her daughter habitually called her "mama," but that when she took her daughter to McDonald's the little girl would address her mother as "mami," a word Chinese children have picked up from picture books and imported television cartoon shows. As this linguistic switch and the T-shirt story show, the dietary relevance of food can be eliminated, or at least become subordinate to children's pleasure at the demonstration of parental love in being taken to a fancy restaurant or the excitement of competing for a publicly recognizable symbol of consumption.

Eat, Drink, and Cultural Transmission

Cultural knowledge is acquired, and it depends on the transmission of ideas, values, and symbols across generations. It is in this sense that the accumulation of dietetic knowledge has a multiplicity of implications for cultural transmission. To clarify what I mean by "cultural transmission" in the context of our research findings, one clear expression of the traditionalist attitude toward food among the grandparent generation is the belief that traditional festivals entail the consumption of special foods. Many of the households we studied not only celebrated the lunar New Year, but also the Lantern Festival (the fifteenth day of first lunar month), the Dragon Boat Festival (the fifth day of the fifth month), the Autumn Festival (the fifteenth day of eighth month), and the Winter Festival (the eighth day of twelfth month). The urban parents we interviewed tended to have a casual attitude about festival food. Some even said that serving and eating festival food should be a matter of personal preference, not tradition. But if the urban household was a three-generation unit, we learned, the grandparents often made sure that there would be *yuan xiao* (sweet dumplings made of rice flour) at the Lantern Festival, *zongzi* (pyramid-shaped buns made of glutinous rice and nuts wrapped in bamboo or reed leaves) for the Dragon Boat Festival, *yue bing* (moon-shaped cakes often with nuts inside) for the Mid-Autumn Festival, and *laba zhou* (rice or refined maize porridge with mixed nuts and dried fruit) for the Winter Festival. The grandparent generation understood why certain foods were associated with specific festivals. The schoolchildren we talked with knew what foods would be consumed at a particular festival but did not know why. These children's parents had only vague ideas about the religious basis for festival foods.

While the religious significance of traditional festival food was declining, providing special treats to celebrate a child's birthday gained unprecedented popularity. Most of the Beijing households we studied celebrated their children's birthdays by buying a birthday cake, preparing a special meal, or going out to a restaurant. Birthday gifts from parents, grandparents, aunts, uncles, and older cousins included books and toys, and sometimes money and a trip to an entertainment center. The celebration of children's birthdays not only became an annual family event but also entailed a considerable increase of household expenses. In the Jiangsu village as well, celebrating children's birthdays had become more popular. In responses on a questionnaire I distributed at the village school, 70 percent of the fifth-graders listed their own birthdays as a family event that must be celebrated. Only half of them mentioned the Dragon Boat Festival and the Mid-Autumn Festival as necessary.

Also diminishing in importance is the traditional use of food in moral education. Chinese literature is filled with moralizing stories about food that emphasize respect for the elderly, courtesy to equals, economic prudence, and respect for food as a product of hard work and as a medium of communication between the living and the dead. A grandfather said emotionally that these messages can no longer be heard today. "This new generation never had to worry about a lack of food or clothes," he said.

> When I was a child, the Japanese came and caused trouble. My parents starved to death while hiding in a mountain to escape a Japanese mopping-up operation. I was a teenager then. I ran away to Tianjin and Zhangjiakou in search of food to survive. By the time I had children of my own, there came the period of three bad years. People were so starved that they began to suffer from dropsy.

The "three bad years" refers to the famine that resulted from the economic turmoil of the Great Leap Forward (1958–60). As many as 30 million people perished in the famine from 1959 to 1961 (see Becker 1996; Jowett 1989:16–19; Yang Dali 1996).

To many of the parents of contemporary schoolchildren, this famine, easily the worst in modern history, has remained seared in memory. A 44-year-old father said that when he was a primary school student, Beijing was experiencing food shortages. His grandfather came from the countryside to help his hungry grandchildren in the capital. "It was deep winter when he arrived," the man recalled of his grandfather's visit.

He was wearing a cotton-padded coat and trousers. Even after he came into the room, he kept saying he was terribly cold. I was puzzled. Before getting into bed to rest, he washed himself with hot water. As he took off his clothes, I realized that the cotton pads of his coat and trousers had been taken out to hide grains from inside. At that time, the government prohibited individuals from taking food from the country to the cities.

When the adults we interviewed were asked if they had recounted such stories to their school-age children, the usual reply was that food-related tales of past suffering were irrelevant to children's dietary concerns these days. They feared not a lack of food but losing face in front of their classmates if they had not yet tasted certain popular brands of foods. Even when their parents or grandparents tearfully recalled their experience of famine and the deaths of family members, their children either found these stories too horrifying to be credible or failed to relate to them at the emotional level. To today's children, a parent said, the older people's past hardships "are like books coming down from heaven," meaning that the stories are incomprehensible.

In addition, the images of choice food and personal happiness that children constantly see on television have served to contradict and even nullify the effect of telling personal accounts of starvation and other forms of suffering. The food companies operating in China have no interest in reminding young people that not until the early 1980s did the average Chinese family have enough to eat. Food industry executives are well aware that the creation of a thriving market for new food products requires shaping children's eating habits and visions of the good life. As indicated earlier, television is one of the most effective media for accomplishing this goal.[2]

Television-viewing, the most popular leisure activity — as measured by the amount of time an average Chinese spends on it after work or school — has a unique impact on personal consumption. A sociological survey found that a cultural fad was created in the late 1980s when schoolchildren became so attracted by what they saw on television that they started to mimic the narration, key phrases, and song lyrics of popular commercials (Wang Jiangang 1989; see also Zhao Bin 1996:639–58). Teachers complained in interviews that some schoolgirls became fixated on television commercials in which movie or pop music stars made appearances to promote food products. Described by one teacher as the "star-chasing tribe"(*zhui xing zhu*), these girls were said to adore the entertainment industry's celebrities to the extent of craving the food featured in the commercials.

Television has affected parents as well. A 1987 nationwide survey found that urban residents spent an average of two hours a day in front of the television set, which accounted for nearly half the available leisure time then (Wang Shaoguang 1995:149–72). With the 1995 adoption of a five-day work week in cities, the amount of time that urban residents spent watching television on weekends increased sharply. Many parents we interviewed in Beijing claimed that they never believed what the commercials said about those food, drinks, and nutritional supplements that were constantly depicted on television as "health-enhancing." On closer inquiry, however, we found that some of the parents bought these products based on what they saw on television and in response to their children's requests. Their rejection of these products took shape only after they discovered that the products were not as good as advertised. China still lacks strict state regulations against exaggerated product claims on television.

As far as schoolchildren are concerned, another venue for learning about food involves peer competition for status in neighborhoods and schools. We were told by both teachers and parents that a child's failure to recognize and consume popular new food products could lead to ridicule within his or her peer group, because a central form of childhood association was the sharing of food and food-related information. Sharing food and eating together, teachers said, is a common practice at schools, usually with classmates of the same sex. Since students are allowed to bring a small amount of food and snacks from home to eat during lunchtime, sharing these foods is also a means of exchanging information on what is good to eat.

The sharing of food-related information can sometimes become a competitive demonstration of one's familiarity with the trendiest foods on the market. Peer group pressure to consume trendy foods became so intense at one Beijing primary school that one student, according to his father, told his friends that he had eaten Wall's ice cream, while in fact he never had. Supposedly, all the boy's classmates had themselves tasted this popular treat, produced by a Sino-British-Dutch joint venture. So when the subject of Wall's came up in a chat, the boy felt that he had to lie to avoid losing face. Teachers said they were keenly aware of the competitive nature of children's food discourse; the problem was created, they said, by parents who provided their children with too much pocket money, which in turn helped create the economic foundation for the students' competition for status and prestige through food (see Chapter 2 above, in which Bernadine Chee gives a fuller account of the problem of competitive consumption among schoolchildren).

Pocket money also gave schoolchildren an opportunity to consume secretly foods that their parents prohibited on health and safety grounds. Most of the parents we interviewed were well aware of this consequence of pocket money but said that it would be unrealistic not to give children any pocket money at all. In urban areas, the 4-2-1 relationship — meaning four grandparents and two parents to one child — meant that youngsters receive a varying amount of money from at least three sets of relations: their parents and their maternal and paternal grandparents. Uncles or aunts are also likely to provide their nephews or nieces with cash presents and pocket money. We found in our Beijing study that a child could receive an allowance of as much as five yuan a day and more than 100 yuan in gifts during the lunar New Year. Most of these children were given pocket money on a daily or weekly basis. Some of the money at their disposal also came as birthday presents or rewards for academic achievement. The largest cash gifts were usually given during the lunar New Year. In the Jiangsu village, most of the children in the fifth grade I interviewed also had pocket money. The lowest amount was 50 *fen* per day and the highest, three *yuan*. As with the schoolchildren we interviewed in Beijing, these rural children's pocket money was spent, more often than not, on snacks, soft drinks, dried fruit, ice cream, or nuts.

Conclusion: Food and Childhood

Growing up in a culture normally means inheriting a body of knowledge from the past and learning to replicate existing behavioral norms. Since a family's elders, especially parents, usually have the earliest influence on a child's socialization, it stands to reason that they usually are the first and vital link in the transmission of knowledge in any society. The imperative to transmit knowledge across generations is to prepare young people to assume adult roles. This preparation involves the inculcation of appropriate values and attitudes as well as the development of practical skills. To this end, an important element of child development is learning what and how to eat.

In China, grandparents have long maintained an active relationship with their own children and their children's children. Thus, the transmission of social values goes beyond the confines of the nuclear family and involves all the stem family's older living members. Our analysis of the interview data suggests that teaching a youngster to understand the health consequences and social ramifications of food has remained an important element of child education. The passing down of this knowledge involves the participation of both parents and grandparents. We recognize that there is still a strong correlation between the traditionalist dietetic knowledge of the grandparent generation and the modernist dietetic knowledge of the parent generation. Although the specific contents of their dietetic knowledge are quite different, they overlap in the sense that both are concerned with achieving a healthy diet.

However, these older generations are now running into

difficulties trying to pass on what they know about food to the school-age generation. This problem bears out the impact of economic reforms and the commercialization of Chinese society. As Charlotte Ikels points out in her Guangzhou-based study of China's transition to a market economy: "Equipping young people for the future is a formidable task under the best of circumstances, but when a society is undergoing rapid change, the challenge can be almost overwhelming" (1996:140). Our interviews show that the challenge is indeed enormous and that it may be very hard to meet.

With a steady stream of manufactured food products entering the market since the introduction of urban reforms, many Chinese adults have felt swamped by consumer information. In describing how their children reacted to this information explosion, a Beijing parent said: "Today's children have learned a lot of things. When we were growing up, we knew nothing. It was only when I got into middle school that I saw a television set. Children nowadays habitually express their wants by declaring which television commercial said this and which classmate said that." Elderly people find this state of affairs extremely confusing. They are unfamiliar with new consumer products; they have to be told by their grandchildren what new foods are on the market, how much they cost, and why they should be consumed. Thus, with regard to manufactured foods, the traditional educational relationship between the oldest and youngest members of the stem family is being reversed.

What also needs to be stressed is the differences in childhood experiences from a historical perspective. Most of the current grandparent generation grew up in a time of severe economic hardship exacerbated by one national crisis after another. They suffered through the Sino-Japanese War (1937–45) and the Chinese civil war (1946–49). When they were children or young adults, food consumption was an issue of physical survival. For those Chinese who are now the parents of today's schoolchildren, their younger years were indelibly shaped by Mao's experiments with radical state socialism and Soviet-style economic development. Many were affected by the famine following the Great Leap Forward and the chronic shortages of basic necessities during the Cultural Revolution (1966–76). In the countryside, how this generation manages the household economy still reflects a lingering fear of starvation. Wasting food, even a tiny amount, is repugnant to them. Urban parents' attitudes toward food may be less cautious. But they retain vivid memories of the strict food rationing of the Maoist era. They came of age standing in long lines at state stores with food coupons in hand to purchase their family's monthly allotment of wheat, corn flour, bean curd, and cooking oil. Because of these experiences, they know how to suppress their desires and temptations to spend their rising but still limited incomes on faddish foods and exotic thrills.

Today's schoolchildren are growing up in a drastically changed socioeconomic environment. They were born into a society that was beginning to experience a very different kind of revolution — a consumer revolution. Furthermore, they came into being under stricter government controls over the country's population growth. In rural areas, such controls have meant that fewer children are born into each household. In cities, the government's population policy has an even greater impact, since an urban couple is allowed to have only one child. Consequently, many concerns have been expressed in urban areas over the policy and the allegedly numerous problems associated with children without brothers or sisters. The problem of *ni ai*, or "drowning children with love," is one frequently voiced concern (Wu 1994:2–12). One fear is that the singletons are provided with too much material comfort and are therefore growing up without any discipline or the ability to study and work hard. As to whether these single children are becoming spoiled brats, available studies contradict one another, leading to more questions than conclusions (see, e.g., Xingyin Chen et al. 1992; Bin Yang et al. 1995).

What cannot be doubted, however, is that Chinese children, urban and rural alike, are learning about and growing up in a culture of consumerism. Even in the Chinese countryside, young children are exposed by television to the tempting images of the latest food products. During my fieldwork in the Jiangsu village, a little girl made fun of me when she discovered I had never heard of an obviously popular soft drink. "You don't even know this brand?" she asked with only slightly concealed mockery. "It's on television every day."

5

Globalized Childhood?

Kentucky Fried Chicken in Beijing

Eriberto P. Lozada, Jr.

The social ramifications of transnationalism —
the flows of ideas, products, people, capital, and technologies
across national boundaries — have become the staple of recent
anthropological literature. This interest is based largely on the high
visibility of cultural artifacts from transnational corporations,
which have left people in very different parts of the world, as one
scholar puts it, "increasingly wearing the same kinds of clothes, eating the same kinds of food, reading the same kinds of newspapers,
watching the same kinds of television programs, and so on"
(Haviland 1994:675). The growing power of such corporations is
sometimes considered a major cause of cultural disruption in developing countries, mutating local traditions beyond recognition. In
this chapter, I argue that although there are now many visible
markers of homogenization because of a more integrated global
system of production and consumption, there has also been a dramatic expansion in particularism, as competing claims for cultural
identity and authenticity have become more strident. This particularism can be seen in the ways some of the most crucial decisions
affecting transnational corporations are made and then modified
within the confines of local societies, through the participation of
local people and in adjustment to local social changes.

To elaborate on this argument, I will examine how the US-
based Kentucky Fried Chicken (KFC) catered to Beijing children in
the 1990s. This focus is mainly warranted by two considerations.

First, fast-food restaurants like KFC have been especially successful among children in large Chinese urban centers. Children are often the decision-makers in determining whether an urban family will patronize a KFC restaurant. Moreover, what children eat is a fundamental part of their socialization, and changes in children's dietary patterns are indicative of changes in their larger social environment (Beardsworth and Keil 1997). In addition, children's consumption of both material and cultural goods is becoming a fiercely contested domain in many parts of the world and among various social groups seeking to implement their particular visions of the future by shaping childhood experiences (Stephens 1995; see Jun Jing's Introduction above). As an organizational actor, KFC is a part of the social life of Beijing children and influences Chinese experiences of childhood by becoming part of local Beijing life. Before I set up the ethnographic context of KFC in Beijing for analysis, let me make a few remarks about this chapter's theoretical framework.

Transnational Organizations and Chinese Children

Transnational organizations, which provide institutional support for the movement of people, goods, and ideas across national boundaries, have existed as long as there have been nations (E. Wolf 1982; Hannerz 1992; Huntington 1973).[1] However, in the past such organizations were less influential than other social organizations, for example, the nation-state itself, in shaping the social practices of local communities (Nye and Keohane 1973). Today, local communities are more fully integrated by global communication networks, world trade and market networks, and labor migrations into a global system of interdependence (Sassen 1996; Appadurai 1996; Featherstone 1990). As a result, understanding the social fabric of everyday life now more than ever requires an understanding of how transnational organizations connect local communities with global forces of economic development and social change (Moore 1994, 1987; Strathern, ed., 1995).

In social analyses of transnationalism, scholars have emphasized one of two perspectives. Some studies have focused on what the anthropologist Marilyn Strathern calls the "concrete models of globalization" (Strathern, ed., 1995:159), that is, the structural implications arising from the "world capitalist system" (see, e.g., Wallerstein 1974; Frank 1969; Vallier 1973; Hanson 1980). Studies based on this type of organizational analysis are often problematic because they assume a high level of cultural homogeneity in the organizations being studied and a high degree of passivity in the adaptation by the host cultures. Also, these studies do not fully account for the influences of informal networks within institutional frameworks. A second group of studies has focused on the cultural implications of transnational processes, in such areas as development, public culture, and diaspora identity (see, e.g., Morley and Robins 1995; Gupta 1992; Escobar 1995). However, these studies tend to underestimate the political asymmetries between nation-states and their ability to define and shape transnational issues. They also tend to homogenize the various transnational institutions such as world religious organizations and international business companies.

In this chapter, I will try to avoid the aforementioned problems by combining the strengths of both perspectives and by focusing concretely on a single transnational organization. My basic approach is identifying Kentucky Fried Chicken in Beijing as an entry point of transnationalism into a specific city and, I might add, literally into the gastronomy of the local people. This approach requires an examination of KFC restaurants in Beijing as socially constructed localities of consumption,[2] the commercial success of which depends on understanding how the local society operates. Since the opening of the first Beijing branch in 1987, KFC operations in China have been gradually "domesticated," in the sense that a formerly exotic, imported food has been transformed into a familiar and even intimate type of cuisine. This domestication process bears the accumulative effects of "localization," which in this chapter refers to innovations and modifications made by KFC in reaction to local competition and to a growing understanding of the special place of children in urban China. Localization also refers to the transformed attitudes of KFC patrons, whereby the once-foreign KFC product is incorporated into everyday social life.[3]

Whether or not they have actually eaten at KFC, Chinese boys and girls know about it from various sources, including television and classmates (see chapters 2 and 4 in this volume). This awareness does not mean that an opportunity to eat at KFC is equally available to all children, but it does result in KFC's becoming a desired taste, a lifestyle aspiration, and even a measure of "distinction" (Bourdieu 1984:6).[4] In addition, catering to Chinese children has placed special demands upon KFC, one of which originates in the children's less-than-enthusiastic response to KFC's most recognizable symbol — the white-bearded, elderly-looking Colonel Sanders. Chinese children rejected this figure in favor of "Chicky," a youngish, fun-loving, and child-specific KFC icon specifically developed for the Chinese market and introduced there in 1995. Chicky will be further discussed below in analyzing the roles of children, parents, schools, and Chinese mass media in the localization of a transnational implant such as KFC in Beijing.

Chicky or Colonel Sanders?

The first KFC restaurant in China opened in November 1987 at a heavily trafficked and highly visible location at the Qianmen area of Beijing, just south of the Mao Zedong Mausoleum and Tiananmen Square. At that time, this Qianmen KFC was the world's largest fast-food restaurant, seating 500. In its first year, the Qianmen KFC drew between 2,000 and 3,000 customers a day, and subsequently set numerous KFC records. In 1988, for example, it fried 2,200 chickens daily and topped all KFC restaurants in turnover at 14 million yuan. By 1994, KFC had seven restaurants in Beijing, located in high-volume tourist and shopping areas, and 21 other restaurants in cities throughout the country. The KFC restaurants in China became a major source of profit for the international restaurant division of KFC's parent company, PepsiCo, Inc. Based on its success in China, as well as on its overall achievements in East Asia (KFC Asia-Pacific in 1993 provided more than 22 percent of all KFC sales, including those in the domestic United States market), KFC announced in 1994 that it was investing an additional $200 million over the next four years to expand the number of KFC restaurants in China to 200.

My study of KFC in Beijing began in 1994 and continued with visits to Beijing during the following four years while I conducted research in southern China. On a Saturday afternoon in the summer of 1995, I visited a KFC restaurant in Dongsi, a popular shopping and dining area in downtown Beijing. Inside the restaurant's foyer, two children crowded around a KFC-uniformed "children's hostess," trying to tell her their preferences in "flying sticks" — a toy children can spin to make fly. "I don't want the green one, I want the red one," one boy shouted.

It was a busy afternoon for the hostess, as she stood by the door, greeting all the children and handing out flying sticks to each child. She had been standing for several hours, but her easily recognized KFC uniform, the trademark red-and-white shirt with black pants, looked crisp and clean, as if she had just put it on. She hesitated in exchanging the boy's toy. His companion also wanted a red one too, in place of the yellow one. Not wanting to disappoint the children, she reached into her bag and brought out two red ones and gave them to the children. They scampered happily back to their tables, and the hostess, having satisfied two more children, turned to look for others in need of a toy or a smile.

KFC, like other fast-food restaurants, has discovered that children love eating at its restaurants and are its regular customers.[5] Adult customers at its Dongsi branch, who most often came with their families, told me that they visit KFC mainly because their children like it.[6] Parents, when asked what they thought about the food in comparison with other fast-food choices, said that they themselves did not really care which fast-food restaurant they patronized, but that their children chose to come to KFC. Their impression of KFC as a place primarily for children was in line with the company's own promotion of itself among children in China as a "fun and exciting place to eat." This is why the company added special hostesses for children.

The most salient symbol of this focus on children is Chicky, known in Chinese as *Qiqi*, a cartoon character that KFC hopes Chinese children will associate with KFC. Chicky is a white-feathered chicken dressed in big red sneakers, red-and-white striped pants, a red vest marked with the initials KFC, and a blue bow-tie. His blue baseball cap (also with KFC logo) is worn pulled to one side, as is the rage in hip-hop pop culture of the United States; Beijing children see such images in music videos regularly aired on local television. Chicky embodies what KFC hopes is the dining experience of its younger clientele. He is obviously fun-loving, as he winks and dances around, with his baseball cap askew. Chicky is exciting, as he waves from his plane in one restaurant mural. But he also works hard in school. On a back-to-school pencil case given to customers ordering the KFC children's meal in August 1995, Chicky exhorts the young customers to "study hard, play hard" (*renzhen xuexi, kaixin youxi*).

The Chicky character provided a strong contrast to Colonel Sanders, the dominant symbol of KFC on its arrival in China in 1987 — whose statues stood like guardians at the entrance of the first Beijing restaurant. It gradually became clear to local managers that Beijing children had problems relating to the Colonel. They identified him as an elderly and dour grandfather, with his white suit, white hair, and goatee. One general manager reported that children would come into KFC restaurants saying "Grandfather sent us." Managers at KFC's regional headquarters in Hong Kong decided to develop Chicky to set a more playful tone for the place.[7]

The physical layouts of KFC restaurants in Beijing also have been designed with children in mind. Many KFC restaurants are built with a play area for their young customers (though not the Dongsi restaurant, due to space limitations). Furniture is built with children's small scale in mind; the sink for hand-washing is low enough that most six-year-olds can use it without assistance. Also, a space is set aside for a childhood ritual only recently introduced to China, the birthday party. The Dongsi KFC had a raised seating area on the second floor, separated from the other tables by a wooden railing. On one wall, a mural depicted Chicky singing "Happy Birthday" and kicking up his heels. The area could seat about 56 customers, and for birthday parties it was decorated with balloons.

During my visits to Beijing between 1994 and 1997, I found that fast-food restaurants, including KFC, were becoming desirable places for children's birthday parties, and staff members and areas within the restaurants were specially designated to help celebrate these events. Partygoers included parents, relatives, and especially "little friends," as children are often called in China. That KFC restaurants were becoming an integral part of conspicuous consumption in the celebration of children's birthdays is one of many indications that youngsters in Beijing and other Chinese cities were acting as consumers in their own right. Chinese and Western firms were finding more commodities specifically designed for and targeted at this new consumer market.

Eating Kentucky Fried Chicken Versus Glorious China Chicken

The KFC restaurant in Dongsi was a two-story establishment, seating around 250 people. The neighborhood has long been an active market area and is home to a wide variety of retail outlets. On a summer Saturday in 1994,[8] I saw a line of people waiting patiently to be admitted by a restaurant employee wearing a pink-collared polo shirt with the KFC logo. This orderly scene starkly contrasted with the mobs that crowded around nearby bus stops, pushing and shoving to board. The restaurant had large windows allowing passersby to see into the kitchen; the stainless-steel counters and tiled floors reflected high standards of cleanliness. There was a take-out window, for those on the move in Beijing's new fast-paced entrepreneurial environment, with a full menu and pictures of selected items. The menu was comparable to American KFC restaurants, with fried chicken, potatoes and gravy, coleslaw, sodas — including Pepsi Cola, of course, as KFC is a PepsiCo subsidiary. A regular two-chicken-piece meal cost 17.10 yuan ($2.14), while a children's meal went for around 8.80 yuan ($1.10). Inside the air-conditioned, brightly lit restaurant, many people gathered around the counters to place their orders, while another crowd clustered around the two sinks toward the back of the restaurant, where signs pointed out the sanitary facilities where customers could wash their hands. Upstairs was a larger seating area, with windows overlooking the street and signs pointing to another set of sinks where patrons could wash up. Uniformed KFC employees were constantly wiping counters, emptying garbage cans, and mopping the walking areas — no easy task given the stream of people walking through the restaurant. On this day, the place was crowded with families — nearly every table had at least one elementary school-aged child. Managers said in interviews that the restaurant was busy serving an army of children almost every weekend.

Across the street from the Dongsi KFC was "Glorious China Chicken," or *Ronghuaji* in Chinese. Here, too, there was also a line, but it was much shorter. There was a hostess, too, but unlike the one at KFC, she looked bored as she smiled and opened the door for customers. The Ronghuaji restaurant was also air-conditioned, but its decor was more reminiscent of a night club. Although the menu did not have as much variety as KFC's, a standard meal was considerably cheaper (8.80 yuan, or $1.10) and the customers got more food (fried rice, soup, and some vegetables). There were also alternatives to fried chicken, such as baked paper-wrapped chicken. Draft beer, a popular item in Beijing restaurants this summer, was also available here. Both the food and the service seemed more "Chinese"; one patron complained in a letter to the editor of a local newspaper about the absence of bathrooms to wash hands after eating greasy chicken, bad service with rushed "hostessing,"[9] and the manager's unpleasant attitude when the customer complained.

Nonetheless, Ronghuaji staff (like those at KFC) emphasized cleanliness, or at least the appearance of cleanliness; Ronghuaji staff members were constantly mopping the floor and wiping counters. On that same Saturday afternoon, there were fewer families with children and more groups of young adults eating at the Ronghuaji than at the KFC.

Chicken Frying and Transnational Politicking

The differences between these two restaurants extend beyond such aspects as the age of their customers. Ronghuaji, a Chinese corporation set up in 1989, had strained to emulate the American KFC,[10] whereas in fact KFC in China, as in many other countries, had been introducing changes to adapt to local consumer demands. Although corporate standards of quality, cleanliness, and management have been applied internationally by KFC, there is, in fact, no standardized way of selling chicken. In China, KFC has had to respond to the demands of different local actors (including many levels of Chinese government)[11] within a shifting political economy. Local managers are given a great deal of operational autonomy by Louisville, Kentucky (KFC headquarters), and Purchase, New York (PepsiCo headquarters), to determine the relationship between KFC restaurants and the Chinese government, as long as they achieve "results with integrity" — standards that are spelled out in the KFC Code of Conduct. This localization of authority, providing the means to respond quickly to consumer demand, may be the key to KFC's (and PepsiCo's) international success. PepsiCo has more than 25,000 units and annual sales exceeding $25 billion (KFC accounts for more than 9,000 of the 3,900 units outside the United States), and oversees the world's largest restaurant system. With the reopening of the Chinese market to foreign investment in the early 1980s, KFC became the first Western restaurant company to enter the People's Republic with the February 1987 establishment of the joint venture Beijing Kentucky Co., Ltd.[12]

Unlike many other American joint ventures in China, KFC

launched its operations from the political power center, Beijing, instead of the economic centers of Guangzhou and Shanghai — a difference that Timothy Lane, who was KFC Asia-Pacific president at the time, called the key to KFC's success in China (Evans 1993). One result of this decision, however, was to link KFC's business in China to events in Beijing. For instance, in 1989 in Beijing, the reopening of KFC's Qianmen restaurant, adjacent to Tiananmen Square, occurred just one week after the military suppression of pro-democracy demonstrations in the square on June 3–4 sent many other foreign investors fleeing or sharply curtailing operations in China.[13] After the crackdown, the KFC Qianmen restaurant was used by Chinese troops occupying Tiananmen Square. American popular consciousness of the failed democracy movement, stirred by its dramatic unfolding and then suppression on television, put many American businesses under domestic pressure to cease operations in China. However, KFC reopened its Qianmen restaurant, citing "contractual obligations." In this tense period of US-China relations, there was still an arena less constrained by state control that allowed KFC and its Beijing partners to continue doing business. According to Saskia Sassen (1996), this arena of global capitalism exists only with the complicity of states; in this case, China's commitment to modernization and economic development (and the American desire to expand the capitalist market) created the conditions for KFC to continue selling chicken. In other words, although transnational organizations have a degree of maneuverability in the arena of global capitalism, they are still greatly constrained by state involvement.[14]

KFC is very much decentralized in its operations. On the most local level, its restaurants are either franchises, joint-venture operations, or company-owned stores. Although the franchises and joint ventures retain greater autonomy from KFC control, even the company-owned stores have a good deal of latitude in the way they conduct their business. The devolution of the decision-making process in KFC is driven by the pressures of the fast-food business: chicken goes bad quickly, and there is little time for KFC staff to consult with superiors about decisions. Marketing plans are driven by local assessments of potential consumers and are also executed on the local level. In our discussions, KFC executives consistently recognized the heterogeneity of local markets.

KFC's flexible structure reinforces the attitude that there are many ways to sell chicken, and that for KFC to succeed in any given society it must be firmly grounded in that society. This is not to say that KFC restaurants are not supported by its transnational networks — Beijing's KFC restaurants draw heavily on PepsiCo's support services. In fact, with the 1995 restructuring of PepsiCo, KFC restaurants now share such services with other PepsiCo restaurants (including Pizza Hut and Taco Bell), with headquarters in Dallas, the home of PepsiCo's snack-food subsidiary Frito-Lay. However, local managers decide how to draw on these support services. They remain important decision-makers in day-to-day operations and in planning of local strategies.

"Cock Fight": Competing and Learning

With the success of the Beijing KFC restaurants, Chinese companies in other major cities such as Shanghai sought to form joint-venture operations with KFC; after 1988, more than 100 companies across the country wanted to open KFC restaurants (Hua 1990). With plans by a Shanghai group to open a KFC in 1989, as the story goes, two Shanghai entrepreneurs went to Beijing to see what was behind the "KFC Fever." After waiting for more than an hour in line at the Qianmen KFC, they gave up and went to the Dongsi KFC, where they were able to taste some fried chicken.[15]

They concluded that the reasons for KFC's success in Beijing, in addition to advanced processing, quality assurance, and management techniques, were tied to the region itself: northerners were used to eating foods similar to the standard KFC fare, such as potatoes and bread. These two entrepreneurs decided that they would emulate the social and technical practices of KFC, but for Shanghai they would offer fried chicken that was more appealing to the southern Chinese palate. In 1989, they opened the Ronghuaji restaurants in Shanghai to compete head-on with KFC. Chinese newspapers (see, e.g., Qian and Li 1991; Niu 1992; *Liberation Daily* 1990) picked up on the rivalry, labeling it a "cock fight" (*dou ji*), and praised Ronghuaji for scoring its first victory when, in February 1990, under competitive pressure, KFC reduced its prices. This Geertzian "deep play" became a symbol of the cultural struggle between local Chinese foodways and the American fast-food invaders.

With the opening of a Ronghuaji in Beijing in Dongsi in October 1992, the "cock fight" story changed tenor, and instead posed the problem in terms of adapting to a new lifestyle; namely, what are the social costs and benefits of a fast-food culture? Ronghuaji's success in competing with KFC demonstrated that Chinese entrepreneurs could employ Western technology and create an industry with "Chinese characteristics." Moreover, there had been a growing recognition that the mass consumption of KFC and other non-Chinese products served as a marker of China's and, more important socially, individual consumers' success in the world market (Wen Jinhai 1992). Later articles (see, e.g., *Beijing Bulletin* 1994a, 1994b) commenting on the "cock fight" noted that KFC was changing its strategy as domestic conditions changed. For example, when the first KFC restaurant opened in China in 1987, 40 percent of the raw materials for its menu were imported. By 1991, thanks to the local development of the fast-food industry, only 3 percent of the raw materials had to be imported — namely, the Colonel's eleven secret herbs and spices.

These assertions of China's successful adaptation of Western business techniques, made in different ways by entrepreneurs such as the Ronghuaji managers, Chinese joint-venture managers, and government officials, ring like a 1990s version of Chinese reformers' calls a century earlier of "Chinese learning for the essence, Western learning for utility" (cf. Wei and Wang 1994). The point is that KFC did not obliterate China's culinary traditions; instead it stimulated a local discourse on national heritage. Since Ronghuaji opened its first branch in Beijing, competing explanations for the origins of fast food have been offered in the media coverage of the "cock fight." Some claim that the origins of China's fast-food industry can be found thousands of years ago in such foods as stuffed buns (*baozi*) and glutinous-rice rolls (*zongzi*); others trace the origins to more recent traditional foods such as spring rolls, fried dough sticks, and other foods that once could be bought on the streets of any market town. Others argue that fast food is an idea wholly imported from the United States, and is something unique to American culture that has spread throughout the world. Another claim is that fast food in China is linked to the recent explosion of economic development and increased personal consumption.

With the reforms begun in the late 1970s, all economic sectors including agriculture have experienced tremendous growth — resulting in increasing levels of individual consumption. One of the most cited reasons for patronizing fast-food restaurants is the desire to eat Western food — to have a taste of modernity. For Chinese visitors to Beijing, eating at a fast-food restaurant is part of the experience of visiting the nation's capital; the Dongsi KFC made this explicit, by mapping out KFC restaurants and tourist sites in Beijing on a large display outside the restaurant. Out-of-town visitors are readily distinguished from native Beijingers when they pose for family pictures standing next to a life-size statue of Colonel Sanders.

Whatever the origins of fast food in China, the beginnings of a fast-food craze in Beijing were apparent in 1984, when the first Western-style fast-food restaurant opened in the city's Xidan district. The Chinese-owned and operated Yili Fast Food restaurant, which used Donald Duck as its symbol, claimed to be "the first step in solving the food service problem."[16] The restaurant charged 1 yuan for a hot dog, 1.20 yuan for a hamburger, and 4 yuan for fried chicken with french fries. About the same time, Huaqing Snack Food Restaurant opened across from the Beijing railway station, making Chinese-style fast food. Both of these early ventures stood out from other Chinese restaurants that simply served food fast by using updated food-preparation technology imported from abroad — Hong Kong and the United States. The arrival of KFC in 1987 further defined the characteristics of the modern fast-food restaurant: high standards of hygiene and a standardization of food quality and menus. By 1994, fast-food restaurants, both Chinese and foreign, had multiplied in Beijing: McDonald's, Pizza Hut, Brownies (Canadian), Café de Coral (Hong Kong), Vie de France (French), Yoshinoya (Japanese), Million Land House (Chinese), and so on. All are marked by standardized, mechanized cooking and an explicit concern for hygiene; the uniformed staff member mopping the floor, no matter what the style of food, is always highly visible in Beijing fast-food restaurants. The flourishing of these fast-food restaurants coincided with a growing concern among Beijing residents about hygiene when eating out. In summer 1993, soon after the outbreak of the "cock fight," there was a food-poisoning scare in Beijing. KFC and similar fast-food restaurants had the advantage in this situation of offering anxious Chinese consumers a predictable product. Furthermore, with the ability to reliably produce a large amount of food, KFC has also been commissioned by businesses and government agencies to cater large banquets. An American economics professor recounted that whenever he visits Beijing, the Chinese Academy of Social Sciences is sure to give him at least one banquet with KFC products. In summer 1994, KFC began providing free delivery within central Beijing (inside the city's Third Ring Road) for orders of more than 500 yuan ($62.50).

The wide variety of fast-food restaurants with international links like KFC have provided a space for Beijing residents to exercise choice: whether sampling exotic, non-Chinese cuisines, choosing which style of fast food to eat, or selecting items from a menu. Beijingers, for the most part, no longer struggle just to obtain life's necessities. With the maturation of the economic reforms, they can now choose from a wider range of goods and services. The new phenomenon of food "neophilia" reinforces Beijingers' sense of being modern, of having progressed well beyond subsistence (Beardsworth and Keil 1997; also see Chapter 3 by Maris Gillette above). The ability of Beijing residents to choose, especially choosing to eat fast food, can be seen as marking their entry into modernity.[17] At the height of the "cock fight" controversy, one writer lamented: "It is said that the pace of modern society has quickened. Pushed by a rapidly advancing way of life, people hardly have time to pant, let alone to enjoy life. Perhaps it is worth the sacrifice in quality to add to the quantity so that everyone has a chance to enjoy the fast-food culture" (Zhang Xia 1993). The accelerated production of a vast array of consumer goods and services, associated with the capitalist market and modernity, has fostered an ideology of consumer choice in Western societies: "Choice has become the privileged vantage from which to measure all action" (Strathern 1992:36). This ideology means more than having a number of different commodities to choose from; it emphasizes the shift of emphasis from producers to consumers. The former's profit depends on the latter's satisfaction — an idea that is gradually spreading in China's transition to a free-market economy.

Working with Schools and Finding Young Consumers

As mentioned earlier, KFC's most important Chinese customers have been children. To further its recognition among children, KFC has worked to develop partnerships with schools, teachers, and parents. Throughout China, KFC sponsors numerous children's sporting events, essay competitions, and other contests. These events have in turn helped KFC lure more of these young customers (and their parents) into its restaurants: KFC set a one-day sales record on June 1, 1993, International Children's Day.[18] The journalist Susan Lawrence describes the welcome given in May 1994 to John Cranor, then president and chief executive officer of KFC, by 110 Shanghai schoolchildren. Dressed in white wigs, fake goatees, and string ties, they performed the "Colonel Sanders Chicken Dance" at a ceremony marking the opening of the world's nine-thousandth KFC outlet (1994:46). Schools, as KFC appreciates, have a major impact on the socialization of children and in defining ideal forms of childhood. But today's Chinese schools cannot be seen as the extension of the nation-state in shaping students into ideal citizens (in the eyes of the Chinese government) or as a homogeneous system defining cultural standards of childhood (cf. Shirk 1982). The variety of schooling options for Beijing children today reflects the increasing social disparities arising from the booming growth of the Chinese economy (Yan 1992, 1994). The emergence of private schools, catering to a new elite, suggests that Chinese children participate as subjects in these processes of social stratification but are also themselves symbolic objects for adults.[19]

It can be argued that KFC plays an important role in this stratification of Chinese childhood. Meals at fast-food restaurants, while an enjoyable family event from the child's perspective, are considered expensive by average consumers. In 1993, a typical meal for a family of three cost between 18 and 48 yuan, when the average monthly income of a wage-earner was about 400 to 600 yuan (Evans 1993:3). John Cranor of KFC described the company's customers as "aspirational consumers," people with enough disposable income to spend the money for a fast-food meal. However, with the enforcement of the one-child policy, Chinese parents are willing to spend more money on their "little emperors" (*xiao huangdi*) or "little suns" (*xiao taiyang*) for fast-food meals, snacks, and toys. Commentaries abound in the Chinese press on how parents and grandparents are focusing too much attention and too many resources on single children, spoiling them to the point that they grow up without discipline. The popularity of fast food, despite its expense, and changing patterns of consumption must be understood in light of these changes in children's social relationships.

KFC is only one of a number of foreign and domestic organizations competing for children's attention in China.[20] In summer 1994, Yoshinoya distributed prizes such as rulers with magnifying glasses to any customer who purchased at least 25 yuan worth of food. McDonald's (there is one across the street now from the

Dongsi KFC) was the leader in the distribution of toys, in Happy Meals, and assorted other souvenirs; at the McDonald's on Wangfujing Street in central Beijing, there was even a separate counter for toy and souvenir purchases. Fast foods were not the only items that children were demanding; children recognize a whole range of brightly packaged snacks by brand name. In a *Beijing Weekly* article discussing changing food consumption patterns, one mother complained that "Every month we spend a third of our income on our child's food, and snacks maybe cover a larger percentage" (Qiu 1994:8). According to the same report, Chinese children spent (or their parents spent for them) $1.25 billion in 1993 on snack food, a category that included KFC chicken.

Besides fast-food restaurants, there are a number of other domains where children and their parents can spend money today that are a recognized aspect of Beijing childhood. Video-game parlors (such as the SegaWorld in Qianmen) are scattered throughout Beijing's shopping districts, including the Dongsi area. Each game cost between one and two yuan in the mid-1990s. Just down the street from the Dongsi KFC were two "Mickey's Corner" stores, the local retailers of Walt Disney products. The Dongsi McDonald's was in the basement of a four-story department store filled with toys, computers, and other wares for children, and bookstores all along Wusi in central Beijing sold books, computer programs, and magazines to help children with their schoolwork. In a survey on children's consumption in Beijing, marketing experts James McNeal and Wu Shushan (1995:14; see also McNeal and Yeh 1997:45–59) discovered that urban children in China influence 69 percent of decisions about consumer purchases and have direct control (through allowances, gifts from parents and grandparents, etc.) of more than $5 billion per year (25 percent of which goes toward the purchase of snacks).

Television is yet another medium that draws Beijing children's attention. Many non-Chinese children's shows (like *Captain Planet*, *G.I. Joe*, and *Inspector Gadget* from the United States and other cartoons from Japan) are part of the local experience of Beijing children. The influence of these shows is further reinforced with toys, clothing, and other products based on the show. Late-afternoon television is dominated by these children's programs, including locally produced children's game shows in which teams of children compete in various obstacle courses, athletic challenges, or information quizzes with children-only audiences screaming *"Jia you"* (literally "add oil," a phrase that translates into something like "Rah, rah" or "Go for it"). And many commercials airing during children's programming advertise drinks, snacks, computers, and other mostly local products targeted at young consumers.

Children also watch television shows not directly aimed at them as a group, including popular serial dramas, sporting events, musical shows, and news reports. These become part of the local experience, symbolic resources that children can draw upon for their own use.[21] For example, in the summer of 1995, students from several Beijing senior and junior high schools, in conjunction with the China Wildlife Conservation Association, mobilized to save the Wusuli tiger from extinction.[22] They set up booths throughout the city to publicize the danger of extinction and to solicit donations to support a wildlife center. After seeing the students on the news, I went to a shopping area, where I saw young people wearing "Save the Tiger" T-shirts, handing out flyers, and collecting money. When reinforced by children's television shows like *Captain Planet* that promote a similar message, and by news reports of other children's social activism around the world, this kind of campaign becomes part of the socialization of Beijing children in the 1990s.

Conclusion: Globalized Childhood?

The most telling marker of KFC's localization in Beijing is that the company eventually lost its status as a "hot topic" (*remen huati*), meaning that it was no longer a major focus of cultural wars. By 1995, "cock fight" articles had become less salient in media discussions, and Glorious China Chicken had expanded, albeit slowly, with food choices that appealed more strongly to young adults. The novelty of "having a taste of modernity" faded. KFC patrons were more likely to say they ate there because it was convenient (*fangbian*), the children liked it, and it was clean. Symbolically, the Dongsi KFC no longer enjoyed equivalency with Beijing landmarks. In August 1995, the KFC map marking KFC restaurants and Beijing's tourist sites was replaced by a new one sponsored by a Chinese non-fast-food restaurant, which omitted any mention of KFC. Eating at KFC represented a change of eating habits. One man who was accompanied by his young daughter told me, "You can't make KFC chicken at home," in a manner suggestive of Americans eating take-out Chinese dishes. It was still a treat, but not a special one. To some Chinese, particularly older people, KFC products would still would "taste foreign," but for children, KFC simply tasted good.

As KFC gained more experience in China, it expanded its offerings to continue attracting customers and to distinguish itself from the growing number of fast-food alternatives. Being Western was no longer enough to ensure success, as KFC became a routine part of the local environment. For example, in 1995, Beijing KFC restaurants offered a spicy chicken sandwich that was not available in KFC restaurants in the United States. With the proliferation of international fast-food restaurants, companies begun to stress the uniqueness of their products. An outlet of the South Korea–based Lotteria chain advertised the "Koreanness" of its fast food in a placard outside the restaurant. There was also a constant bombardment of Lotteria commercials on television, in Korean, showing scenes of happy South Korean customers. The menu highlighted Korean fast-food specialties, such as the bulgogi burger (barbecued beef) and red-bean frozen dessert. Beijing customers became more selective in their consumption, more aware of the differences among fast-food offerings.

In retrospect, Chinese children have played a key role in the "localization" of KFC restaurants, influencing many of the changes in KFC business tactics. KFC has become a fixture of the local environment in the sense that it is part of the local children's experiences and embedded in local social relations. In one sense, children do draw parents into KFC restaurants, to eat fast food, taste modernity, and have fun. In the process they are drawing their elders into an intersection of local society and transnationalism. The children's special relationship with KFC restaurants is reinforced by television shows and other popular media and by their schools, as each enhances awareness of the world outside China and the relationship between their lives and global capitalism.

But this is not a passive relationship in which a transnational organization like KFC dictates lessons to be mastered by the natives. Both local residents and KFC are linked in a network of social relations that include manifestations of the nation-state (through schools, bureaucracies, and so forth), the media, and rival fast-food restaurants like Ronghuaji. As a result, KFC has had to adapt to the expectations and demands of its customers in ways that are not necessarily standard throughout the world KFC organization. In this case, the "periphery" talks back to the "center." With the increased consumption of goods and services for children, KFC has had to ensure that people are interested and supportive of their message. Rather than reflecting a fixed set of practices originating in its world headquarters in Louisville or its regional headquarters in Hong Kong, KFC's branches in Beijing are the sites of consumption where transnational forces are "domesticated," that is, localized with the input of local people, including local managers and young consumers. The invention of the mascot Chicky is a case in point, in that this character was invented specifically for Chinese children. Staffing requirements have also been adjusted, to introduce hostesses catering to young people. Additionally, KFC's outreach programs linked to schools and children's holidays incorporate local employees' understanding of the Chinese educational system.

Beijing children, just as children in most parts of the world, live in a deterritorialized space that can be viewed as a sort of globalized childhood culture; Chicky pencil-boxes with a pinball game on top can appeal to first-graders, whether in Beijing or in Boston. Fast-food restaurants like KFC are favorites among children, and like school they are part of children's social experiences. Many of the same cartoon characters continue to attract young television viewers in both China and the United States. The resulting "culture" is not a single, homogenized global children's culture, because these childhood experiences with consumption exist not in a vacuum but embedded in particular networks of social relations and historical contexts. Particularism becomes possible despite seemingly worldwide practices such as eating at KFC because specificity is produced in the consumption process. At first glance, KFC restaurants in China, as part of a transnational corporation, might seem to be one of those hallmarks of globalism that the anthropologist Daniel Miller refers to as the "new massive and often distant institutions" that catalyze the politics of differentiation (1995:290). On closer inspection, however, the success of KFC restaurants in Beijing has depended on its ability to become local, to become an integral part of Beijing children's social life.

Modernist descriptions of transnational organizations, as discussed earlier, are clearly not reflected in KFC's own business structure. In its decentralized organizational structure, businesspeople are well aware of the organizational traits necessary to succeed in today's globalized economy and the shift of emphasis from production to consumption. Even with global linkages, international support networks, and an arsenal of both financial and symbolic capital, the ability of transnational organizations to succeed in various locations, whether in Beijing or Delhi, hinges on their ability to become intelligible to people in their local social context.

Food, Nutrition, and Cultural Authority

in a Gansu Village

Jun Jing

This chapter deals with the cultural ramifications
of children's food consumption in Dachuan, a village in northwest
China's Gansu province.[1] In the pages that follow, "food" and
"nutrition" are broadly defined to include not only grains, vegetables, animal protein, and sweets and beverages but also vitamin
supplements, therapeutic food recipes, and a variety of items in the
category of health foods and tonics.[2] At the outset of my discussion, it may be helpful to recall two catalysts of social change in
post-Mao China. One was the economic reforms[3] and the other the
government's one-child policy.[4] Both developments, begun in the
late 1970s, have contributed to a dramatic rise in prosperity and
smaller families. Consequently, Chinese parents in general now
have more money to spend on fewer children. Although academics,
in China and abroad, have made the question of China's continued
ability to produce enough to feed its people the focus of intense
debate (see Brown 1995:38; Liang Ying, ed., 1996; Smil 1995:801–
13), a very different question is being asked by Chinese parents,
namely, what food is good for children to eat?

This question is often raised with great anxiety. With more than
170,000 food companies now operating in China, the appearance
of a dazzling variety of dietary products on the market has been
accompanied by an equally dazzling variety of commercial claims.[5]
Not surprisingly, identifying healthy food for children has become
a special concern. In Dachuan, this concern is entangled with a local

discourse on a wide range of complex issues affecting children's health. We will look at why and how the local discourse has been shaped by three forms of what I call "cultural authority." I shall explain the exact meaning of this term after we take a look at the economic changes that have taken place in Dachuan since the breakup of the communes.

Food, Children, and Economic Development in Dachuan

Dachuan is a relocated community; its original site was flooded by a dam project in 1961. In the following years, most villagers experienced the misery caused by land shortages and chronic food scarcity. As soon as the central government showed a willingness to reform the agricultural sector in 1981, Dachuan dismantled its collective farming system, turning the primary responsibility for production over to individual households. The purpose of the reforms was to spur productivity, which had languished under the commune system for decades. As villagers hoped for, productivity increased at an amazing pace, but widespread poverty persisted. During my first visit to Dachuan in 1989, the local diet was heavily dependent on potatoes through much of the year; meat was consumed mainly during the lunar New Year festival. By 1992, a few households could afford to buy slices of pork each week and to supplement their potato-based diet with wheat. For nearly 40 percent of the local households, however, meat remained a rare luxury and potatoes remained the staple food. These households fell below the poverty line, set by the central government at an annual per capita income of 300 to 400 yuan, or $50 to $65 according to the official exchange rates in 1992. By 1995, however, even these poorer households were able to meet minimum caloric requirements by supplementing potatoes with wheat, eggs, vegetables, cooking oil, sugar, and animal protein. The local diet was shifting to one of real variety.

This dietary change was brought about by a marked increase of per capita income, thanks to a village-wide effort to grow tomatoes and strawberries in greenhouses, to sell in nearby cities during colder seasons. Together with the construction of over 100 fish ponds around the village, the new cash-crop economy boosted Dachuan's per capita income to 800 yuan by the end of 1996. But with the move from acute food shortages to a degree of prosperity for some households, and a full stomach for many, came the realization that choices could be made and that children in particular should be better fed.

But how? To ask this question in Dachuan is to encounter different, and sometimes conflicting, answers. Particularly when children's health is at stake, food can provoke highly emotional debates. A case in point is a family discussion I witnessed in the summer of 1997, involving Kong Defang, the daughter of one of my key informants in Dachuan. Defang had gone to Beijing, where she worked in a bakery shop, married a migrant worker like herself, and gave birth to a son. When the boy was six months old, the couple decided to take him to see his maternal grandparents. After arriving in the village, the baby began crying loudly, continuing right through the night. The baby's grandmother thought that he was hungry because his mother's health was poor and she therefore did not have enough milk to nurse him. She suggested taking her daughter and the baby to a local temple to offer incense and food to a goddess who is believed to be especially responsive to female supplicants seeking guidance in caring for their babies and their own health. An older sister-in-law offered a simpler solution, suggesting that the baby be weaned and fed with milk powder and rice porridge; she insisted that the best brand of milk powder sold at a nearby store was one that she had seen on television. The baby's father and grandfather were against weaning the baby at only six months. The father suggested seeing a doctor of Western medicine; he believed that the instant noodles his son ate on the train from Beijing had gone bad and made him sick. The grandfather also considered the noodles to be the cause of the baby's discomfort, but he urged his daughter to treat the boy with a recipe of traditional Chinese medicine, which involved boiling reed roots and dried dates with millet. Defang finally broke down in tears as the question of what to do about the crying baby continued to be debated through a late family dinner. She did not know whose advice to follow. In the end, she decided to follow everyone's. Although she did not stop breastfeeding the baby, she did buy milk power, choosing the brand that her sister-in-law had recommended.

It might seem at first that Defang simply obeyed the people whom she was supposed to obey by custom. After all, it was her traditional superiors — her parents, older sister-in-law, and husband — who were telling her how to deal with the crying baby. Yet this explanation does not apply to Defang, who is an intensely independent woman. After all, she had moved to Beijing against her parents' wishes, married a colleague without first telling her family, and, because she did not have a birth permit, secretly hired a doctor to deliver her baby in a rural county near Beijing. Defang's own explanation for why she broke down crying during the family meeting was that she found "sound reasons" (*you dao li*) in all the suggestions:

> County doctors have cures for my baby. Deities can protect
> him. Milk power is a good supplement for breast milk. My
> father's food therapy could invigorate the baby's health. But I
> could not figure out how to do all these things at once with
> the baby crying in my arms. Finally I decided to take him to
> the county hospital first and then visit the local deities' temple
> with my mother. And now I am using milk powder and my
> father's medicinal food recipe.

Defang's explanation suggests that her eventual actions had little to do with power relations but arose from her perceptions of "sound reasons," even though they were in conflict. In other words, she was faced with several different but persuasive recommendations, making it hard for her set priorities.

My interviews with other villagers suggest that Defang's experience was not untypical. In searching for solutions to the delicate problems of child care, the local people were exposed to a variety of ideas that they found sensible and authoritative. Many of such ideas were derived from the state-sponsored promotion of modern science and Western medicine, the practice of popular religion and traditional child-rearing methods, and the impact of market forces as conveyed most powerfully through television advertising. Considering their profound effects in shaping the attitudes of Dachuan villagers toward children's health and diet, I shall examine the persuasive capacities of modern science, popular religion, and market forces below in a discussion of the analytical concept of "cultural authority."

Defining "Cultural Authority"

It can be argued that questions of how to feed children are questions about authority because they deal with what advice is deemed persuasive and worthy of acceptance on a voluntary basis. By emphasizing persuasion and voluntary compliance, this way of looking at authority differs from the classic definition offered by Max Weber. In his writings on *Herrschaft* (variously translated as "authority" or "domination"), Weber distinguished among legal-rational authority, traditional authority, and charismatic authority. Legal-rational authority involves obedience to formal rules established by regular public procedures. Adhering to quasi-legal norms in formal bureaucracies is the principal example of this type of authority. By contrast, deferring to traditional authority involves the acceptance of rules that embody custom and ancient practices. In the case of charismatic authority, commands of a religious leader are obeyed by followers convinced of the extraordinary character of their leader, whose authority transcends existing rules or customary practices (see, esp., Weber 1968).

But authority, as we use this term in English, involves more than giving commands or obeying rules. Theologians and scientists may be authoritative when speaking of religion and nature, and yet they are often constrained from regulating, much less dictating, specific choices and actions. A physician may advise a patient to change his diet for medical reasons. The patient may very well take this as an authoritative judgment of the facts but decline to follow the advice. In modern society, opinions with regard to nutrition and health are issued in great numbers by medical professionals, pharmaceutical companies, government regulators, and the news media. However, they are not regarded as authoritative representations of reality unless they are persuasive. Authority in this sense is the capacity to influence people's behavior by influencing how they think; it refers to the probability that particular definitions or interpretations of reality will be perceived to be valid. This form of authority is defined by the historian Paul Starr (1982) as "cultural authority" to distinguish it from the three basic types of "social authority" that Weber had in mind. To be specific, Starr's definition of cultural authority (1982:13) is in keeping with a familiar, though always troubling, distinction between culture as the realm of meaning and ideas, and society as the realm of relationships among social actors. According to Starr, cultural authority has the potential to shape and reshape people's ideas, values, and attitudes without resorting to commands or rules. Since its influence is dependent on persuasion and voluntary compliance, cultural authority may be accepted without being exercised; typically it is consulted, even by people in powerful positions, often in the hope of resolving ambiguities. In real-life situations, cultural authority is delegated by particular people or institutions and represented by different forms of specialized knowledge (1982:13–17).

To apply the concept of cultural authority as defined above, it is important to stress again that my discussion of the Dachuan material is concerned with the impact of modern science, popular religion, and television advertising upon children's consumption of food. To this end, the following steps are taken to put my analysis in a coherent framework. First, I discuss the connection of the Chinese state's public health agendas and children's food consumption by explaining why the Chinese government has undertaken numerous education campaigns to make children's nutritional well-being a key component of the country's one-child policy. Second, I examine the role of traditional child-rearing practices by looking at how the worship of deities in Dachuan affects the application of Chinese medicine and the family's use of traditional food therapy. And third, I analyze the impact of food advertising on children in light of the proliferation of television sets and retail shops in Dachuan.

The main purpose for bringing the state, modern science, popular religion, traditional child-care methods, and market forces into my analysis is to point out that in this case the state-sponsored promotion of science and the influence of popular religion embody two contradictory forms of cultural authority. Although the tension between them has long antecedents in China, it is intensified in the sphere of rural child care by the convergence of the government's population policy and the resurgence of popular religion during the post-Mao era. This convergence of conflicting cultural authorities is complicated by China's commercialization, which has enabled businesses to turn television advertising into a new force of cultural authority over the question of how children should be fed. In short, the Dachuan material suggests that children's diet cannot be viewed simply as a matter of individual choice. Rather, what Dachuan children eat embodies the collision of three different forms of cultural authority in a community that has undergone rapid social and economic change since the early 1980s.

Science: A Governmental Attempt to Claim Cultural Authority

The Chinese government is fully aware that its one-child policy would be undermined if couples feared that their children's chances of surviving into healthy adulthood were threatened by disease or malnutrition. The one-child policy thus has been accompanied by publicity campaigns and public health programs aimed at fostering children's health. The impact of such efforts has been deeply felt in Dachuan. In interviews during the summer of 1997 as part of a 24-hour dietary survey of 30 six-year-olds, I found that 25 of these children had taken manufactured calcium supplements.[6] In each case, the supplements were taken at the recommendation of township or county-level doctors, who believed that the health of local children was suffering because their diet did not contain enough calcium.[7] It is noteworthy that suggestions for taking calcium supplements were usually received during visits to local clinics or county-level hospitals and during the central government's annual immunization drives.

Let us focus on immunization, a nationwide effort to prevent four epidemic diseases: measles, diphtheria, whooping cough, and polio. For polio, for example, from 1993 to 1996 the central government organized a total of six rounds of inoculations for children under four years old; each round involved 80 million children. In Dachuan, the yearly immunization was the responsibility of doctors and nurses sent down to the village from the local township and county seat. They were helped by local officials and village cadres, who would round up the village children to wait in lines to be injected with various vaccines. Mothers or grandmothers usually accompanied the children during the immunization process; they often used this opportunity to ask the doctors for advice on childcare. I learned that a common recommendation given to the local women by the doctors and nurses was to buy calcium supplements if they had not yet done so. In a Shandong village, Huang Shu-min and two other scholars also discovered that it was from doctors that local villagers learned that they should provide their children with calcium and other mineral supplements (Huang Shu-min et al. 1996:335–81).

This recommendation was in response to a nationwide health problem. According to *China Health and Nutrition* (1997a:53) — a magazine published by China's Commission of Science and Technology — a series of studies in the 1980s found calcium deficiency to be a main cause of rickets among Chinese children. Even in Beijing, a health organization found in a 1982 survey of 1,154 preschoolers that 37 percent suffered from rickets.[8] In response to these findings, circulars about children's calcium needs were issued by the Ministry of Health, along with numerous directives to medical institutions throughout the country to urge them to help improve children's physical well-being by publicizing the importance of modern nutrition. Subsequently, production of calcium supplements and multivitamins was increased in China with imported technology and through joint-venture pharmaceutical companies.[9]

The Chinese government's ability to embark on large-scale programs to deal with children's health problems has a direct bearing upon the one-child policy. Since its formal adoption in 1979–80, this policy has been meant to apply first to all urban areas and eventually extend to the countryside. In explaining the need for the policy, the government has tried to convince the public not only that China has too many people; moreover, its "population quality" badly needs improvement through "preventive eugenics" (*yufang youshengxue*), meaning that marriages of mentally retarded people, close relatives, and patients with hereditary diseases must be prevented to avoid births of children with severe medical problems. The government claims its promotion of preventive eugenics is based on scientific principles, and it has tried to demonstrate the advantages of adopting allegedly "superior childbearing methods" (*yousheng cuoshi*). These include the selection of physically and mentally fit marriage partners, a premarital medical examination, the timing of conception, and prenatal testing, as well as physical exercise and nutritious food during pregnancy and exposing the fetus to music and other beneficial influences.[10] To persuade the public that the official appeal for fewer children and preventive eugenics will enhance the physical well-being of the next generation, the government has launched a series of publicity campaigns promoting what it considers to be "superior child-rearing methods" (*youyu cuoshi*). These include voluntarily studying child psychology, testing children's intelligence, responding to a crying child appropriately, determining suitable sleeping arrangements, and, above all, learning about breastfeeding, weaning, and good nutrition. The standard venues of the officially recommended methods for producing "children of superior birth" (*yousheng wawa*) are the usual means of state-society communication: state-controlled radio and television stations, wall-posters, work-unit meetings, community blackboards, newspaper columns, popular health magazines, and parent-teacher meetings at day-care centers.

The government has repeatedly emphasized that rural residents are most urgently in need of "scientific" methods for producing "children of superior birth." This official opinion is reflected in a book published after a government-run, nationwide essay competition (Guo, ed., 1991). The submission of essays was organized by the State Family Planning Commission, the Ministry of Health, the All-China Women's Federation, and the All-China Patriotic Hygiene Movement Commission. The specific task of selecting, editing, and publicizing the prize-winning essays was assigned to the Chinese Science and Technology Association, China Central Television, Central People's Radio Station, the Chinese Medical Association, and three leading newspapers and magazines on public health.

The winners addressed topics ranging from pregnancy, hereditary ailments, and disease prevention to marriage customs, breast-feeding, and children's food. More than 10,000 letters and 2,000 essays were received by the Chinese Medical Association; its Popular Science Society was in charge of evaluating the essays for publication and broadcast. Finally, the selected essays were broadcast by the China Central Television through the popular *Hygiene and Health* program. The organizers claimed that 100 million people watched this program and that more than one million copies of newspapers and magazines containing the prize-winning essays were printed. The writers of the prize-winning essays were identified as "mostly from grassroots work-units." This is a clue that the essay writers were mostly medical personnel, family-planning officials, and child-care professionals who were working in state-run institutions. Published by the China Population Press in Beijing, the book contained 90 short essays and 30 dealt explicitly with child-rearing issues in rural areas.

Nutrition is the central topic in ten of the published essays. Three criticized an allegedly popular belief in rural areas that pregnant women must eat a great quantity of fish and pork to produce healthy babies. One essay traces a boy's mental retardation to his mother's overconsumption of fatty pork during pregnancy. The baby inside her grew too big, this essay asserts, to be delivered naturally. The boy experienced oxygen deprivation and brain damage before he and his mother were saved by a hastily performed Cesarean.

Another essay on overeating in pregnancy cites the case of a boy named Xiaoming. Everything was fine with this boy at birth except for a harelip. His mother told a doctor that she was bewildered by her baby's deformity because she had strictly followed the guidelines in a fertility handbook. The doctor, after inquiring into what she ate in pregnancy, concluded that her son's harelip was caused by taking excessive cod-liver oil while pregnant. That is to say, she had ingested too much vitamin A.

The problem of overfeeding is a target of reproach, also. In an essay about chocolate, the author claims that many well-to-do people in the countryside buy too much chocolate for their youngsters, regarding it as a nutritious food. The author notes that chocolate is rich in sugar, calories, and iron but should not be consumed in great quantities by young children, especially those who are overweight or have bad teeth. Another essay takes on a far more serious issue of overfeeding, the common practice among rural parents of giving their young children "invigorating tonics" (*buyao*) in the hope of improving their health. For example, a kindergarten boy is said to have taken a commercially produced flower pollen tonic (*huafen koufuye*). The polliniferous substance of this drink is extracted from the stamens of flowers. After four months of taking this drink, the boy developed what the author called "premature sexuality," indicated by frequent penile erections. In another essay, a grandmother is said to have given a homemade ginseng-based broth (*renshen tang*) to her four-year-old grandson for three days to cure the child's coughing and to restore his *qi*, or "vital energy."

The child had to be rushed to a hospital when blood began oozing from his nose and mouth. The author of the essay pointedly adds that this is not an isolated case and that one fruit farmer he knows once bought as many as eleven kinds of "invigorating tonics" for his children.

At first glance, the central message of these essays is that too much of a good thing is bad. On closer examination, the essay writers are condemning what they perceive to be widespread ignorance of scientific matters in rural areas. The same sentiment is expressed by a country doctor, who reports that a mass hysteria seized a village when three newborn infants abruptly died within two days. These babies, the doctor concluded, died of a vitamin B deficiency because their mothers had come to rely on refined rice as a staple food after the village acquired electric-powered threshers.

In these essays, the popularization of scientific approaches to nutrition is mixed with vivid dramatization, including tales of a boy's early sexuality, mysterious deaths of village babies, and the detrimental effects of overfeeding. By tapping into public anxieties, these narratives illustrate the relevance of the government's promotion of scientific child care to people who might otherwise be unconcerned with what the government says about children's diet. Most of all, the essays render the state a measure of cultural authority to influence behavior by persuasion. In contrast to the state's heavy-handed childbearing policy, its advocacy of scientific child-rearing methods is not threatening. On the contrary, it seems to combine neatly a public cause with private concerns. By using modern medical science to educate the rural people about child care, the state is a position to depict its one-child policy as the first step to "superior childbearing," which in turn is projected as an ideal condition for "superior childrearing." When these two steps are taken, the promised result is "children of superior birth and superior upbringing." In this way, modern science is characterized as an ultimate yardstick of what is good for the family while the state casts itself in the double image of compassionate proponent of both modern science and children's welfare.

Religion: An Alternative Force of Cultural Authority

To find out how national policies affect ordinary people, such as those living in the village of Dachuan, it is necessary to mention that the Yongjing county government, which has jurisdiction over Dachuan, began in the early 1980s to impose a limit of two births per rural couple and a three-year interval between the first and second birth. In spite of widespread resistance by local farmers, the annual birth rate in Yongjing dropped sharply. In 1979, the county's annual birth rate was 17 newborns per 1,000 population. By 1982, it had fallen to 13 per 1,000. And by 1992, there were only 10 births per 1,000. A key factor contributing to these significant fertility declines was the county government's organization of local doctors, officials, and policemen into special task forces to enforce the use of contraceptives, birth quotas, the spacing of births, and the sterilization of young women who had given birth to two or more children.[11] Meanwhile, the county government stepped up pressure on township-level officials to devote more time and manpower to implementing the state's rural birth-control policy. It did so by linking the promotions of township leaders with their contributions to fertility declines in areas under their jurisdiction. This deliberate linkage of career advancement and population control helps explain the harshness of penalties imposed by local officials against the parents of unauthorized babies. The penalties often involved beatings, heavy fines, and confiscation of private property. In the eyes of the villagers, the most severe punishment was the forced sterilization of women who had exceeded the official birth quota but still had no son.

In Dachuan, the county government's tough measures were deeply resented. A community of about 3,600 people in 1997, Dachuan is dominated, politically and numerically, by a lineage surnamed Kong. Claiming to be descendants of Confucius, these Kongs represent about 85 percent of the local population. Surname exogamy is strictly practiced by the Kongs; thus, most Kong daughters leave at marriage to settle in other villages while a few marry into the households of non-Kong villagers. With the departure of married daughters, sons are the only source of security and support for aging parents in this village, where there are no pensions or medical insurance at this writing. Consequently, the safety net for old age is the begetting of at least one son, who must be brought up with a strong sense of obligation to his parents and must be healthy to be able to care for them in the future. This filial obligation is in fact the moral foundation of the Chinese family system. As Charles Stafford has put it, Chinese parent-child reciprocity follows a seemingly simplistic formula: first, a married couple must *fu yang* ("rear and nourish") children, and then children must *feng yang* ("respectfully nourish") parents. In both cases, the original meaning of the Chinese word *yang*, which in written form has the "food" radical, presupposes "nourishing" to be a reciprocal act of feeding. When this act is interrupted, the family breaks down (Stafford 1995:77–111).

With fear spreading that the state might subject Dachuan to the one-child policy (already applied to all the urban residents in Yongjing county), thereby threatening security in old age and the continuance of the family line, the reconstruction of local temples, particularly those dealing with fertility, became an urgent matter. Dachuan used to have six temples, but they were destroyed in the 1960s and 1970s. In 1982, central authorities adopted a more tolerant policy toward religion. In subsequent years, a wave of religious fervor swept the Chinese countryside (see, e.g., Cai 1992; Anagnost 1987:147–76; Harrell 1988:3; MacInnis 1989; Luo, ed., 1991; Shen Zhiyan and Le Bingcheng 1991), leading to the reconstruction of temples and the revival of large-scale temple festivals. As of 1998, five of Dachuan's six temples had been rebuilt. One, inside the village, venerates Confucius and the more immediate ancestors of the local Kong lineage (see Jing 1996). The other four temples, on a mountain behind the village, are devoted to one god and six goddesses. Each of these goddesses is associated with fertility. On the top of the mountain is the Temple of Lady Jinhua (*Jinhua niannian miao*), a rain-making and child-providing deity. Halfway up the mountain is the Palace of One Hundred Sons (*Baizi gong*), rebuilt for a trinity known as the Three Heavenly Mothers (*Sanxiao niannian*), who are fertility goddesses worshiped in many parts of rural China. At the foot of the mountain is a Buddhist shrine where the Goddess of Mercy, Guanyin, is enshrined; Guanyin is known for her fertility-enhancing powers and is also believed to be capable of performing many other miracles. At the entrance of a footpath leading to the mountain is the Local Deities Temple (*Fangshen miao*), devoted to the worship of Lady Jinhua, General Yang Lang, and the Mystic Woman of the Ninth Heaven (*Jiutian xuannu*). General Yang is a flood-control god while the Mystic Woman of the Ninth Heaven is believed to be particularly responsive to prayers for the recovery of sick women and babies.[12]

An ultimate expression of the close relationship between religion and health is the presence of two booklets of medical prescriptions on an altar inside the Local Deities Temple. One booklet is for male adults and the other for children and women. Each has fifty poems; under each of these poems — numbered from one to fifty — is a prescription for traditional Chinese herbal medicine. A particular prescription is selected after a simple rite of divination in which a patient or a relative of the patient offers incense and then picks up a brush holder containing a bundle of chopstick-sized sticks. Each of the sticks is also numbered from one to fifty. The temple visitor holds the brush holder with both hands and shakes it with its opening toward the front until a stick falls onto the ground. The first stick falling out, it is said, represents a medical tip from the enshrined deities. The number on the head of the fallen stick is then used to locate the prescription by finding the poem with a matching number in the appropriate booklet. If the visitor is illiterate, he or she can ask a temple watcher to copy the prescription on a piece of paper to take home. Based on my observations at this temple, the booklet for women and children was used more than the one for male adults.

This and the other temples on the mountain where six goddesses are enshrined play an important role in how adults, especially women, care for young children — not just because of the two booklets of prescriptions.[13] The food offerings at the temples are considered blessed by the goddesses and thus to possess a therapeutic effect on ill children and adults alike. The idea that the food offerings are blessed is based on the popular belief that people and deities enjoy a reciprocal relationship. Temple rituals suggest that deities depend on regular worship and offerings to maintain their power. Thus, when food offerings to deities are ample and regular, supplicants can hope for a favor in return, which includes taking home some of the food offerings from the temple. There are many expressions of this belief. For example, worshipers often hear from others at the temple that they should take the offerings home for the children to eat to "ensure peace and safety" (*bao ping an*).

But the most important religious activity in terms of its impact upon children's diet is the food-therapy advice offered at the temples by elderly women when worshipers gather on the first and fifteenth day of the lunar month. The most active participants in these gatherings are elderly women, who spend hours, sometimes the whole day, at the temples. There they burn incense, chat in the side halls, sing hymns, clean the altars, and rearrange the food offerings. These regular temple gatherings give the village's elderly women a fixed time and space to pass on their child-care experience to younger women who visit the temples seeking help from the goddesses. In a village where participation in nearly all formal social gatherings, such as weddings, funerals, banquets, excursions to sweep tombs, ancestral rites, and birthday parties, is determined by kinship ties or particular interpersonal relationships, the bimonthly temple gathering represents an all-inclusive communal event. Very much like the deities who protect the local people but demand continued food offerings in exchange, the older women give child-care advice to young women with the expectation of receiving "special favors" in return — for example, that the younger women will carry bricks up the mountain to build additional temple chambers.

The typical response of elderly women to children's physical distress of any kind is to immediately alter what they are eating. A child suffering from digestive problems, they often suggest to young mothers, should eat radish pies cooked with slices of fresh ginger and lean pork, or take millet porridge with dried dates and rock sugar. An alternative remedy for a sick child is to grind and toast radish seeds and hawthorn flakes, which are eaten with a bowl of millet porridge. A child with a cold should drink water boiled with ginger slices or cabbage roots. For fever, hot soup of mung beans, lotus seeds, and reed roots is a common recommendation. Children afflicted with tapeworms and hookworms are to chew the uncooked seeds of pumpkins, sunflowers, and black sponge gourds on an empty stomach. The list goes on, but it is significant that all of these medicinal recipes make use of locally produced, inexpensive edibles that can be prepared at home. The emphasis is on self-reliance, on curing sick children with commonly available and affordable food therapy.

Also noteworthy about these recipes is their relationship with traditional Chinese medicine. Doctors of traditional medicine habitually classify a wide range of foods into "five flavors" (pungent, sweet, sour, bitter, and salty) and "five energies" (hot, cold, warm, cool, and neutral). The different flavors and energies are thought to produce different effects within the human body. Perspiration, for example, can be induced by pungent foods — for example, ginger, green onions, and peppermint. The heat-producing effects of greasy foods can be balanced by foods known for their cooling effect, such as bamboo shoots, water chestnuts, and bitter gourd. The necessity to rely on inexpensive dietary sources for medical help means that many adult villagers have some idea of the therapeutic values of various foods.[14]

It is worth noting that traditional Chinese medicine, with its strong influence over the local family's use of food therapy, is founded in religion; it is closely related to the traditional Chinese concept of *yin* and *yang* — that is, the primordial dual forces of hot and cold, day and night, male and female, positive and negative. If the forces of *yin* and *yang* can manipulate the natural order, they must also exert their power on the human body and what it consumes. The five flavors and five energies of foods are therefore classified by doctors of traditional Chinese medicine into *yin* and *yang*. Cooling and cold energies are *yin*; hot and warm energies are *yang*. Sour, bitter, and salty flavors are *yin*; pungent and sweet flavors are *yang*. Ordinary Chinese, such as most Dachuan residents, may not fully understand the *yin-yang* theory or precisely why different foods are classified into different categories. But they are more or less aware of the medical values of certain spices, vegetables, fruits, gourds, herbs, and grains. This awareness comes from encounters with doctors of traditional Chinese medicine, from talking with neighbors, from praying for healing at temples, or by living near people whose health returned after using traditional food therapy. The connection of food therapy, food classifications, and the *yin-yang* theory implies that a traditional belief system endows Chinese medicine with cultural authority and profoundly affects the manner in which food is used for its medicinal values and to treat ill children.

The Market: A Competing Force of Cultural Authority

In 1985, Dachuan had only four black-and-white television sets. When I first visited the village in 1989, there were four color and 86 black-and-white sets. At the end of 1992, there were twelve color and 107 black-and-white sets, meaning nearly one-sixth of local households were receiving in their homes broadcasts from Beijing, Lanzhou, and Tianshui, a city in southeastern Gansu. By summer 1997, about one-third of the local households owned a television set. Although Dachuan is a rather remote village, television now links the socialization process of local children with the overall commercialization of Chinese society. Every evening, after the prime-time news, children as young as two or three were often the ones who decided what to watch next and when to switch channels. In 1997, local teachers said in an interview that primary school pupils spent up to three hours a night watching television. Children under six who did not yet have to go to school spent even more time before the set. For these children, television functioned much like a playmate during the day when parents and grandparents were busy and therefore let their children watch what they wanted.

Long before the child has a full set of teeth, he has become the television food advertisers' representative in the home. Highly impressionable, the child holds opinions of what is good to eat that sometimes contradict those of his parents or grandparents. Take, for example, the cheap instant noodles that children in Dachuan break into small pieces to eat as if they were more expensive biscuits. A mother complained in an interview in 1997 that her three-year-old son always preferred instant noodles to the fresh noodles she prepared. "But how can I blame him?" she asked.

When he sees another child eating a bag of Master Kang instant noodles, he wants some, too. From watching television, he thinks that all mothers buy Master Kang for their children. And he cries if I refuse to buy it for him. This child has quite a temper. When he really cries, he chokes and loses his breath. Then, when his father sees that, he gets angry and blames me for being too strict with our son. Then I become upset and get into a loud argument with my husband.

The brand that this mother mentioned, Master Kang (*kang shifu*) instant noodles, is produced by the Taiwan-based Tinghsin International Group. In 1995, the company's sales exceeded 5 billion yuan ($602 million) and represented more than a quarter of China's instant-noodle market. Although Chinese news media reported in 1996 that some packages of Master Kang noodles failed to meet the Chinese government's hygiene standards, aggressive advertising has overwhelmed any bad publicity and an effective sales network has kept profits strong. Far from feeling any damage, in 1996 Tinghsin expanded its production lines with new investments worth $30 million to increase its China-based subsidies to 42.[15]

Aside from television advertising, local children's consumption of commercial foods has been affected by the increase of village shops. It used to be that Dachuan villagers could only buy manu-factured foods by going to a market street serving the urban fami-lies of a large nearby fertilizer plant. In 1992, the village's first gen-eral store opened, and three more followed the next year. By 1997, Dachuan had twelve stores selling commercial foods. The store owners fully appreciated that selling these foods to children could be very profitable. In 1995, I asked four store owners in Dachuan if they were selling or had sold what they considered to be "baby foods" (*ertong shipin*) and "child nutrients" (*ertong yingyang pin*). Without hesitation, they named eighteen kinds: a Chinese medici-nal tonic made of chicken embryos and called Baby Essential (*wawasu*), a digestive drink known as Baby Laughter (*wahaha*), a honey-based tonic called Royal Jelly (*fengwang jing*), small bottles of ginseng tonic (*renshen koufuye*), pollen water (*huafen koufuye*), cod-liver oil, orange juice, chocolate, milk powder, almond pow-der, ice cream, lotus-seed powder, chewing gum, milk powder mixed with malt, sweetened fruit jelly, salted fish and beef in tiny plastic bags, vitamin C tablets, and instant noodles.

While Baby Essential and Baby Laughter were the best-known dietetics for children, especially babies, the store owners insisted that most of the other commercially produced foods were bought for youngsters as well. They reminded me that Baby Essential, Baby Laughter, Royal Jelly, chocolate, ice cream, chewing gums, or instant noodles were not yet available in Dachuan when I was doing research there in 1989. These commodities entered Dachuan only when one store began to experiment with selling what was billed as children's food. Sales were modest but showed a profit at the year's end. The other stores followed suit. The most profitable items sold at these stores were alcohol and cigarettes. The second-ranking goods — convenience foods and soft drinks — were mainly purchased for children. Salt, vinegar, soy sauce, and cooking oil were also sold in great quantities.

In 1997, the four store owners who had been in operation in 1995 told me that they stocked a small quantity of relatively expensive tonics such as Baby Essential and Baby Laughter with which local children and parents had become familiar from television. But inexpensive manufactured foods still sold best. Although children were easily influenced by what they saw on television, most of the advertised foodstuffs and drinks were too expensive for most couples to purchase for their children on a regular basis. In keeping with their purchasing power, parents preferred to buy the cheapest kinds of food at the stores, such as instant noodles, to at least partially satisfy their children's craving for what they saw advertised on television.

Unlike the urban children whose consumption behavior is analyzed by Guo Yuhua and Bernadine Chee in this volume, the children of Dachuan had little pocket money. Nor could they eat commercial foodstuffs every day. Their say over their family's food consumption was much weaker than that of the urban children studied by Guo and Chee. This weak influence was acknowledged by the mothers of the 30 six-year-olds in my 1997 survey. Within the 24-hour period under study, these children's dietary intake consisted mostly of potatoes, maize, and wheat, supplemented by small amounts of vegetables, instant noodles, popsicles, and local pears and watermelons. Not a single child ate meat. The day before the survey, only three mothers had allowed their children to buy what they referred to as "between-meal snacks" (*ling shi*) from the village stores.

But I should make two further observations. First, over most of the year, these children ate meat about twice a month. Their meat consumption then picked up dramatically for a period of two months once pigs, sheep, and chicken were slaughtered for lunar New Year celebrations. Second, most of these children consumed commercial foods and soft drinks at least once a week. Furthermore, allowing children to have store-bought food was common on special occasions. One of these occasions was the wheat harvest, when busy parents and grandparents gave children money to buy food, especially instant noodles, from the village stores. And when a child suffered from a minor ailment such as a skin rash, low fever, or broken wrist, his parents would often go to a village store to buy candy, soft drinks, and even rather expensive slices of dried beef as a special treat to cheer him up. The child's birthday was another special occasion for commercial foods from the village stores.

Although a considerable gap still remains between what they might want to eat and what they actually consume, the children of Dachuan are linked by the proliferation of village shops and televisions to the broad range of ideas, images, and values of China's emerging consumerist culture. The impact of television advertising is especially noteworthy. Never before has an entire generation of rural village children been raised watching television and being exposed to an onslaught of commercial information. This exposure is a relatively new human condition not just in Dachuan but throughout China. During its first two decades, from 1958 to 1978, Chinese television broadcast not a single commercial. The country's first television commercial, in 1979, advertised alcohol (Chen Pei'ai 1997:80). In the early 1980s, commercials began appearing regularly, but most promoted sales of machinery and appliances for industrial enterprises. By the early 1990s, however, personal consumption became the dominant theme of television advertising. A clear sign that television advertising has become a new force of cultural authority in the debate over what children should eat is the increasingly refined promotion of a material-goods-make-happiness ethic, associating food with the achievement of a high IQ, family harmony, good health, and a carefree childhood. The images and scenes in food commercials often involve the consumption of faddish foods by babies and schoolchildren in happy home settings, on family outings, and at birthday parties. For example, in the televised commercials of such baby foods as infant formula, vitamin-enriched cereals, and digestive tonics, advertisers often rely on cute-looking children, film stars, and sports celebrities to emphasize the fun of eating trendy foods. These attempts to commercialize children's consumption confirm the anthropologist Igor Kopytoff's argument that "the production of commodities is also a cultural and cognitive process: commodities must be not only produced materially as things, but also culturally marked as being a certain kind of thing" (1988:64). Plainly stated, production for mass consumption involves manufacturing "cultural goods" — ideas, symbols, images, expectations, and knowledge — for the explicit purpose of persuading people to accept a particular type of cultural authority that endorses the consumption of certain goods as important for an individual's happiness. As elsewhere, television advertising in China is an ideal medium for selling foods as cultural products; television has the capacity to reach the vast Chinese countryside, where, however limited the individual family's purchasing power, the sheer number of families represents a huge market. Around 20 million babies are born in China each year, the great majority to rural families.

Conclusion: Authority, Conflict, and Convergence

The Dachuan material suggests that the consumption of food by local children bears the accumulative effect of interactions among the power of the state, commercial interests, and popular religion. The discussion above demonstrates that the people of Dachuan have been exposed to at least three different, sometimes conflicting, forces of cultural authority with regard to the issue of how to raise healthy children. These are state-sponsored modern science, popular religion, and market forces transmitted by television advertising. One of the Chinese government's primary means of winning support for its population policy is the launching of publicity campaigns to demonstrate that its efforts to improve children's health are based on the scientific principles of modern nutrition and Western medicine. By contrast, the worship of deities in Dachuan provides a very different form of cultural authority; it seeks the intervention of supernatural beings to influence the precarious fortunes of childbirth and child care. And while the religiously informed emphasis on curing sick children with traditional food therapies is on inexpensive, homemade recipes, television advertising advocates the consumption of expensive, factory-made foods to achieve personal happiness. As a developing art of persuasion in

China that is certainly biased toward the food-processing industry, television advertising represents yet another form of cultural authority; its power to persuade hinges on the transmission of commercial information to inculcate the idea that a happy, healthy childhood is determined by buying consumer goods in general and manufactured foodstuffs in particular.

My discussion, however, is not meant to suggest that these three forces do not accommodate one another. They definitely do so in Dachuan, for some very important reasons. One is the wish to have at least one heir to continue the family line. Another is the dominance of patrilocal residence and surname exogamy, which means that sons remain in Dachuan while most daughters leave the community at marriage. The persistence of patrilocal residence and surname exogamy in Dachuan cannot be explained simply by local people's unwillingness to tamper with tradition. Official policy perpetuates rural customs through a household-registration policy that prevents young men from moving to live in another village. Local officials fear, often correctly, that they would create a burden for themselves if they permitted a young man to settle in a different village, where he would almost certainly stir resentment among local residents fearing that he might insist on a share of their land. In addition, Dachuan has no social welfare programs akin to urban China's retirement pensions and medical insurance. Children, especially boys, who will stay in the village after marriage, are the sole source of support for their aging parents.

Under these circumstances, the parents' one hope for security in old age is children. The necessity for offspring requires Dachuan parents to pay close heed to different forms of cultural authority over the management of childhood in the hope that they will all contribute to the mutually dependent bond between children and parents. Here let me emphasize that Dachuan is not an exceptional case; in thousands of similar Chinese villages, male children are seen by parents as their best investment in the strict sense of the word, partly because the longstanding anxiety over one's welfare in old age has yet to be eased significantly in rural China.

Finally, we might ask if traditional beliefs and practices regarding children's health or diet will fade soon. After all, modern nutrition is being vigorously promoted by government agencies while commercial agencies are trying to cultivate a secular, pleasure-oriented attitude toward food. Both types of agencies represent powerful institutions with great influence over ordinary Chinese. However, Taiwan and Hong Kong have shown that traditional Chinese medical and nutritional beliefs are resilient enough to thrive in the face of modern science and intense commercialism. The medical anthropologist Arthur Kleinman (1980), studying a large sample of Chinese on Taiwan, found that in 93 percent of incidents of illness, diet was altered — usually as a first resort, initiated by the patients themselves or families who acted on their belief in the effectiveness of traditional medicine and nutritional recipes. Eugene N. Anderson reports that his sketchier figures from Hong Kong are even higher (1988:230). In mainland China, traditional medical beliefs are in no danger of disappearing in the near future. On the contrary, considerable numbers of people in China proper continue to cherish traditional healing practices. The vibrant revival of popular religion in the post-Mao period has only reinforced the cognitive foundation and the cultural authority of these practices.

7

A Baby-Friendly Hospital

and the Science of Infant Feeding

Suzanne K. Gottschang

After a drastic decline in breastfeeding, the importance of feeding babies with breast milk is being rediscovered in China. Key to this rediscovery is the Chinese government's promotion of scientific knowledge of the nutritional and psychological benefits of breastfeeding (Chen Ya 1996:15–16). In the mean time, however, the official encouragement of breastfeeding faces challenges arising from the country's integration with transnational economic forces. Foreign companies such as Nestle and Borden are now market leaders in producing and selling baby food and breast milk substitutes in China (*Eurofood* 1996:3).

In this chapter, I will investigate how a prenatal care unit acts as a site of convergence for both the new emphasis on breastfeeding in urban China and the penetration of commercialism into the sphere of infant feeding.[1] Based on my extensive fieldwork at a hospital in Beijing and visits to the city's other hospitals, I will demonstrate an ironic situation: namely, that the promotional efforts of foreign infant formula companies are readily apparent in urban hospitals despite Chinese laws restricting the sale and advertising of breast milk substitutes. The main argument I make is twofold: on the one hand, that the Chinese government's promotion of breastfeeding has the effect of compelling individuals to relinquish their private judgment on infant care to medical authority; on the other hand, that the penetration of commercialism into Chinese hospitals has obstructed the effectiveness of the government's measures to promote breastfeeding.[2]

Science and the Baby-Friendly Hospital Initiative

Since 1992, the Chinese government, in cooperation with the World Health Organization (WHO) and United Nations Children's Fund (UNICEF), has reorganized more than 4,957 urban hospitals into "Baby-Friendly Hospitals" (*aiying yiyuan*) to promote breastfeeding. The goal of the Baby-Friendly Hospital initiative (hereafter BFHI) as defined by UNICEF and WHO is to promote the practice of breastfeeding by reorganizing hospital routines, spaces, and knowledge in maternity wards and obstetrics clinics (UNICEF Beijing 1992). This initiative represents China's response to a dramatic decline in the rate and duration of breastfeeding in urban areas. For example, in spite of supportive policies for breastfeeding implemented before the economic reforms initiated in the late 1970s, the number of urban Beijing mothers who breastfed their infants for six months declined from 81 percent in 1950 to 10.4 percent in 1985 (Zhu 1994; Yuan 1997). Nationwide, the rate was 30 percent in 1990 (Chen Ya 1996:15). Following the BFHI, however, this trend may have begun to reverse. According to one official source (Yuan 1997), rates of exclusive breastfeeding for four months in large and medium-sized cities in China rose to 64 percent in 1994.

In the pages that follow, I will explore the use of science in the promotion of breast milk and explain why infant formulas can be regarded as "bearers of commercial ideologies" (M. Lee 1993:39). In their decisions about using either breast milk or infant formula, urban Chinese women function as individuals in a social environment in which the one-child policy places a premium on the health of single children for both the family and the future of a modern nation (Anagnost 1995). At the same time, the cultural-economic milieu of these women's lives marks them as participants in a fast-changing society where the absorption of scientific information and the consumption of goods that are marketed as "scientific products" signifies one as modern.

Women's use of one feeding method over another involves a complex decision-making process, and certain aspects of the process may be better understood in the urban hospital, where issues related to infant-feeding practices form an important part of women's prenatal care. Considering this linkage of individuals and institutions, I will explore how the notion of science is used in the urban hospital setting to promote breastfeeding, how the notion of science is employed by infant formula companies to promote their products, and the ways in which women responded to these efforts.

To this end, I will highlight key moments in the prenatal health care process at which women are confronted with the symbolic importance of the science of infant feeding through breastfeeding education classes and through the foreign formula promotional pamphlets that were disseminated in these classes. I will then focus on two women's narratives about their decisions to use foreign infant formula or breast milk. My analysis is primarily intended to illuminate how and why the use of science and commercial products in infant feeding forms a "basis for reflection on and reproduction of social relations" (Good 1994:113). Before I discuss these points in detail, however, I want to mention why locating my analysis in the hospital is useful.

Limiting my focus to the hospital serves two purposes. First, all 30 women in my study sample received their prenatal and postnatal care in the same hospital. Therefore there is a certain continuity in their encounters with hospital discourses dealing with representations and practices related to infant feeding and with the hospital's policies on breastfeeding. Analyzing encounters in a common location is particularly important when one conducts research in an urban area where people are constantly interacting and responding to a variety of cultural and social contexts. Even though many other factors shape women's experiences and their interpretations of these encounters, they all experienced the hospital environment, and thus this location provides an important aspect of continuity and context for my study. The second purpose for limiting my focus to the hospital setting is that it enabled me to have conversations with the women participants in the obstetrics clinic. I accompanied them to their classes on breastfeeding, to their check-ups, and occasionally to other types of appointments in the hospital. In the process, I was able to witness their reactions as they were presented with texts, images, and information about infant feeding. These encounters facilitated many impromptu conversations and comments in later interviews.

Beyond the methodological usefulness of locating my analysis in the hospital, the urban hospital setting has been described as an important location where women's decisions about breastfeeding are formed, shaped, or changed (Hull et al. 1989; Popkin et al. 1986). Generally, scholars have viewed urban hospitals in developing countries as discouraging of breastfeeding, since the routines and practices of the maternity ward often separate mother and child and thus limit opportunities for breastfeeding (see, e.g., Van Esterik 1989). In addition, hospitals are viewed as centers conveying powerful representations of what is "modern" and "scientific" (see, e.g., Jelliffe and Jelliffe 1981). According to the health economist Barry M. Popkin and others (1986), decisions by women in third world countries not to breastfeed often can be traced to health professionals' lack of knowledge of infants' nutritional requirements, their transmission of negative attitudes toward breastfeeding, patients' use of health professionals as role models, and the influence of the infant food industry (1986:9).[3] I will describe precisely how infant feeding is linked to the ideology of science as a part of the Baby-Friendly Hospital Initiative and how international companies promote and define images of the allegedly "scientific" nature of infant formula. To do so, I will focus on how special training classes on breastfeeding are conducted as part of prenatal care.[4]

The Beijing hospital where I conducted my research is a microcosm of the larger development of the Baby-Friendly Hospital

Initiative.[5] According to Yuan Xiaohong of the Chinese Ministry of Health (1997), since the BFHI began in China in 1992, some 800,000 obstetricians, gynecologists, pediatricians, nurses, birth attendants, and maternal and child health workers, as well as 360 village and township doctors, received training on breastfeeding. Guidelines for a hospital to become a certified baby-friendly hospital include observance of such routines as putting the infant to the mother's breast within a half-hour of birth, rooming-in infants with mothers after birth, providing breastfeeding education classes prenatally, and offering breastfeeding education during the postpartum hospital stay (Xie 1992). This program represents an impressive, national-level campaign to increase the rate of breastfeeding, and it indicates the special role played by the state in the protection of children's health. However, the state-sponsored promotion of breastfeeding may not be as effective as hoped for, partly because China's market reforms have brought an influx of foreign formula companies, which have employed various marketing methods to compete for a dominant market share for infant formula products, maternal nutrition supplements, and toddler food products.[6] And this competition has penetrated some of the baby-friendly hospitals that are expected to be the very sites where the government's promotion of breastfeeding takes place.

Inside a Baby-Friendly Hospital

I conducted much of my fieldwork in a small, 300-bed hospital in southwestern Beijing primarily serving local residents and a few large work units in the area. The name of the hospital as well as the real names of the staff and patients have been withheld to preserve confidentiality. The hospital's obstetrics clinic enjoys a local reputation of being as good as or better than some of Beijing's larger, more famous hospitals. When I arrived to begin my research, the hospital had recently achieved certification as a baby-friendly hospital by UNICEF and the Chinese Ministry of Health. The hospital had reorganized its obstetrics clinic and maternity wards, and it offered training courses for staff to follow criteria for certification set by the UNICEF and WHO in conjunction with the Ministry of Health.

Specifically, the hospital renovated areas of the maternity wards to create private rooms for mothers, and had eliminated the practice of keeping all infants in one nursery. Consequently, babies are roomed in with their mothers throughout their hospital stay. In addition, all women who receive prenatal care in the hospital are required to attend three breastfeeding classes that are taught by a specially trained nurse. The certification process required that at least one obstetric nurse, one physician, and one pediatrician attend a special training seminar in breastfeeding. These staff members were put in charge of the hospital's effort to facilitate breastfeeding among new mothers and to educate pregnant women about the benefits of and techniques necessary for successful breastfeeding.

As one ascends the steps to the hospital, it is difficult not to notice the brass placard with red lettering announcing in English and Chinese that this is a baby-friendly hospital. In addition to the Ministry of Health's authorization, the placard mentions the World Health Organization and United Nations Children's Fund as sponsoring organizations. Inside the main lobby, large boards display brightly colored posters promoting breastfeeding. The centerpiece of the lobby is a poster of a smiling woman clad in a lacy negligee in the act of breastfeeding her infant, with a nurse in a crisp uniform standing behind her. The poster reads, "Helping Mothers Achieve Breastfeeding."

The obstetrics clinic, located in a hallway, contains wooden folding chairs for patients waiting to be seen by the nurse or doctor. Behind a small desk is a receptionist who registers patients as they arrive. Here, women first encounter promotional messages on breastfeeding as a scientific feeding method. Posters and pictures explain why breastfeeding is the best source of nutrition for infants and best for fostering their physical and mental development. A room is designated for prenatal breastfeeding education; there, each woman is required to attend three classes. Ideally, women attend these sessions at four months, seven or eight months, and nine months of pregnancy. A woman reaching her third or fourth month comes in for a check-up, registers and, after paying a small fee, is given a receipt and instructed to go to the end of the hall for breastfeeding education. Let us look at three breastfeeding classes in detail to highlight how the ideals of science were presented by Nurse Bai, my chief informant at this hospital, and how she invoked medical authority in relation to infant feeding during her classes.

Session One: Introducing Breastfeeding

Nurse Bai greeted Mrs. Li, a 23-year-old small-business owner, and asked her to sit down on the bench next to her. Nurse Bai asked for her receipt for payment for the class (three yuan) that Mrs. Li obtained from the clinic receptionist. She recorded Mrs. Li's name, age, anticipated date of delivery and noted the date and that this was Mrs. Li's first visit to the class. I use the phrase "breastfeeding class," but in fact these were not systematically scheduled. Rather, they were ad hoc and conducted by Nurse Bai as women arrived in the breastfeeding education room. Record-keeping details completed, Nurse Bai told Mrs. Li that, as part of her prenatal care, she would attend three sessions where they would discuss the importance of breastfeeding and practice breastfeeding and other infant care techniques with a doll. The nurse said that she would respond to any questions or concerns Mrs. Li may have about feeding an infant. Nurse Bai began her brief summary of the benefits of breastfeeding. She told Mrs. Li about the health, psychological, developmental, and economic benefits of breastfeeding. She described why breast milk is not only the most natural but also the most scientific method of feeding an infant, and explained that breast milk contains complete nutrition for the infant up to the age of four months. She also outlined the immune properties of breast milk that protect infants from illness. In addition, she noted that breastfeeding provides an opportunity for psychological bonding with the infant and thus promotes the child's physical and mental development. Furthermore, Nurse Bai said that breast milk makes babies more intelligent. Finally, she said, breastfeeding is much more economical than using infant formula or milk, which are expensive but not as nutritious for the baby. After outlining the benefits of breastfeeding, she asked to examine Mrs. Li's breasts. As she examined Mrs. Li's nipples, she demonstrated how Mrs. Li should massage and wash her breasts to prepare for breastfeeding. Nurse Bai first demonstrated the massage techniques and then asked Mrs. Li to try. After a few corrections, Nurse Bai recommended that Mrs. Li massage her breasts and nipples twice a day throughout the pregnancy. This portion of the session took about ten minutes. After Nurse Bai completed the massage lesson, she asked if Mrs. Li had any questions. Mrs. Li said that she understood everything and had no questions.

Then Nurse Bai began telling Mrs. Li about the importance of good nutrition during pregnancy. At this point, she handed her visitor a glossy, full-color pamphlet outlining pregnant women's nutritional needs. The pamphlet was published by a Western formula company to advertise a nutritional supplement for pregnant women.[7] Nurse Bai explained that the pamphlet had important information but that Mrs. Li did not need to buy the advertised supplement. By simply eating a balanced diet, she would receive all the nutrients she required during pregnancy.[8] During this encounter, Mrs. Li did not talk much and Nurse Bai did not attempt to engage in conversation beyond her instructional obligations.

In other observations, I found that while the content of the instruction varied little between encounters, the interpersonal dynamic between Nurse Bai and the pregnant women did. Some women chatted and interacted in a more conversational way; others were not talkative, only answering direct questions, and in these situations, the encounter took on a more didactic tone.

The first session, Nurse Bai pointed out to me, is geared toward introducing the idea and the benefits of breastfeeding. The goal is first to explain the importance of breastfeeding and to wait until women are further along in their pregnancy before discussing the practical aspects of breastfeeding. These include how to hold the infant, help the infant suckle properly, and manage breast engorgement and other aspects of the process. When asked why she handed out the informational pamphlets from foreign formula companies, she said that many women did not realize how important good nutrition is during pregnancy. She explained that the hospital had no pamphlets of its own on nutrition and that the foreign formula company's representatives gave them to her free of charge. She acknowledged that the companies used these pamphlets to encourage the use of their products and that their motive conflicted with the purposes of the breastfeeding education program; nonetheless, in her opinion, it was important to ensure that women had information on nutrition during pregnancy. She also mentioned that giving them a small present such as a pamphlet made women feel good about coming to see her and encouraged them to return for the additional education sessions. During my study, I collected sixteen pamphlets produced by three different foreign formula companies that Nurse Bai had handed out. I will discuss the content of these pamphlets later.

Session Two: Teaching Breastfeeding

Mrs. Wang, a 27-year-old elementary school teacher, entered the education room one day and announced that she was there for her second class on breastfeeding. Nurse Bai, who was busy talking to another woman, asked Mrs. Wang to sit on the bench next to me. As she was talking, Nurse Bai turned on the television and VCR at Mrs. Wang's right and told her to watch a video on breastfeeding. I watched it with her as Nurse Bai continued to talk to the other woman. The video, entitled *Breastfeeding* (Shanghai Educational Television 1994), begins with a shot of a chubby, healthy baby as the female narrator states that breastfeeding is the most natural and scientific way to feed infants up to six months. The narrator goes on to say that unfortunately in the modern world, people are not aware of the importance and benefits of breastfeeding. A montage sequence of workers in a laboratory examining what is presumably breast milk fills the screen as the narrator outlines the more than one hundred beneficial substances contained in breast milk. The film then cuts to an infant's head, and an animated picture of the brain appears as the narrator states that these nutrients are essential for proper development of the brain. Later, the video shows a smiling couple in a park with their infant; the narrator explains that breastfeeding also benefits mothers by helping them to lose weight and preventing uterine problems during the post-partum period. Finally, the film moves in for a close-up of the smiling mother holding her infant, and the narrator states that breastfeeding also encourages bonding and love between mother and infant. The next scene is an outpatient clinic where women are attending a breastfeeding class. The class, according to the narrator, helps pregnant women understand the "mysteries" of breastfeeding; the video then cuts to a diagram of the breast and describes the process of milk production and the relation between nipple stimulation and the hormonal responses that encourage breast milk production.

The dialectic of motherhood and medical science is expressed throughout the video. To convince the viewer of this dialectic, it shows pictures of laboratory workers making slides of breast milk, lists of the many nutrients available in breast milk, and animated images of the hormonal-physiological aspects of milk production. Medical authority is depicted in the form of health professionals interacting with patients throughout the video, with images of nurses and doctors educating both women and men about breastfeeding, helping women learn the correct positioning of the baby, teaching them how to express breast milk, and correcting mothers-in-laws who try to bottle-feed the baby by showing them the nutritional value of breast milk. The message is clear: breastfeeding requires medical (read scientific) assistance. In a larger sense, the video conveys the idea that mothers need assistance in developing their mothering practices and medical knowledge. Medical professionals are presented as the best means to achieve this ideal.

I have so far highlighted several aspects of the 45-minute video, but it contains many images and information I have not described. The aspects I have described illuminate a variety of messages about the scientific nature of breast milk that are being conveyed to pregnant women in the breastfeeding class, which I will discuss in depth in my analysis of the educational sessions below. For now, let us turn to the final educational session for pregnant women.

Session Three: The Practice of Breastfeeding

The third session of the breastfeeding education program emphasizes the practical aspects of breastfeeding. Mrs. Zhou and four other women in their ninth month of pregnancy attended the class one day, and each practiced different ways of holding an infant for breastfeeding after observing Nurse Bai's demonstration with a model of a breast and a plastic doll. They each tried several times; as they practiced, Nurse Bai corrected their positioning and discussed some of the common mistakes women make as they learn to breastfeed. As the class was ending, Candy,[9] a Chinese representative of a foreign formula company, entered the room.

A well-dressed young woman in her thirties, she greeted the group and asked if she could talk to us about some nutritional information and products for pregnant women and nursing mothers. No one answered her question directly, but none of the women left the room. Nurse Bai told everyone to move down on the benches to make room for Candy. Candy took several colorful brochures about nutritional drinks for pregnant and nursing women from her briefcase and handed them out. As she did so, she told us that she was a doctor (a cardiologist) who had decided to work for this company to expand her opportunities. Then she began a rapid sales pitch to the women and Nurse Bai. Leaning toward them, she started by saying:

> I am a mother too; my son is two years old. But, we all know
> how busy we can get and sometimes you don't have enough

time or energy to make or eat a balanced meal. Especially when you are a new mother, your baby needs a lot of attention. Research studies have shown that many women do not get enough vitamins during or after pregnancy when their bodies need them most. Our drinks provide a convenient way to make sure you receive all the good nutrition you need.

One woman interrupted Candy to ask why she would need this drink if she ate vegetables, fruits, and meat. Candy replied that it was possible to do this but may be more difficult when one is busy or too tired to cook a meal. The women all looked at the pamphlets, and no one said anything for a few minutes. Finally, one woman asked her if her company also made formula for infants. Candy replied that, yes, it did and that these were the most scientific types of infant formula on the market. At this point, Nurse Bai interrupted Candy to say that this was not a topic that she could talk about. As Nurse Bai was admonishing Candy, one of the women turned to me and Mrs. Zhou and said, "Chinese milk formula is as good as these foreign products." Candy overheard her remark and started to reply, but Nurse Bai stopped her by asking her to leave some information with her about the maternal nutritional drinks. This was clearly a signal to Candy to leave, and she dug out some more pamphlets from her bag and handed Nurse Bai some samples of the nutritional drinks. She said good-bye to everyone and left the room.

With Candy's departure, the room erupted as all the women started speaking at once. Nurse Bai, putting the samples in a cupboard, told them that they all were very healthy and that there was no need to buy any special products. The woman who had made the comment earlier about Chinese milk being as good as foreign milk made a point of repeating her remark to the whole group. One of the other women responded that with so many fake or poorly made products on the market, it was hard to say whether a Chinese product is as "good" as a foreign company's.[10]

This educational session and Candy's visit raised a number of issues that resonated with other conversations and classes I attended with women in the hospital. A major concern about the quality of food products was expressed by the women when they were talking with Candy. The concern is not misplaced. Recent laws and popular news stories indicate that consumers face the real possibility of purchasing counterfeit or poor-quality food products. The Food Hygiene Law passed by the central government in 1995 represents an attempt to regulate the problem (Kan 1996). The Chinese State Administration for Industry and Commerce also launched a quality-control campaign focusing specifically on health-food industries (Chen Qiuping 1996). Women in my study at various moments during my fieldwork expressed concern with the quality of Chinese-produced food products and medicines, especially whether they should consume these products during their pregnancies and whether their infants should consume them. I will discuss later how the foreign companies producing maternal nutrition drinks and infant formula promote their products as scientific ones in ways that intersect with women's anxieties about the quality of Chinese food products.

In addition, these women's concerns with the quality of food products extend to their own bodies as sites of consumption. When Candy introduced the maternal nutritional drinks, she used the medical authority of scientific studies that indicate that most women during pregnancy and the post-partum period do not receive enough essential nutrients. The comment made by one woman that a balanced diet should provide these nutrients indicates an awareness of the necessity of good nutrition during the perinatal period. The women's conversations, questions, and statements after Candy left the room revealed that nutritional well-being for both mother and child is a worry shared by these women. This point was corroborated throughout my research, with women often admitting that they knew that they should be eating more of a certain food in order to maintain good nutrition, but were not, for numerous reasons. In addition to citing medical studies as an authority to prove the usefulness, and even necessity, of a maternal nutritional drink, Candy tried to appeal to the image of the busy, concerned mother who simply had no time for her own needs. By consuming the convenient nutritional drink, a mother would be able to maintain her own health and her busy schedule — and attend to her baby's needs. These concerns are mirrored later in this chapter when I turn to two women's narratives about their infant-feeding decisions. Before doing so, however, let us examine more closely the issue of medical authority as it was presented in these educational sessions.

Teaching the "Science" of Infant Feeding

In the sessions described above, four types of medical authority emerge: that of Nurse Bai; that of the 45-minute educational video; that of the formula pamphlets; and that of Candy, the cardiologist-turned-formula-company-sales-representative. The medical authority invested in Nurse Bai by the hospital structure is implicated in any understanding we have about the transmission of representations of the scientific aspects of infant feeding. Indeed, the power dynamic that was established by holding a class with a teacher and students also plays a role in the development of medical authority about feeding infants (Freire 1996). The science of infant feeding was imparted in the class sessions, and, while the language Nurse Bai used relayed representations of nature as well, the overall message was that breastfeeding requires special knowledge.[11]

Requiring a class on breastfeeding as a part of women's prenatal care in the hospital imparts the idea that medical knowledge and authority are essential to successful breastfeeding. The video presentation on breastfeeding in the second session reinforced the idea that there are scientific and medical advantages to breastfeeding. Further, by presenting images of other women attending similar classes led by doctors and nurses, the video supported the notion that a class on breastfeeding is an important means for women to learn about effective breastfeeding techniques. Moreover, it suggested that the most qualified individuals for imparting this information would be medical professionals.

The importance of the medical professional as an authority on breastfeeding was also apparent in the way Candy, the formula representative, presented herself to the women in the class. She told them that she used to be a cardiologist as a way of conveying to them that she too was a member of the professional medical community rather than a mere salesperson with no special background in medicine or health. Her presentation of self and the comments that her presence inspired from women at the session she attended also highlighted women's responses to the educational sessions.

The women in my study reacted in complex ways to the breastfeeding education classes. However, the importance of medical personnel as authorities in terms of infant feeding was clear when we consider women's preferences in seeking advice. When I asked women during the prenatal period to whom they would first turn for advice if they had a question about feeding their infant, 20 women out of 30 told me that they would seek information from a health professional, either a doctor or a nurse. In post-partum interviews, when I asked if they had sought advice for questions about infant feeding and whom did they ask, of the 25 women who sought advice, 18 had asked a doctor or nurse.

However, several women in my study as well as others I met in the hospital were resistant to the idea of having to attend the classes and to the medical authority they represented. They responded in a variety of ways. Some voiced their resistance to me when I met with them after class. Mrs. Zhang, a 24-year-old factory worker, said to me one day, "Why should I have to attend a class? Breastfeeding and being a mother are natural; I don't need to go to a class to learn anything." When I asked her to whom she would turn if she needed advice, she said, "It would be my mother. She raised two children; she can help me." Mrs. Zhang's response was not unusual, although more than half the women I followed through the fourteen months of my study told me that they would ask a doctor if they had problems or questions about infant feeding. Others resisted the class requirement by cutting short the time they spent in the session, telling Nurse Bai that they had an appointment or that their mother-in-law was waiting for them. Later when I asked them about the classes they would say they simply did not want to stay and felt they did not need the information.

By contrast, seven women in my sample explicitly said to me that they enjoyed coming to class sessions. They felt that they needed information about breastfeeding and were concerned about raising a healthy child. Ms. Yang, a 23-year-old office worker, told me that she felt many aspects of child care were more modern than the traditional practices followed by her mother and mother-in-law. She did not want to raise her child using traditional and "backward" (luohou) practices. She viewed the hospital staff in general and the breastfeeding class in particular as useful sources of modern knowledge about mothering. The seven were also avid consumers of books on pregnancy and child care and believed that more information from professionals external to family traditions was a way of empowering themselves as modern mothers.

In addition to the information imparted by Nurse Bai in the class on breastfeeding, the foreign formula pamphlets represented another source of descriptions of scientific infant feeding. In her role as "breastfeeding educator," Nurse Bai handed them out to pregnant women who attended her classes, and her medical authority lent weight to the claims made by the texts. The act of giving information about commercial products, whether they advertise foreign infant formula or maternal supplement drinks, in the context of the Baby-Friendly Hospital Initiative represents a contradiction of the stated goals and practices of the obstetrics clinic, which aims to discourage the use of infant formula. Nurse Bai, however, said that some of the information, especially on maternal nutrition, was useful. Since she had no access to any other pamphlets, she viewed the pamphlets of the foreign formula companies as necessary but not the best way of providing information she believes important for women's health.

Furthermore, as I described earlier, she wanted to hand out some sort of small present in return for the women's participation in her classes. I see this practice and Nurse Bai's justifications as part of the contradiction established by the assumption that breastfeeding is simultaneously natural and scientific. If breastfeeding is natural, why should women need to attend a class? Nurse Bai, by regarding the pamphlets as small gifts for attending her class, was implicitly acknowledging this contradiction. If breastfeeding is also the most scientific and modern means of feeding infants, then the medical authority of science and the women's consumerist desires to achieve modernity and to be good mothers should prove more powerful than any formula advertisement.[12]

The pamphlets that Nurse Bai distributed in the prenatal education classes varied in content *vis-à-vis* breastfeeding. I analyzed the content of twelve different pamphlets that I received from Nurse Bai and found that about half (seven out of twelve) of them presented detailed information on the benefits and techniques of breastfeeding. The others contained the brief message required by the WHO Code, with the remainder of the text discussing other issues such as maternal nutrition, exercise, and the company's product line.[13] The twofold message in those that extensively discuss breastfeeding was that breastfeeding is the natural and scientific way to feed infants. The cover of one pamphlet depicted a mother in the shape of a pod and a tiny green sprout extending from her belly. Inside, the infant is shown as a human infant resting in a pea-pod shaped plant. From the visual image alone, the message was that "growing" a baby is like nurturing a seed into a plant and in the modern world requires both nature and science (agricultural technology). The "science" of breastfeeding in these pamphlets was often not expanded on in the text. Instead, the text claimed that if for some reason a mother cannot use breast milk to feed her infant, then formula is the most modern and scientific means of feeding an infant. Charts and graphs compared the formula nutrients with those of breast milk. The implied message was that their product had been scientifically proven to be similar to breast milk.

The wordplay of "nature" and "science" is exemplified in another pamphlet, which declares in large characters: "The first natural choice for breast milk replacement" (*tidai muru de tianran shouxuan*). The message continued in smaller characters that stated that breastfeeding is best for infants up to the age of six months, but that if, for some, breastfeeding was impossible, formula should become parents' natural first choice. The word *tian ran* in Chinese is best translated as "naturally produced," as opposed to *ren gong*, or "artificially produced." In this case, the formula company was marketing its product as natural and thus scientific in terms that claim it is like mother's milk, which is a natural rather than an artificial product. In other words, nature was not linked rhetorically to breastfeeding, but rather to the scientifically produced infant formula.

Experiencing the Science of Infant Feeding

Medical authority and knowledge resonated throughout the variety of media and representations I describe above. In the context of the hospital, where women encounter a primarily Western biomedical model of pregnancy and infant feeding, the over-arching authority rests in the use of science and its physiological focus to define these bodily experiences. In the field of biomedicine, where biology is considered to be universal and culture is a limiting construct for individuals, it is particularly important to highlight the authority and knowledge vested in the medical construction of breastfeeding (Strathern 1996:145; see also Martin 1989).

Moreover, the transnational, modern character of this authority and knowledge exists not only in formula advertisements but also in the information from UNICEF and WHO used by Nurse Bai in her classes and in the video, which is based on the same materials and information. These materials presuppose that breastfeeding is a universal, biological capability of women. The goal is then to seek ways to mitigate the limiting factors of "culture" to increase the rate of breastfeeding. Previous multilateral attempts to increase breastfeeding focused on discerning indigenous cultural practices that lead to a decrease in breastfeeding initiation or supplementary feeding practices and then educating women and health workers about the dangers of such practices (see, for example, Gussler and Briesemeister 1980). Chinese researchers promote this notion as well. For example, Xie Jili of Jiangnan City People's Hospital (1992) says that traditions such as not feeding infants in the first few days after birth are based on the erroneous belief that colostrum is bad for the infant, and that this belief should be changed. The assumption is that such traditions are simply a matter of ignorance and that once women know a better way, they will change their behavior.

Since the advent of the Baby-Friendly Hospital Initiative in China in 1992, however, the model of health behavior change has become more sophisticated and acknowledges the more complex facets of implementing such changes. Most interesting for my discussion here is that UNICEF/WHO assumes that modernity is associated with biomedicine and that implementing programs in urban hospitals will provide breastfeeding with the cachet of modernity through medicine (United Nations 1995). The result of this policy and the methods used to implement it thus contain the message that breastfeeding is scientific as a means of articulating a form of social relations linked to modernity rather than tradition. Importantly, Chinese researchers are also expressing these ideas in their research reports. One Chinese article noted how important it is to overcome the image of breastfeeding as a "traditional" practice and to emphasize it as a scientific practice (Wang et al. 1991:3).

Keeping this modernity-versus-tradition advocacy in mind, I turn now to two women's narratives about their infant feeding experiences. My intention is not to determine a causal explanation for their decisions to use breast milk or foreign infant formula. Rather, their stories exemplify how individual women make these decisions in relation to a social context that places a premium on the authority of science and the consumption of modern knowledge and products as markers of modern life (Good 1994).

In the case of Mrs. Wang, a 26-year-old teacher, the decision to use a Western infant formula rather than a Chinese product stands as a moment when symbolic meanings of foreign are situated as superior to Chinese by virtue of being more scientific and of higher quality.

I use a foreign infant formula to feed my baby. It is from Holland. I decided to use infant formula (*naifen*) after one month of breastfeeding. I was sick with a cold and couldn't take any medicine for it because it would affect my breast milk. If I took the medicine, I couldn't feed my baby. Finally my doctor told me I needed to take some medicine, so I did but then I couldn't use my milk to feed the baby. I had no choice. I talked to my husband and a friend who is a doctor. I didn't know whether to use Chinese or foreign formula. I think feeding an infant is the most important aspect of raising a child, so when I talked to my husband, he said that we must use the best substitute we could and that foreigners had been feeding their infants with formula for a long time and that they were a more scientific culture than China.

Even though it costs us 200–300 renminbi (yuan) every month, I think it is worth it. My mother-in-law disagrees and thinks we can use cow's milk to feed the baby. She says she raised two children with cow's milk and they were healthy. She also told me that you can't replace human milk anyway. She didn't support me, you know. But my doctor friend told me that foreign formula has many more nutrients than Chinese brands. Ordinary people, they think that cow's milk is good for infants, they think it should be fresh and fresh milk is more nutritious. They think it can, at times, be better than mother's breast milk but they are ignorant. Foreign infant formula is the most similar to breast milk. It is the most suitable for babies. Even though we spend more money, it is best for our child's health. This is most important.

Mrs. Wang's narrative raises a number of issues related to the authority of science and consumerism. In her words, she believes that since foreigners have been using infant formula for a long time, it must be safe for her infant. Moreover, to garner support for her decision, she sought the advice of a friend who is a medical doctor, a voice of authority. Mrs. Wang's trust in science is especially clear when she describes her mother-in-law's stated preference for cow's milk. Her mother-in-law calls on her own experience with feeding babies as an authority to support her position that cow's milk is good enough for babies. Later in the narrative, Mrs. Wang refers to "ordinary people" as ignorant in their belief that fresh cow's milk is suitable for babies. She also suggests that if one cannot use breast milk, then one should use the most scientific alternative, and in this case the best product is a foreign-produced one, from a place where science has a longer history.

The emphasis placed by Mrs. Wang on the quality of foreign products also reflects a common concern among Chinese consumers that local products may not be of the highest quality or safe. Given that the couple's combined income ranged from 1,100 to 1,400 yuan a month, they were spending approximately 18 percent of their monthly income on infant formula alone. Mrs. Wang was also telling us that she can afford to buy foreign formula and by doing so was acting in a more modern manner than those who use fresh cow's milk or Chinese infant formulas to feed their infants. The symbols of science are embodied in the role of her doctor friend whose medical authority is invoked as she described her decision to go against the "ignorant" thinking of her mother-in-law. Furthermore, in Mrs. Wang's narrative medical knowledge as well as foreign scientific knowledge were ranked over her mother-in-law's experiential knowledge.

A similar sentiment is expressed in the narrative of Mrs. Zhai, a 25-year-old factory manager who started using infant formula as soon as she returned home from the hospital. Her mother had stayed with her during the first month after the birth and helped her take care of her newborn child while Mrs. Zhai was "doing the month" (zuo yuezi): a traditional Chinese post-partum practice of recovery, which is now also known as "birth leave" in urban

China.[14] Like Mrs. Wang, Mrs. Zhai rejected the traditions of her mother's generation as "backward" (*luohou de*) and wanted to raise her son in the most modern, scientific way possible (Anagnost 1995). Her narrative describing her decision to use a foreign infant formula suggests that the symbols of science and modernity were important building blocks in Mrs. Zhai's understanding of child care:

I started using infant formula as soon as I returned home from the hospital. I attended the classes on breastfeeding at the hospital but I knew that I would be returning to work so I researched the infant formulas on the market and compared them. The Chinese products did not have as many nutrients as the foreign ones. I also asked my friends what formulas they had used. They mostly used foreign products as well. I thought if my baby can't have my milk, he should have the most nutritious substitute I could buy. My mother wanted me to breastfeed. She had breastfed me and my sister and believes it is the best for infants, especially when they are very young. I told her that my work was important and that I could not see trying to breastfeed for a few weeks and then have to switch to formula. It would be best for me and the baby if he got used to the formula right away.

I also wanted to raise my son in the most modern, scientific way. China is developing quickly and becoming more modern; I want my son to benefit from these advances. The traditional ways are not good. I will take my son to a nursery school run by a woman who used to work as a psychologist. It is expensive and means I have to work more but I don't want my mother or my mother-in-law raising my son using traditional methods. The foreign brand of infant formula is expensive, but I don't believe that the Chinese formula companies are reliable — who controls them? The foreign companies have international standards that they have developed and they are more scientific. So, I feel foreign products are safer and have better nutrition. Some of them even have more nutrients than breast milk!

Mrs. Zhai's narrative clearly articulates the importance she places on living a "modern" life and that, apart from her logistical reasons for not wanting to breastfeed, she feels she is feeding her son with the product of modernity and science in the form of foreign infant formula. Thus, her son, in his infancy, participates in a modern lifestyle. Her narrative also exemplifies her belief that a nursery school run by a psychologist is a more modern and scientific way of raising her son. She is, in many different ways, trying to avoid what she defines as "traditional" (*chuantong de*) practices of child rearing in order to prepare her son for life in a new kind of society. By literally consuming the products of science and modernity through infant formula, and by scientific child-rearing methods, her son and, by extension, Mrs. Zhai are living a "modern" life that deviates sharply from what she believes is a more "traditional" life. Furthermore, her description of Chinese products as potentially unreliable, in contrast to the international standards of foreign manufacturers, indicates her distrust of Chinese manufacturing standards. Mrs. Zhai's comments reflect larger social concerns about food quality and safety, which may be another factor in her decision to use a foreign formula product. Rather than relying on government measures designed to protect consumers from poor-quality or fraudulent products, she believes that she can safeguard her son's well-being herself by choosing a foreign formula product.

Conclusion: Mother's Love and Medical Authority

As the ethnographic material suggests, the symbolism of science and its conflation with notions of modernity in urban Chinese women's lives act as a powerful force in women's infant-feeding decisions. While science is emphasized *vis-à-vis* tradition, it is presented as a precondition for modernity, an indicator of these women's departure from the liability of ignorance. Viewed in this light, the emphasis on science at the baby-friendly hospital is not merely for physiological reasons but also to convey the idea that a participant in the hospital's breastfeeding program should surrender her personal judgment to medical authority. Of course, this idea is not a uniquely Chinese phenomenon. Andrew Strathern (1996), drawing on Deborah Gordon and Margaret Lock's work (1988; see also Foucault 1994), argues that a cornerstone of modern biomedicine is the medical community's assumption of biological universalism and the institutionalized promotion of this assumption. Phrased differently, culture is assumed to be a secondary rather than a constitutive force in medicine. If culture has any role to play in medicine at all, at least according to the assumption of biological universalism, then it has to do with the patients and their inadequate understanding, not with medicine and physicians as such (Strathern 1996:145).

As the ethnographic material from the Beijing hospital under my study shows, science is also valued for its foreign origin, whereas ideas associated with Chinese provenance are often perceived as "undeveloped" or "backward." The growing importance of foreign infant formula in urban China was brought home to me when thirteen out of the thirty women in my study group decided to switch to a foreign formula rather than to a Chinese-produced one, because they believed that the foreign product was more "scientific." Given that this is a baby-friendly hospital, where the benefits of breastfeeding are emphasized, it is strikingly ironic that all the women participating in my study received pamphlets produced by foreign infant formula companies. These colorful, glossy advertisements are intended, to borrow a phrase from Penny Van Esterik, "as part of a broader semiotic or sign system to communicate something about the user" (1989:175). That is to say, one message conveyed by the promotional literature is that these products are the first and natural choices for an enlightened individual, and especially for a truly caring mother to make when she considers alternatives to breastfeeding. In retrospect, the blatant penetration of infant formula promotional literature into the baby-friendly hospital's special unit, set up specifically for the promotion of breastfeeding, bears out the onslaught of commercialism now occurring in China.

8

State, Children, and the Wahaha Group of Hangzhou

Zhao Yang

In mid-May 1996, the Zhejiang province–based Wahaha Group heard the bad news from its agents that sales of its well-known fruit-flavored milk drink were plummeting in the neighboring province of Anhui. There, the feel-good name of Wahaha — "Baby Laughter" — was mentioned anxiously in connection with the poisoning deaths of three young girls. Two weeks earlier, these girls had died after drinking five small bottles of the Wahaha drink. Two of the girls were sisters, an eighteen-month-old toddler and a five-year-old preschooler. Their four-year-old cousin was the third victim. Although the Anhui provincial government barred the local news media from reporting on this tragedy, word of mouth about the Wahaha Group's possible responsibility quickly spread throughout Anhui, causing sales of the company's aggressively advertised and nationally known milk drink to collapse.

Autopsy results linked the deaths to an arsenic-based rat poison. After traces of arsenic were discovered in the five empty Wahaha bottles, Anhui police authorities decided to hold the Wahaha Group responsible and even acted on behalf of the deceased's families to seek financial compensation. A team of police officers from Zhejiang, who rushed to Anhui and conducted a separate inquiry, strongly disagreed with the Anhui police. They pointed out that commercial sales of arsenic had been banned in Zhejiang for years, and thus no arsenic could have found its way into the five bottles when they were manufactured at the company's factory in

Zhejiang. In addition, the Zhejiang police suggested that the girls might have drunk fake Wahaha, probably manufactured by illegal profiteers in Anhui, where arsenic was still widely used to kill rats.[1]

As the Anhui and Zhejiang police investigators could not agree with one another, the Zhejiang authorities asked the Ministry of Public Security in Beijing to review the evidence. The ministry determined that the Wahaha Group was blameless, but before it informed the Anhui officials of its conclusion, the *Beijing Youth Newspaper* ran a front-page article headlined, "Three Little Girls Die Tragically in Wahaha Poisoning Incident." Jointly written by three reporters (Kong Wenqing, Zhu Qing, and Zhong Jiangguang, June 5, 1996), the article noted that the key question of how arsenic had gotten into the five bottles of Wahaha remained a mystery, and that sales of Wahaha's milk drink remained brisk in Beijing because few people there had heard about the Anhui girls' deaths. The three reporters were immediately reprimanded by the Chinese Communist Party's Propaganda Department, and their article was criticized as having cast a "very bad influence upon society."[2] Thereafter, no Chinese news organization dared to report on the case.

But how could rat poison have gotten into the Wahaha bottles? Was the Wahaha Group really not at fault? If so, who should have been blamed for the loss of three young lives? Was the arsenic an act of industrial sabotage? And why did the police investigators accept the dead girls' families' claim that the five Wahaha bottles were sealed when an older relative bought them from a local store? I expect all these questions to be going through the reader's mind, but unfortunately there is no further information in the Chinese press that might help answer them.

The Answerable Question

One important question that can be addressed, however, is why central authorities were so interested in protecting the Wahaha Group. Prior to this incident, the Chinese news media had reported numerous incidents in which shoddy products or managerial negligence were found responsible for consumers' deaths. Of course, in some cases hastily filed news reports tarnished the reputation of businesses that were ultimately found to be innocent. But in numerous cases, state authorities had intervened to shield companies from bad publicity largely because of their economic or political importance. The official protection of Wahaha after the *Beijing Youth Newspaper* report about the three Anhui girls' deaths falls into the second category, and is the focus of the following discussion.

At the outset, it can be said that there were two reasons why central authorities took a special interest in protecting Wahaha. First, the company was a paragon of the post-Mao economic reforms. It went from a small, three-person retail business in 1987 to national fame by adopting innovative measures to take advantage of China's transition from central planning to a market economy. In an amazingly short period, the company became one of Chinese food industry's leading profit-makers, and was recognized by the state as one of the country's "500 top enterprises" (*qiye wubai qian*). Perhaps more important, Wahaha had become a symbol of nationalist pride. Once it had established itself within China, the central authorities came to regard it as a major force in the domestic food and beverage industry's effort to fend off fierce competition from abroad. The company was so successful in marketing its products and expanding its production capacity that central leaders urged it to develop into China's answer to the US-based Coca-Cola Co. Second, the Wahaha Group had come to see a correspondence between its interests and the state's. It had taken concrete actions to support the government's plans to improve children's health by improving what they ate and drank. And when the central government needed profitable enterprises in well-to-do cities to transfer capital and technology to Sichuan province to create jobs for workers and farmers who would be displaced by the Three Gorges Dam project, the Wahaha Group decided to invest in three factories to create new jobs for resettled workers in Fuling county, the lower parts of which will be submerged in the year 2003.

Thus, for central authorities, the Wahaha Group was no ordinary company; it was a patriotic, public-spirited, politically reliable business — an edifying example of Deng Xiaoping's much extolled vision of "socialism with Chinese characteristics." In the following discussion, I will show how Wahaha went about establishing its reputation in the marketplace as well as in high places of political power. I will then explain why Wahaha eventually decided to merge with a foreign company, thus dashing the government's hope that it might become China's own Coca-Cola-like corporation.

Cultural Strategy: Nationalism and Indigenous Food Cures

The foundation of what has become the Wahaha Group was a small, school-run enterprise in Hangzhou. The three teachers who started it said they had heard constant complaints from pupils' parents that their children were unwilling to eat what the adults considered to be good food. After conducting a dietary survey to investigate this problem, the company drew on traditional Chinese medicine to produce a nutritional drink that would also stimulate children's appetite. The formula for this drink, which turned the company into a household name within three years, was developed from a mixture of medicinal herbs commonly recommended by doctors of traditional Chinese medicine to enhance children's appetites and to treat their eating disorders. The chief collaborator for developing the company's first product was Zhu Shoumin at the Zhejiang University of Medical Sciences. The basic ingredients are dates, haw, wolfberry, and lotus seeds. It also contains calcium, iron, and zinc, as recommended by Professor Zhu and other nutritionists (Meng Yuecheng 1996:1). The product's registered name is "Wahaha Nutritional Drink" (*Wahaha yingyang yinliao*), its effects, according to the company's promotional literature, include "invigorating the spleen and stimulating the stomach" (Zong Qinghou 1996:2). This medical claim was turned into a slogan — "Food Tastes Good After Drinking Wahaha" — that was repeated in its aggressive sales promotions on television.

In my interviews with Wahaha's senior executives, they said their emphasis on their original product's close relationship with Chinese medicine was based on their recognition that traditional medical and nutritional beliefs have persisted in Chinese society as a strong influence upon adults, especially the elderly, who see no sharp separation between diet therapy and herbal medicine. To an adult who clings to traditional medical beliefs, the executives said, ordinary foods contain powerful healing effects. For example, chewing fresh cherries can alleviate laryngitis; celery juice mixed with a little honey helps to lower cholesterol level; and tea with ginger can relieve gastroenteritis. Therefore, although calcium, iron, and zinc are among the ingredients in this drink, it is the benefits of the ingredients from Chinese herbal medicine that the company has stressed in its promotional literature. By turning to the appeal of what the company describes as a "5,000-year tradition" of Chinese medicine, the Wahaha Nutritional Drink has been deliberately marketed as an indigenous Chinese health drink. Its efficacy is said to have been proven by many centuries experience and therefore can not be doubted. This is, of course, a sales pitch, but it is a culturally sensitive business tactic aimed at winning over parents and especially grandparents. In urban areas, the prevalence of families with two parents working outside the home means that grandparents must serve as their grandchildren's caretakers.

The Wahaha Group's decision to emphasize its drink's indigenous character was followed by the company's determination to depict itself as a staunch defender of the domestic food and beverage industry against what Wahaha's executives called an "unhealthy tendency" in mass consumption: the public's fascination with Western and Japanese consumer goods. One senior Wahaha executive (Zong Qinghou 1996:3) criticized it as "worshiping and blindly believing in things foreign" (*chongyang meiwai*). He did not have to try very hard to find evidence to back his statement. In a 1994 collection of case studies illustrating consumption patterns in urban China, the editor raised the rhetorical question: "Do you prefer Chinese consumer goods or foreign?" In reply, the editor wrote this sarcastic passage:

> A survey of 18 Beijing department stores in 1992 found that 40 percent of the goods for infant care were imported, ranging from fashionable clothes to disposable diapers to Nestle baby formula and to talcum powder. . . . A private entrepreneur's wife boasted that since her "little princess" (i.e., her daughter and only child) was born she has been fed on nothing but imported milk powder. Her daughter is now more than two years old but has yet to eat a single mouthful of Chinese rice. (Zhao Feng 1994:11–12)

To Wahaha Group executives, these consumer attitudes were being bolstered by the increasing leverage of foreign corporations, who "enter our domestic market like a swarm of bees" (Zong Qinghou 1996:2). This angry evaluation of the market situation, by Wahaha's general manager, Zong Qinghou, was not without foundation. Take soft drinks, for example. Days after Deng Xiaoping announced China's economic liberalization in 1979, the Coca-Cola Co. came knocking on the door. By 1994, Coca-Cola had thirteen plants in China. In 1996, it had 23 — 16 in operation and 7 under construction (Tuistra 1996). According to a nationwide Gallup poll in 1997, Coca-Cola had replaced Hitachi as the best-known foreign brand in China, with 81 percent of Chinese surveyed recognizing the name (Leicester 1997). In a magazine article published in 1996 — entitled "Will Chinese or Foreign Soft Drinks Dominate This Summer?" — a Beijing journalist reported how seven of China's nine leading soda manufacturers had been converted into Coca-Cola Co. and PepsiCo Inc. subsidiaries. These Chinese factories, the reporter said, had been assured by the foreign companies that their original products would make up at least 30 percent of their output, but that promise was rarely kept (Liu Yun 1996:7–8). It was with these acquisitions in mind that another Beijing journalist wrote a detailed account of how Coca-Cola Co. and PepsiCo Inc. gained 30 percent of the Chinese soft-drink market and as much as 85 percent of the market in four of China's largest cities (Huang Fei 1997). In this fiery article, the writer focused on mergers, takeovers, and superiorly funded advertising campaigns to explain how the foreign companies had "swamped seven armies of Chinese goods." By July 1998, domestic makers occupied only a 21.1 percent share of China's carbonated beverage market compared with 57.6 and 21.3 percent for Coca-Cola and PepsiCo, respectively (*China Daily*, July 27, 1998, p. 8).

Children in urban China are ardent consumers of Coke and Pepsi. Xue Meng, a fifth-grader in Beijing, boasted in 1997 that he had drunk Coke for the past three years but not a single drop of tap water. Trying to end his dependency on Coke, the boy's parents had him read articles from health newspapers and magazines that advised against drinking too much Coke. "Xue Meng finally stopped drinking Coke," his father said, "but it took us a long time to make him do so. It is hard for parents to compete with Coca-Cola commercials. If parents simply tell children what to do, they will never listen. The only solution is to educate them, to let them realize by themselves what is a good dietary habit."[3]

For the Wahaha Group, however, a loftier cause is at stake than mere personal health. At a trade conference on the production of children's food and drinks, Zong Qinghou, the company's general manager, declared:

> Chinese culinary arts and theories of diet therapy have a long tradition. In more than 5,000 years of this tradition, our ancestors left behind many excellent things that must be cherished. . . . We believe that it is absolutely imperative to treat the development of China's own nutritional food industry as a matter of developing our entire national industry. It is imperative that such a stand be taken because the most resilient commodities are usually those that originate in our national cultural heritage. (Zong Qinghou 1996:3)

Although the Wahaha Group expressed this nationalistic sentiment with great passion, it decided to avoid competing with foreign companies like Coca-Cola and PepsiCo in major cities. Wahaha's main business strategy, to borrow one of Mao's military maxims, was "encircling urban areas from rural areas." This explains why 60 percent of Wahaha's revenues for 1996 were generated in the Chinese countryside. By avoiding a rivalry with foreign competitors and making other shrewd decisions, Wahaha managed to maintain a remarkable growth record. By 1997, ten years after the company was founded, Wahaha had increased its inventory to over 30 products and reached an annual output value of 10 billion yuan — a rather impressive achievement for a business that started with three people and a bank loan of just 140,000 yuan.

Political Strategy: Helping the State Helps the Company

To a degree, all Chinese enterprises find it necessary to heed state policies while formulating business strategies. Shifts in state policies often are an important factor in their own production and marketing readjustments. To be sure, this close attention is a longstanding habit. For more than three decades before the urban reforms were introduced in the mid-1980s, managers of China's state-run and collectively owned enterprises had to meet state-set production quotas, and they learned that their careers depended on placing the state's plans ahead of whatever concerns their enterprises might have. After all, their enterprises were operating within the confines of a centrally directed economy where the highest authority for important economic decisions was the central government and its economic planners.

The Wahaha Group sharply differs from many of the enterprises that had operated under central planning. From its very inception, its business strategies bore the hallmarks of the emerging market economy and a fast-growing consumer culture. Founded as a school-run enterprise to generate extra income for teachers, the company did not have state-set quotas to meet. From the development of its first product to pricing and marketing its growing inventory, the Wahaha Group closely followed market trends to guide its existence and expansion.

But it would be wrong to assume that the company ignored the state. On the contrary, it was as concerned with state policies as with market trends. Having originated as a school-run enterprise, it was intensely interested in the linkage between its business prospects and state policies on children's welfare, especially children's health. It can be argued that one of the crucial steps taken by Wahaha in the process of making itself into a nationally renowned enterprise was the tailoring of the company's business decisions to state policies directly concerned with children. For this reason, it is necessary to explain exactly which state policies Wahaha considered important to incorporate into its business decisions.

The first state policy to be considered is China's one-child policy for urban couples and its limits on births in the countryside. After this population program was promulgated in 1979, a series of related legal codes and provisions were enacted in the next fifteen years for the protection of children. These included, most notably, the Law on Compulsory Education, the Juvenile Protection Law, the Law for the Protection of Maternal and Infant Health, and the Adoption Law. To make these legal measures work, monitoring agencies were established under such central organizations as the National People's Congress and the State Economic Planning Commission. In the meantime, the Chinese government worked closely with the United Nations Children's Fund (UNICEF) and the World Health Organization (WHO) to seek international aid to improve children's health. After Prime Minister Li Peng signed the "World Declaration on the Survival, Protection, and Development of Children" (initiated by the United Nations and adopted in 1990), the government worked out its "Program for Chinese Children's Development in the 1990s," whose goals were to reduce the country's infant mortality rate by one-third and severe malnutrition by half by the year 2000.

The legal codes, health policies, and cooperation with international organizations were meant, in part, to send a clear message both in China and abroad that the country's stringent population policy was of a benign nature, devised to protect children and build a livable environment for future generations. But public declarations of good intentions had yet to be followed by actions to remedy some of the serious nutritional problems affecting children's health. One of the government's responses was the establishment of a children's food industry. China's first children's food factory was founded in 1966. But significant growth in the children's food industry occurred only in the 1980s, largely due to state intervention. For example, a "Children's Consumption Committee" was founded in 1981 to serve as an outreach organization for the Ministry of Light Industry. The committee's "Children's Food Working Group" immediately began work by conducting a survey on the nutritional status of children and the production of children's food in fifteen provinces. After the survey revealed an acute shortage of milk, milk powder, and other dairy products, the central government spent the equivalent of $100 million to import 50 production lines to manufacture dairy products. The Ministry of Light Industry then cooperated with the Ministry of Health to establish state regulations for the production of children's food, especially infant formula. In 1986, these ministries recruited more than 200 experts to devise a set of standards, and made them public four year later. By the early 1990s, China had 29 modern factories exclusively producing milk formula and other baby foods.[4]

From its inception, the Wahaha Group regarded its growth as an extension of the central government's policies on children's welfare. Its first product, the appetite-inducing "Wahaha Nutritional Drink," was aimed expressly at the children's market, and it became an instant success, generating in its first year an after-tax profit of nearly 2 million yuan. In the first three years of its operation, the company was heavily dependent on sales of this digestive drink. Thereafter, however, it began to concentrate on the fruit-flavored milk drink that would figure in the Anhui poisoning case. This shift occurred upon Wahaha's realization that the demand for milk, milk powder, and other dairy products increased dramatically in the late 1980s and early 1990s. In this period, China's annual import of dairy products averaged 60,000 tons, but imports still could not meet the growing demand. At the same time, domestic dairy products, and especially milk powder, repeatedly failed to meet state standards and in some cases were discovered to be serious health hazards (Chinese Academy of Agricultural Sciences 1994:271). The tarnished reputation of many of the manufacturers responsible for the shoddy dairy products opened up an opportunity for the Wahaha Group to create and market a new product nationwide: the fruit-flavored milk drink.

If they banked the company's future on children's consumption patterns and market forces, Wahaha's executives did not forget their golden rule: helping the state is helping the company. This understanding of state-company relationships was illustrated by two events that dramatically boosted the company's production capacity. In September 1991, Wahaha made headlines when it acquired the Hangzhou Cannery Factory. The acquisition was described by the Chinese press as the country's first "small-fish-eat-big-fish" takeover. Previously, Wahaha had only 300 employees and a much smaller factory space. The Hangzhou Cannery Factory, one of the city's oldest industrial enterprises, had more than 2,000 workers. It had, however, been operating in the red for three years, could hardly sell any of its products, borrowed heavily from banks to keep its workers from unemployment, and accumulated a debt load of 40 million yuan. The Hangzhou city government finally decided that the best way to save the factory from closing down was to have it merge with Wahaha, which had petitioned city officials for extra land to expand its factory space. Wahaha's initial response was not enthusiastic. It preferred increasing its production capacity by hiring temporary workers and renting additional factory space. Finally, the city government prevailed; it was a case in which officials imposed their will on businessmen. One senior executive revealed that the company later changed its mind in favor of the merger and spent "three months of hard and carefully planned work to persuade employees" that the risky move would eventually turn out to be beneficial (Wahaha Group 1995:3–4). The risk indeed proved to be worthwhile: Wahaha gained a new factory space of 50,000 square meters, allowing it to considerably boost its production, and it managed to pay off half of the cannery factory's debts within a year. Moreover, Wahaha became a nationally known exemplar in the government-initiated restructuring of the ailing state sector.

The next step for expansion was Wahaha's entry into Sichuan province, where hundreds of thousands of local farmers and workers were slated for resettlement to make way for the Three Gorges Dam, now under construction on the Yangzi River and designed to be the world largest hydroelectric project. The first group of generators is scheduled to begin operations in the year 2003, raising the water level of the reservoir to 135 meters above sea level. When the project is completed in 2009, the water will rise to 175 meters. In all, thirteen cities, 140 towns, and 1,352 villages will be submerged. Most of the officially estimated 1.3 million people who have been targeted for relocation are residents of small villages and medium-sized cities in Sichuan province. Never before in China, or anywhere else for that matter, has a single hydroelectric project displaced so many people (see, e.g., Dai and Xue 1996).

To compensate Sichuan for its enormous loss of land and its resettlement burden, the central government called upon enterprises in the country's coastal cities, especially industrial centers downstream on the Yangzi, to contribute money and technology to Sichuan by investing in the creation of new enterprises to hire displaced workers and peasants. Few enterprises responded to this call, but Wahaha took it seriously, partly for economic reasons and partly for political concerns. From an economic standpoint, Wahaha had still wanted to expand production after taking over the Hangzhou cannery. It also wanted to establish a production center in Sichuan, China's most populous province. Politically, the company's senior executives realized that the Three Gorges Dam project had been regarded by central leaders, notably then-prime minister

Li Peng, as a political task in at least three senses. First, the project was said to be fully supported by the local people, who viewed it as an attempt to alleviate poverty and prevent lethal floods and a major contribution to China's overall development. Second, the project was hailed as a memorial built by the second-generation leadership of the Chinese Communist Party to Mao Zedong, Zhou Enlai, and Deng Xiaoping, who allegedly all gave their unreserved blessing to building "a high lake within the gorges," to quote one of Mao's poems. Third, the project was being undertaken as a showcase for national pride, to demonstrate to critics overseas that China was capable of constructing this huge dam (see, e.g., Jing 1997:65–92, Eckholm 1998a:8). Demonstrating enthusiasm for this dam project would be, therefore, a show of allegiance to the central government, dead revolutionaries, and the nation. Thus, after a quick tour of Sichuan's Fuling county in 1994, Wahaha executives invested 40 million yuan to produce mineral water by changing the management and the technology of a candy factory, an alcohol works, and a cannery plant in Fuling county.

Wahaha Takes a Different Tack

Because of Wahaha's commercial success and its considerable help to the state, its top executives were able to meet with national leaders on various occasions. During these meetings they were told of the central government's wish that Wahaha become the Chinese response to Coca-Cola. For a time, Wahaha treated this encouragement from the very top as a matter of great honor, and yet the company failed to follow through. Instead, in 1997 Groupe Danone, the French multinational food corporation, bought a controlling interest in Wahaha. Danone already had other operations in China, including its Lu biscuit plant and its Amoy dairy product, sauce, and dim sum business. However, Danone's leading partner in China, a major overseas market for the ambitious Paris-based company, was Wahaha. In other words, the best-known Chinese children's food company was now partly owned by foreigners.

What led to this somewhat surprising development — which the Wahaha Group does not want to publicize — cannot be fully explained by Danone's financial might or Wahaha's interest in Danone's superior technology. The forces that drove Wahaha into a merger with Danone were domestic. Some Chinese companies, jealous of Wahaha's commercial success and its political privileges, fought back against it, sometimes with dubious tactics. These tactics included faxing the *Beijing Youth Newspaper* article about the three dead Anhui girls to Wahaha's competitors, wholesale agents, and consumer protection agencies, clearly with the intention of ruining the company's reputation.

The Wahaha case thus suggests that state intervention can be crucial to a company's success but that even the state's most favored businesses are vulnerable. Becoming Danone's Chinese partner in China has given Wahaha a new means of securing official protection, since the operation of joint ventures and transnational corporations in China is a matter of international relations that must be handled, in the view of Chinese authorities, with caution, encouragement, and special protection. Although Wahaha has continued to promote its products as Chinese goods and even entered direct competition, in 1998, with Coca-Cola and PepsiCo by marketing a new brand of carbonated drink called "Future Cola," the Wahaha Group's future development is a topic of discussion and planning in a boardroom in France. It will be interesting to see whether or not the company will continue to define its mission as a struggle to defend China's domestic food industry and the country's cultural heritage.

Food as a Lens: The Past, Present,

and Future of Family Life in China

James L. Watson

In 1926, as Jun Jing notes in his Introduction to this volume, Beijing workers spent approximately one percent of their food budgets on snacks and refreshments. Presumably some of these snacks (*xiaochi*) were eaten by adults, which means that most children had only fleeting — and, no doubt, highly intense — encounters with candies, crackers, cookies, and sweet beverages. Children ate essentially what adults consumed; the very notion of children's food, as a distinct category of consumables, did not exist in China prior to the 1960s. When Lu Xun (1881–1936), China's leading chronicler of early twentieth-century life, wrote nostalgically about the tastes of his childhood he did not dwell on food designed specifically for children. Instead, he waxed lyrically about broad beans, water chestnuts, wild rice shoots, and muskmelons. What will future Lu Xuns be writing about when they recall the tastes of childhood? Will it be their grandfathers' beans and their mothers' hand-cut noodles? Or, will they dwell on the Big Macs, pizza, and layer cakes they shared with peers at birthday parties held in fast-food restaurants? If nostalgia is a condition induced by the painful recall of long-lost — and hence romanticized — experiences of pleasure (F. Davis 1979), we might well expect the Big Mac to triumph over the broad bean.

Children as Consumers

In the late 1960s when I first began field research among rural Cantonese in Hong Kong's New Territories, children were not consumers in any active sense of the term (J. Watson 1975). They were passive recipients of consumer goods, primarily food (toys were not yet commoditized; see below). Children ate what was poked into them by adult guardians; few learned to use chopsticks or spoons until they were nearly three years old. Manufactured foods designed specifically for infants did not appear in rural Hong Kong until the late 1970s. In contrast to the scene described by Suzanne Gottschang in Chapter 7, babies were weaned on ordinary adult foods, especially fish and rice, that had been chewed thoroughly by parents — and then transferred, with chopsticks, from one mouth to another. This weaning technique can still be observed in neighborhood restaurants, but most Hong Kong parents now use canned baby foods and formula drinks at home.

A market in manufactured snacks, especially ice cream pops, was just beginning to emerge in the New Territories during the late 1960s. The coveted items were expensive by local standards and were kept out of sight, locked deep in the freezers of village shops; cheaper pops of lower quality were hawked by itinerant peddlers who carried their goods in small ice chests attached to bicycles. Given that children below the age of twelve seldom had any spending money, snacks could be obtained only from indulgent adults — a category that (usually) excluded parents and grandparents.[1] The most sympathetic adults were emigrants on holiday, home for a brief stay after years of work in the European restaurant trade. Big-spending returnees were always good for pocket money (*lingqian*) if caught in a good mood. The best time to accumulate snack money was, of course, Spring Festival (lunar New Year celebrations), three days during which married men were obliged to give red packets of "lucky money" to every child they encountered. Village children went on binges during this period, exhausting local supplies of ice cream and making themselves thoroughly ill in the process.

Research reported by Jun Jing and his colleagues shows that children in today's China have a high degree of decision-making power within the family. Nearly 70 percent of household spending, including food purchases, was dictated by children in mid-1990s Beijing.[2] The idea that a child could dictate what the family ought to eat at mealtimes would have astonished my New Territories neighbors of the 1960s. Children ate what was presented to them or they went hungry. Alternatively, a disgruntled child could troll the neighborhood, searching for something more appealing. Villagers often carried cooked food outside and sat on stools in front of their houses, eating as they chatted with passersby. At these strategic moments children would suddenly appear, with mouths wide open, expecting to sample whatever was on offer. I do not recall ever seeing a villager ignore one of these open mouths; adults simply fed the little foragers, absent-mindedly, and continued talking or eating. Adults did not, however, share food with other adults; only children under age four were granted this license.

The late 1960s was not a particularly affluent period in the New Territories, which leads me to conclude that this communal feeding behavior probably had a long history and was not a twentieth-century innovation. In recent decades (1980s and 1990s), childhood foraging has disappeared, except among close kin. Concern for sanitation is one reason for the change, but, perhaps more significantly, there has been an erosion of neighborhood cohesion in the New Territories as more and more residents have moved to urban areas and their houses have been rented to immigrants from China.[3]

Meanwhile, the great grandchildren of my 1960s neighbors are every bit as assertive and commanding as their Beijing counterparts. A full-scale market in children's food emerged in the New Territories by the late 1980s, a period corresponding to the appearance of transnational fast-food chains. McDonald's opened six restaurants in urban centers within easy bus rides of the villages where I have conducted most of my ethnographic research. Pizza Hut, KFC, and a host of local (Chinese-style) fast-food outlets followed in rapid succession. Elsewhere I have described the process by which McDonald's transformed itself from an exotic import into a routine purveyor of "local" cuisine in Hong Kong (J. Watson

1997). Children played a central role in this transformation and converted their neighborhood McDonald's into after-school clubs and leisure centers. A similar process of localization appears to be under way in Beijing, though at a slower pace to judge from Eriberto Lozada's account of KFC in Chapter 5 and Yunxiang Yan's work on McDonald's (Yan 1997b).

Today the balance of decision-making power within the Chinese family — at least in respect to food — is shifting from senior to junior generations. Evidence for this claim abounds in chapters by Georgia Guldan, Guo Yuhua, and Bernadine Chee. Lozada argues that KFC empowers the younger generation by forcing parents to participate in a domain of transnational culture that privileges children. In effect, the young act as guides and instructors for older consumers who are less sure of themselves in this new terrain. I witnessed a similar process of generational inversion during my mid-1990s study of McDonald's in the New Territories. Village children were often far more sophisticated — and confident — than their adult chaperons. Six-year-olds ended up showing their grandparents what to order, where to sit, and how to behave.

The consumer power of Chinese children is reflected in KFC's decision to abandon Colonel Sanders and replace him with Chicky — a carefree, youthful chicken who wears an American baseball cap. Chicky, like Ronald McDonald (known as "Uncle McDonald" in Chinese), appeals directly to children who are educated, via television, to appreciate the antics and the fantasy lives of cartoon characters. Most adults in China have little understanding of Chicky's or Uncle McDonald's drawing power. Both of these characters embody the notion of "fun," a concept that is very difficult to translate into Chinese. According to Daniel Ng, the impresario of Hong Kong McDonald's, Chinese parents did not encourage playfulness and frivolity as acceptable pursuits until recently. Mr. Ng and his colleagues made a conscious decision to promote McDonald's as a place where Hong Kong children could "have fun" and enjoy themselves in an environment catering specifically to young people.[4] Birthday parties, toys, and child-sized seating made this new category of consumer feel welcome. In Hong Kong, and increasingly in other Chinese cities, fast-food chains and snack companies are commoditizing the notion of fun and highlighting it in their advertising campaigns.

Why do children consider McDonald's and KFC to be fun places to eat, in contrast to their own family kitchens or school canteens? The answer, in my view, is choice: At McDonald's even the youngest consumer can select his or her own food.[5] Literacy is not a requirement, given that everything on the menu is illustrated in vivid color. Freedom to choose implies an absence, or at least a standing-down, of adult supervision.

Elderhood, Childhood, and Public Ritual

One of the more intriguing aspects of globalization is the export, and subsequent domestication, of American-style celebrations: Mother's Day, Father's Day, Halloween, Thanksgiving, and of course birthday parties complete with cakes, candles, and gifts. Anthropologists have explored the transnationalization and localization of Christmas, which has a long history of cultural migration (Miller 1993). There can be little question that Greater China (PRC, Taiwan, and Hong Kong) is a hotbed for research of this nature. American-style weddings, which feature white bridal gowns (an inversion of traditional Chinese color symbolism — white being the color of mourning), and large, lavishly decorated cakes became the rage in Taiwan and Hong Kong twenty years ago; the style took off in the Chinese mainland during the 1980s and 1990s (Gillette 2000). Halloween has metamorphosed in Hong Kong as a child-center celebration for the promotion of pizza. The latest American holiday to make a splash in Hong Kong is Father's Day; Mother's Day has not done so well, for reasons that have yet to be explored.

What these new celebrations have in common is a preoccupation with children's food, combined with child-focused entertainment. Father's Day, in its Hong Kong guise, is promoted as an occasion for family meals in restaurants, with children acting as hosts to their fathers (even though parents pay the bill). Menus for the occasion feature hot dogs, hamburgers, pizza, and ice cream sundaes. It may be called Father's Day, but it is, in fact, a celebration of childhood. The first such American import, and by far the most important, was the birthday party. There is a special irony in this story, given that, until recently, most Chinese did not know — and certainly did not celebrate — their birth dates in the Western calendrical sense. A record of one's birth according to lunar reckoning was kept for divinatory purposes (used primarily at marriage and death), but few were interested in converting the complex lunar notations to a standardized Western date. By the mid-1980s, however, children in Hong Kong and (urban) Taiwan were not only aware of their Western calendrical birthdays; they expected to celebrate the occasion as the major event of the year. Birthday parties are now the rage in China, according to Guo and Lozada. Seventy percent of fifth-graders in Guo's Jiangsu village research site celebrated their birthdays (see Chapter 4). In Beijing, KFC has constructed special party enclosures for children; Chicky's most important role is to sing "Happy Birthday" to the celebrants (see Chapter 5).

Jun Jing notes in his Introduction that the rise of the birthday party reflects a profound shift in generational power. Rituals of longevity have been superseded by celebrations of youth. This is certainly true in the New Territories, where children now stand in the center of every family celebration. The scene was strikingly different in the 1960s: Elders, men and women over 60 *sui* (lunar reckoning of years), dominated the ritual life of the community; children, by contrast, were almost completely ignored.

Male elders were automatically invited to attend all wedding banquets, housewarmings, and lineage rites. They were expected to "eat for" their families, thereby conferring legitimacy on marriages, adoptions, and claims to leadership (J. Watson 1987). People over 60 formed banqueting clubs based on their (lunar) year of birth; these groups gathered in a nearby restaurant for an annual meal, paid by membership subscription. There were also ascension-to-elderhood ceremonies for male elders who had reached their sixtieth years in the lunar calendar. The only parties focusing on children were "full month" (*manyue*) banquets held to mark an infant's survival for 30 days after birth. The newborn may have been the focus of attention, but the celebrants were exclusively adults. Children who congregated at village banquets were tolerated as onlookers but were not treated as formal guests (seats were not reserved for them at tables); they hovered on the fringes, waiting for someone to take notice of them. A graduation ceremony was held each year at the local primary school but this event was not paralleled by family celebrations or by special banquets. The ritual invisibility of childhood does not imply that New Territories villagers of the 1960s considered children to be unimportant. Children gave meaning to life in the sense that they perpetuated patrilines and conferred a kind of immortality on their progenitors. Children were sources of both anxiety and joy. Nonetheless, villagers did not formalize this preoccupation by creating a set of recurrent and standardized rituals that celebrated childhood.

Toys, Childhood, and the Commoditization of Play

It is no coincidence that toys and children's food emerged as commodities at approximately the same time in the New Territories. Toys and food are closely associated in the experience of contemporary children, so much so that the boundaries between these two categories of consumables are often blurred (visit any candy store and behold the racks of edible toys). Toys are also the most common prizes offered by fast-food, snack, and soda companies. Hong Kong has long been a center for the production and design of manufactured toys, but the finished products rarely appeared in New Territories homes until the mid-1980s. In earlier decades village children sometimes fashioned makeshift toys and games from castoff materials; my slides from the 1960s and 1970s bear witness to the remarkable creativity of these efforts. The only manufactured items that served an entertainment function in the community were mahjong tiles, small dice (for various gambling games), and playing cards (referred to locally as *hakka-pai*, "Hakka cards") — all of which were used primarily by retired people.

Returning for a visit in 1986, I discovered that the homes of New Territories villagers were suddenly awash with manufactured toys, making it dangerous to walk without extreme care (a problem not observed during previous visits). Children had also begun to acquire pet dogs, a real shocker for those who recall the traditional role of dogs in Cantonese villages.[6]

Something important had obviously happened among New Territories families in the mid-1980s. This was a period of rising affluence and increasing exposure to cultural influences emanating from urban Hong Kong. Village children had become "personalities" who expected to perform in public and have their opinions heeded by parents — a radical break with the past, when children were severely disciplined for intruding into adult conversations. In other words, a new notion of childhood had emerged, paralleling in some respects the process documented for early modern Europe (Aries 1962). Prior to this period village children were not treated as completed individuals, with unique personalities or personal tastes worthy of serious consideration. Children were *sailoujai*, colloquial Cantonese for "kids"; there was no linguistic category, and hence no conceptual frame, for a distinct stage in the life cycle translatable as "childhood." Only at marriage was a child transformed into a ritually recognized adult; the marriage rites were, in fact, a set of symbolic acts that converted social infants into responsible, community-oriented persons (see R. Watson 1986).

New Territories shops began to carry a wide range of children's food and toys in the mid-1980s. Another manifestation of these changes is the commoditization of play, exercise, and recreation. In many Chinese cities, including Hong Kong, commercialized play centers — such as Whimsy International — opened in the mid 1990s. Parents at Shanghai's Whimsy spend an average of 15 yuan (US$1.70) per child for entry fees; 30,000 people visit every weekend.[7] Inside these centers children play arcade games, jump into rooms filled with balls, and try their hands at various athletic skills — winning snacks and small toys in the process. Commercialized play centers first appeared in the United States in response to parental fears of urban violence. Perhaps the best known of these companies, Discovery Zone, was founded in 1989; by early 1995 it had become a transnational corporation, with 300 outlets scattered around the globe.[8] Chinese parents I spoke with in Hong Kong share (to a certain degree) their American counterparts' anxieties about street violence, but they stressed another concern: Many believed that the play centers helped their children adapt to the demands of Hong Kong's high-pressure schools, which privilege conformity and peer group cooperation. Play centers in Shanghai and Beijing serve an additional function: They provide safe arenas where singletons (only children) can interact with age peers. Chinese urbanites increasingly find themselves confined to apartments in alienating, high-rise buildings — miles from family or friends. In such settings it is difficult to find suitable playmates for one's little emperor or little empress. It is not surprising, therefore, that the commoditization of children's play has taken hold so rapidly in Chinese cities.

Contrary to common belief, children's play is not a "natural," spontaneous activity. People learn to play, just as they learn how and what to eat. Furthermore, when children are socialized to eat whatever and whenever they wish, and when they are encouraged to play in a manner that preserves rather than burns calories, it should not be surprising that so many are overweight and physically inactive.

A Social History of Fat: Prosperity Versus Pathology

Thirty years ago most Chinese people celebrated plumpness as a sign of prosperity and robust health. Many Hong Kong businessmen of my acquaintance worked hard to put on extra body weight, consciously eating high-caloric meals at every opportunity. Similarly, plump babies were much admired as symbols of good luck and were depicted as such in popular art and religious iconography. The opposite condition — thinness — was avoided at all costs, given that an emaciated body represented bad luck, illness, and early death. Chronic food shortages were imprinted in the living memories of most adults who lived in the New Territories during the 1960s and 1970s. The Chinese famine of 1958–60, known euphemistically as the "three bad years," killed more than 30 million people and was directly responsible for a huge influx of refugees into Hong Kong (D. Yang 1996).

The stigma of emaciation was such that even during affluent years thin people had difficulty finding marriage partners. It was assumed that they would not live to bear or support children. If special bulking diets did not help, villagers consulted shamans (*wenmipo*, "ask rice women") to determine if supernatural forces were causing a secret affliction (see J. Potter 1974). The culprits usually turned out to be aggrieved ancestors who were "eating" the health and vitality of a descendent in retaliation for neglect or mistreatment. Plumpness, by contrast, was perceived as a clear indication that the person so blessed was in harmony with the supernatural world. Until recently, therefore, ordinary people in Hong Kong, China, and Taiwan worried more about increasing their body weight than reducing it. Obesity did not become a recognized pathology in popular consciousness until the late 1980s; prior to this time, in fact, it was rare to see individuals who fit the modern clinical guidelines of obesity. As Georgia Guldan shows in Chapter 1, however, this is no longer true, especially for Chinese children. Guldan notes that among certain subsets of Beijing (male) children the rate of obesity exceeded 20 percent in 1995; 21 percent of Hong Kong eleven-year-olds were obese in the mid-1990s. It also comes as a shock to learn that Hong Kong has the world's second-highest level of childhood cholesterol, trailing only Finland.[9] The Chinese government now recognizes obesity as an emerging health crisis and launched a propaganda campaign to encourage exercise; in May 1998, 2,300 children (aged three to six) performed "kid-friendly" calisthenics in Tiananmen Square for a national television audience.[10]

In one respect, the epidemiological transition from under- to overnutrition marks a major achievement in Chinese history. The specter of famine is no longer a major concern for ordinary people, at least among urbanites.[11] How did China reach this point? The answer, as Guldan shows in Chapter 1, lies in the dietary implications of rising affluence. In only two decades (dating from 1978, the beginning of Deng Xiaoping's reforms), China moved from a diet rich in grains and vegetables to one laden with red meat, sugar, and edible oils (see also Huang Shu-min et al. 1996; Popkin et al. 1993). During the heyday of socialism (1949–78) the state provided urban residents with mountains of low-grade cabbage for cooking, pickling, and storage. Often there was little else to eat during the long winter months. By the early 1990s the consumption of cabbage had dropped sharply and other, more expensive vegetables and fruits were readily available in urban markets.[12] At the same time, as Guldan and Jing note, the proportion of meat and edible oils in the diet increased dramatically. In spite of these dietary improvements, however, many Chinese parents still believe that their children are not getting enough to eat. These anxieties fuel a national craze for appetite stimulants such as Wahaha, the saga of which is outlined by Zhao Yang in Chapter 8.

Does this mean that the battle against obesity is lost before it begins? Are recent trends among American children any guide to China's culinary future? In both societies young people increasingly dictate their own diets and control their own food money. Formal meals (breakfast, lunch, dinner) are irrelevant to many American teenagers who eat whenever, and wherever, they wish. Market researchers note an important linguistic shift in the United States: For most young people a "home meal" refers to any food that has been heated in a microwave or a toaster oven (O'Neil 1998). One cannot help but note similar developments in Taiwan and Hong Kong, where the market in convenience foods and take-out cuisine has exploded in recent years.

Spoiled Singletons Versus Demanding Retirees: China's Future?

This book is perhaps unique in the sense that it tracks a profound historical transformation in social attitudes toward children during the early stages of that transformation. Parallel studies of European and North American childhood are, of necessity, based on historical research that enjoys the benefits, and suffers the pitfalls, of hindsight (see, e.g., Aries 1962; Demos and Demos 1969; Kett 1977). We have no way of knowing whether the changes described in this book, including the appearance of a singleton subculture, will transform China in ways that would make family life unrecognizable to Lu Xun, Mao Zedong, and Deng Xiaoping. Readers who have lived or worked in China prior to the 1990s will indeed find much that is new in these chapters; some changes are disturbing (rising obesity rates, ferocious peer pressures, decreasing play time), but such problems are by no means restricted to China (cf. White 1994).

Jun Jing challenges a key element of received wisdom regarding childhood in late twentieth-century China: Are singletons in fact "spoiled"? In his introduction to this book, Jing defines a spoiled child as one who is "showered with too much attention and material comfort by overindulgent parents and grandparents." Evidence presented in this book both supports and refutes the spoiled singleton hypothesis: Bernadine Chee demonstrates in Chapter 2 that the emotional costs of parental indulgence are heavy indeed. Research by psychologists and sociologists hints that singletons in China may be no more spoiled than their counterparts in Europe and North America (see Falbo et al. 1989:484–85; Wan 1996). What we are observing in China is a shift in decision-making power within the family, from senior to junior generations (summarized in Yan 1997a). In Chapter 4, Guo Yuhua proposes a three-generation model for understanding attitudes toward food and consumption practices; members of each generation find it difficult to appreciate the concerns of those who did not share similar life experiences. The expectations of children and parents, the latter being veterans (victims and/or perpetrators) of the Cultural Revolution (1966–76), are strikingly different. As Guo and Chee demonstrate, the current generation of parents is determined to give their offspring every possible advantage, in part as compensation for hardships endured during four decades of Maoist socialism. Their children, in turn, are being socialized to expect advantages and to consume in a conspicuous, competitive manner.

In the late 1990s, China's first wave of singletons entered the adult worlds of business, university, and military service. Research among these young people will answer many of the questions posed by this volume: Are China's little emperors and empresses really different? Will they emerge as conscientious, caring citizens capable of leading China into a market-oriented, globalized, and increasingly more democratic future?

There can be little doubt that China faces an even more daunting generational transition in the not-too-distant future: Who will pay to support an aging, complaining cohort of retirees who are expected to live into their eighties and nineties? Will China's "boomers" be as demanding (and as irresponsible) as their counterparts in the United States?

Confucian norms dictated that Chinese parents were expected to "rear and nourish" (*fuyang*) their children and, in return, adult offspring were required to "respectfully nourish" (*fengyang*) their aged parents (Stafford 1995:79–111). The symmetry of the bargain has long since broken down in many parts of the Chinese world. Private nursing homes constitute a booming business in Guangzhou, the first Chinese city to legalize such facilities (Eckholm 1998b). In 1998, 10 percent of China's population was over 60; by 2050 the figure will rise to 25 percent. Compared to the United States and Japan, two societies that face similar demographic crises, the Chinese government has made few provisions for the support of older citizens. It is assumed that, as in times past, the family will take care of its own (D. Davis 1991; Ikels 1996:128–

36). In the future, therefore, Chinese wage-earners will have to choose between the demands of their children and the expectations of their retired parents. If the balance of consumer power shifts again, and seniors reclaim their hegemonic position within the family, the sequel to this volume — 30 years hence — could well be entitled "Feeding China's Retired Emperors."

Appendix to Chapter 3

Food diary of Peng, an eleven-year-old

Hui boy, June 7–14, 1997

Peng kept a food diary for one week at my request. During this week, Peng was in school. He was asked to record the time of day he ate, the foods he ate, where the foods came from, and their price, if known. The record of intake is complete, but for some entries Peng did not provide a price, or indicate where he procured the food. At this time, one yuan, or Chinese dollar, was equal to about one-eighth of an American dollar. A mao is one-tenth of a yuan.

June 7, 1997

9 A.M.: Two fried cakes, one made from rice flour, the other from wheat. Purchased from a food stall operated by his father's maternal uncle's daughter. 5 mao per cake. One soda. Purchased from his paternal aunt, who runs a restaurant outside the entrance to his home. 3 yuan per can.

3 P.M.: One bowl of steamed noodles (*liangpi*) at his mother's father's restaurant. 2.5 yuan per bowl (free for Peng).

7 P.M.: Stir-fried vegetables and rice purchased from a restaurant on the street where his family lives. Eaten at home. 34 yuan total cost (for four persons).

June 8, 1997

7:00 A.M.: One package of instant noodles (*fangbian mian*), at home. 8 mao per package.

Noon: Red bean and rice porridge. At his mother's father's restaurant. No price.

Between 6 and 6:30 P.M.: Three pieces of chocolate, several pieces of candy made from sugar, orange peel, and plum (*huahuadan*), one piece of pineapple candy, and several slices of watermelon. At home, from family cupboards. Price unknown.

7 P.M.: Noodles with egg and tomato. At home, prepared by his mother.

June 9, 1997

7 A.M.: Meat and vegetable steamed stuffed buns (*baozi*). Purchased from a food stall. 3.5 yuan total.

8 A.M.: One container of juice drink, at 5 mao per box, and chewing gum (*paopaotang*) at 3 mao per package, purchased from the convenience store at the entrance to the school. Total 8 mao.

12:30 P.M.: Three pieces of chocolate, six pieces of candy, at home from the family cupboard. No price. One ice cream bar (brand name *shiziwang*) from a convenience store on his street.[1] One yuan. Fried eggplant and squash, at his mother's father's home, prepared by his aunt. No price.

5 P.M.: Two packages of juice drink, purchased at the convenience store outside the school's entrance (note: this brand of juice drink comes in plastic bags). 1 yuan. Two packages of dried fruit (*wuhuaguo*), 4 mao. One bag of candy (*lilixing*), 5 mao. One ice cream bar (*baipanggao*), 1 yuan.

7 P.M.: Fried egg and rice. Eaten at home. Prepared by his mother.

June 10, 1997

8 A.M.: One bottle of soda, no price. One package of crisps (*guoba*), 1 yuan. Purchased from store outside school gate.

12:30 P.M.: Sandwich (cooked beef inside a locally prepared flatbread). Prepared by his father. Eaten at home. Three pieces of chocolate and some candy, from family cupboards. Eaten at home. One ice cream bar (*baipanggao*), purchased from store on the street. Eaten at school. 1 yuan.

5 P.M.: One ice cream bar, purchased from store on street. One yuan. One banana, no price.

7 P.M.: Fried eggplant and fried egg and tomato with local bread. Purchased from restaurant down the street. Total 11 yuan.

8:30 P.M.: One package of crisps (*guoba*). 1.3 yuan.

June 11, 1997

7 A.M.: One bowl of meatball soup (*hulatang*) and one local flatbread. Purchased from his father's brother's wife's food stall. 3 yuan.

12:30 P.M.: Eggplant and cucumber, prepared by his father. One piece of local bread, 5 mao. One bottle of soda (*bingfeng*), 1 yuan.

5 P.M.: Packaged puffed rice snack with toy. Purchased from local store. 1 yuan.

7 P.M.: Mixed vegetable stew (*shaguo*), with rice. Purchased from restaurant down the street. 5 yuan.

June 12, 1997

Noon: Steamed noodles, one bowl. From his mother's father's restaurant. 2.5 yuan (no charge). One local bread, 5 mao.

2 P.M.: One ice cream bar (*zhanwangshen*). Purchased at convenience store outside school, eaten in school yard. 1 yuan.

4 P.M.: One ice cream bar (*bingwang*). Purchased at convenience store outside school, eaten in school yard. 1.5 yuan.

7 P.M.: Frozen popsicle. Purchased at local store. 1 yuan.

June 13, 1997

9 A.M.: Fried cakes made from rice flour. Purchased from street stall, eaten at home. 5 mao per cake.

9:30 A.M.: One ice cream bar (*baipanggao*). 1 yuan.

Noon: Fried meat and vegetables stuffed in local bread. Prepared by his father. One bowl of rice porridge. Eaten at home.

Afternoon: One bottle of soda. 1 yuan.

7:30 P.M.: Cucumber, squash, and cured meat. Prepared by his father.

8 P.M.: One bottle of soda. 1 yuan.

June 14, 1997

11 A.M.: One fried rice cake, 5 mao. Purchased on street and eaten at home. Some melon. One bottle of soda, 1 yuan. Eaten at home.

1 P.M.: One bowl of steamed noodles from his mother's father's

restaurant. 2.5 yuan (no charge for Peng). One bowl of mung bean porridge, prepared by Peng's father. One bottle of soda, 3.5 yuan.

6 P.M.: One bowl of noodles fried with egg and tomato. Prepared by Peng's father. One bottle of soda.

Character List

aiying yiyuan　愛嬰醫院
baipanggao　白胖高
Baizi gong　百子宮
baojian shipin　保健食品
bao ping an　保平安
baozi　包子
bingfeng　冰峰
binggan　餅乾
bingwang　冰王
bu xiguan　不習慣
bu　補
buyao　補藥
chaoji shichang　超級市場
chi bubao　吃不飽
chongyang meiwai　崇洋媚外
chou doufu　臭豆腐
ci hai　辭海
dalu mian　打鹵面
Damaishi jie　大麥市街
dazi bobo　韃子餑餑
dongshi　懂事
douji　鬥雞
douzhi　豆汁
duan nai　斷奶

ertong jiankang shipin yinliao　兒童健康食品飲料

ertong shipin　兒童食品

ertong yaoshan　兒童藥膳

ertong yinshi　兒童飲食

ertong yingyangpin　兒童營養品

fangbian　方便

fangbian mian　方便麵

Fangshen miao　方神廟

fenjie　分解

fengwang jing　蜂王精

feng yang　奉養

fu yang　撫養

ganjing weisheng　乾淨衛生

gaodanbai yingyang mifen　高蛋白營養米粉

gaodian　糕點

gaogan mian　高乾面

gao pan　高攀

guanchang　灌腸

guanxi　關係

guandong tang　關東糖

guoba　鍋巴

Haixing haiwai gongsi　海星海外公司

hakka-pai　客家牌

hao wan　好玩

hei haizi　黑孩子

hulatang　胡辣湯

huafen koufuye　花粉口服液

huahuahdan　花花蛋

huashengsu　花生酥

Huizu　回族

jia you　加油

jian　健

jiangle weixin hua　講了違心話

jiaozi　餃子

Jinhua niangniang miao　金花娘娘廟

Jiutian xuannu　九天玄女

kang shifu　康師傅

kexue weiyang　科學喂養

kexue xiandaihua　科學現代化

kuai　塊

laba zhou　蠟八粥

lao da ta　老打他

laomi mian　老米面

lao shouxing　老壽星

lilixing　粒粒星

liang fen　涼粉

liangpi　涼皮

ling qian　零錢

ling shi　零食

ludougao　綠豆糕

luohou　落後

manyue　滿月

mei sha　沒啥

mumin　穆民

muru　母亂

naifen　奶粉

naizi cha　奶子茶

nan tang　南糖

ni ai　溺愛

ni zhen hui tiao　你真會挑

pagao　爬糕

panbi　攀比

paopao tang　泡泡糖

qi　氣

qifen hao　氣氛好

Qiqi　奇奇

qiye wubai qiang　企業五百強

qianjiu　遷就

qingnian　青年

qingzhen　清真

ran 染

remen huati 熱門話題

rengong 人工

renkou suzhi 人口素質

renkou weiji 人口危機

renshen koufuye 人參口服液

renshen tang 人參湯

renzhen xuexi, kaixin youxi 認真學習, 開心游戲

sailoujai 小老仔

Sanxiao niangniang 三霄娘娘

shaguo 沙鍋

shangpin jingji 商品經濟

shiziwang 獅子王

shouxuan 首選

shuo bu qing 説不清

si xiao long 四小龍

si-yi-er zonghezheng 四一二綜合症

suanmei tang 酸梅湯

tebie ganjing 特別乾淨

tian 添

tianran 天然

tianshi 甜食

tongnian 童年

tuotuo mo 飥飥饃

wahaha 娃哈哈

wahaha yingyang yinliao 娃哈哈營養飲料

wawasu 娃娃素

wandou huang 豌豆黃

weisheng su 維生素

wenmipo 問米婆

wotou 窩頭

wuhuaguo 無花果

xigong mizhou 西貢米粥

xi guo da jing 洗過大淨

xiaochi 小吃

xiao er fushi　小兒輔食

xiao huangdi　小皇帝

xiao huanghou　小皇后

xiao shouxing　小壽星

xiao kang　小康

xiao taiyang　小太陽

yi shui wei zhu　以水為主

yinliao　飲料

yin yang　陰陽

ying er fuzhu shipin　嬰兒輔助食品

ying you er shipin　嬰幼兒食品

you dao li　有道理

youshenmo chishenmo　有什麼吃什麼

yousheng cuoshi　優生措施

yousheng wawa　優生娃娃

youzha hui　油炸燴

yufang youshengxue　預防優生學

yuan xiao　元宵

yue bing　月餅

zhanwangshen　丈王神

zhui xing zu　追星族

zilai hong　自來紅

zongzi　粽子

zuo yuezi　坐月子

Notes

Introduction

1. Apparently believing that the problem of parental indulgence is serious and widespread, the Chinese government has created a nationwide system of "schools for parents" to offer courses on the proper ways to bring up a healthy, disciplined, and patriotic generation of young people. The exact number of such schools is unknown, although a regional source indicates that they quickly snowballed after parent education was formalized in 1983. According to William Meredith (1991), Guangzhou, the capital of Guangdong province, had 13,000 parenting schools in 1987, with an enrollment of 2.3 million participants and an approximately 80 percent rate of attendance on a voluntary basis. Newlyweds and young parents meet at these schools at least once a month. Even in the rural areas within the vicinity of metropolitan Guangzhou, efforts were made to let village women take child-rearing courses.

2. Of course, hunger has yet to be eradicated in many rural areas and in some pockets of urban centers in China. According to latest government figures, about 6 to 7 percent of China's total population still needs to be lifted from dire poverty.

3. At the beginning of this transition, reformers in China tactically described it as the development of a "commodity economy" (*shangpin jingji*), rationalizing it with Marxist theories about economic development to deflect its critics.

4. The childhood foods in Lowe's account are the following: "noodles with jellied stew" (*dalu mian*), "fried doughnuts" (*youzha hui*), "glutinous rice cake" (*zongzi*), "Saigon rice porridge" (*xigong*

mizhou), "buckwheat cakes" (*pa gao*), "cold starch jelly" (*liang fen*), "starch-filled sausages" (*guan chang*), "bean juice" (*dou zhi*), "yellow bean cakes" (*wandou huang*), "sour plum tea" (*suanmei tang*), "Tartar pastry" (*dazi bobo*), "milk tea" (*naizi cha*), "stinky bean curd" (*chou doufu*), "Manchurian candy" (*guandong tang*), "south China candy" (*nan tang*), "Naturally Red Moon Cakes" (*zilai hong*), "dried cake powder" (*gaogan mian*), and "old rice powder" (*laomi mian*).

5. One of the earliest official pronouncements about China's lack of human capital for economic development was made by the Guangdong Province Family Planning Office in a 1979 newspaper article that declared: "Planned control of population growth would also help in raising the scientific and cultural level of the nation. . . . The ordinary worker in Japan has finished upper middle school, but in China there are 100 million young people who are illiterate or semi-illiterate, and five million of them are in Guangdong. . . . we need not only workers in quantity but, more important, workers of quality, that is, ones who have a degree of culture and the ability to be expert at one thing and good at many others" (Ebrey et al. 1981:413).

6. Interview with Zhang Xiaogang conducted on March 5, 1997.

7. Of course, fancy dinner parties have been a central form of Chinese social communication for centuries. Even the famine of 1959–61 and the long period of austerity thereafter failed to bring about a conservation movement at the government banquet halls. Now suddenly there is so much to eat, the expense of official feasts is reportedly 100 billion yuan a year (Zha 1995:122).

Chapter 1

1. For more information on infant care in traditional China, see Hsiung Ping-chen (1996:73–79) and Liu Yongcong (1997:60–79).

2. For a review of both nutritional and social issues of complementary feeding worldwide, see World Health Organization, *Complementary Feeding of Young Children in Developing Countries*, 1998.

3. For a more detailed account of these contests, see *Beijing Review*, Feb. 28–March 6, 1994, p. 7.

Chapter 2

Acknowledgments: The generosity of The Henry Luce Foundation supported the research for this project. I also gratefully acknowledge the Chiang Ching-kuo Foundation for International Exchange, The Fairbank Center for East Asian Research at Harvard University, and the Department of Anthropology and Faculty of Social Science at The Chinese University of Hong Kong for sponsoring and funding the conferences that were the impetus for this chapter. I especially want to thank the children and the parents whom we interviewed, who made this endeavor possible. James L. Watson, Rubie S. Watson, Michael Herzfeld, Bai Nansheng, Guo Yuhua, Jing Jun, Wang Muzeng, Wang Shan, David Arkush, C. Fred Blake, Yan Yunxiang, Malcolm G. Thompson, Hilary A. Smith, Michael Laris, Mary Jacob, Anthony Kuhn, Lu Gang, Wang Xiaofeng, Eriberto Lozada, Jr., Karl Ruiter, and Christine Chee Ruiter all aided me at various stages in the writing of this chapter, and I am indebted to them for their kindness and constant support. I would like to dedicate this chapter to my parents, Bernard L. K. and Loretta S. K. Chee.

1. It is important to note that, as with decisions about other commodities, food selections themselves were expected to change over time, especially choices about novelty items (Campbell 1992: 58). A Beijing snack shop owner I spoke with in May 1997, for example, divulged that children were no longer "interested" in the shrimp chip snack that seemed so prevalent in 1995; he observed that children were most eager to buy a recently imported fruit candy and dried seaweed.

2. That is, eating decisions share qualities with decisions made about other aspects of daily life such as those about clothing, transportation, education, work, and recreation. Such decisions are often repetitive, high in volume, and unremarkable to the people making them.

3. Specifically, we believed that inquiring about these children's daily diets would serve as a path to understanding their everyday lives, especially since Han Chinese have traditionally been sensitive to the symbolic value of food (see K. C. Chang's excellent anthropological and historical study, 1977). For example, studies of Chinese society have shown that food sharing and division distin-

guishes *inter alia* family units and lineage relationships (J. Watson 1975:210; Parish and Whyte 1978:133).

4. We made this request because we sought to interview children who had diverse experiences and backgrounds, thereby providing more perspectives on the array of forces affecting children's lives.

5. In addition to the social factors discussed in this chapter, biological and psychological factors may also influence human food preference. See Rozin et al. 1986, Birch 1980, and Pliner 1982 for studies on the biological and psychological factors that influence human food preference.

6. The ten children whom we interviewed from the northwest Beijing school were selected from several grades by the principal. They performed well in school, and their discussions about food resembled to varying degrees those of the three families discussed later in this chapter.

7. The children's names have been changed to protect their identities. Because I make multiple references to individual children throughout the chapter, I have provided English translations of their names to facilitate understanding.

8. Wall's is owned by Unilever. Many of the parents whom we interviewed expressed their opinion that Wall's ice cream had a high content of milk. Wall's popsicles, however, cost significantly more than those of most other brands. For example, eleven of Wall's thirteen varieties of popsicles cost two yuan (US$.25) or more, and the "Magnum" popsicle cost 7.50 yuan, the equivalent cost of a lunch plate.

9. Note that some Han Chinese parents have been observed to give to their children in the hope that the children remember their generosity and consequently take care of them when they reach old age (Milwertz 1997; M. Wolf 1972; Ikels 1993). However, in our investigation, when we asked parents, "What hopes do you have for your child?" they replied that they hoped their child would go to college or that their child would manage to take care of themselves in a highly competitive environment.

10. Only two of the other ten children's parents expressed as much attention to the nutritional content of foods, and one of them was a nurse. Both mothers knew about vitamins and traditional notions of "hot" and "cold" foods.

11. According to this mother, the regulations stipulated that after 5:00 P.M. when children returned home, they should not have to do more homework; they should just play in order to ensure their healthy development.

12. More than a few of the parents we interviewed expressed skepticism toward food products advertised as beneficial to children, citing the controversy over the drink called Wahaha (see Zhao Yang's Chapter 8 in this volume). However, the sheer volume of false advertisements and fraudulent products that were exposed on state-run television and in newspapers during 1996–97 indicates that private and state consumer protection agencies are as yet insufficient to help parents safeguard their children.

13. Georgia Guldan's substantial research and contributions toward the assessment of Chinese nutritional knowledge point out that modern nutritional knowledge was low in both rural and urban areas of China during the 1990s, as illustrated by research conducted in Sichuan province (Guldan et al. 1995:164). On March 28, 1997, in Hong Kong she said to me that this overall insufficient nutritional knowledge may be the result of the Ministry of Health's low ranking in terms of government subsidies.

Chapter 3

1. Based on discussion with my informants, I have chosen to use personal names without family names in this chapter. Xi'an is a city of about two million in Shaanxi Province, one of the five provinces that comprise northwest China.

2. Other meanings of *qingzhen* that residents of the Muslim district reported included honesty in business, belief in Islam, and observance of a Muslim lifestyle.

3. While Hui refuse Han hospitality, Han accept Hui food and drink, freely consuming Hui foods and using Hui cookery. See Pillsbury 1975 for a discussion of this issue with reference to the Hui on Taiwan.

4. A *fen* is one one-hundredth of a yuan.

5. These "cakes" do not resemble Western oven-baked cakes at all. They are made of seeds and nuts compressed into squares, and are not baked.

6. One *mao* is one-tenth of a yuan. See Appendix for prices of mass-produced Western foods.

7. The annual mourning for what is known as the "Hui Uprising" (*Huimin qiyi*) takes place in the Muslim district on the seventeenth day of the fifth lunar month of the Chinese calendar. See Gillette n.d. and Ma Changshou 1993 for further information on this late nineteenth-century massacre. The Prophet's Birthday occurs on the twelfth of the third lunar month of the Islamic calendar, but was always celebrated in January in Xi'an.

Chapter 4

1. A comparable case is Hong Kong children's knowledge of fast food. As James L. Watson points out, "Grandchildren [in Hong Kong] often assume the role of tutors, showing their elders the proper way to eat fast food. . . . It is embarrassing, I was told by an 11-year-old acquaintance, to be seen at McDonald's with a grandfather who does not know how to eat properly" (J. Watson, ed., 1997:102).

2. That Chinese television has become a major medium of consumer information is definitely a recent phenomenon (see Lull 1991). As late as the mid-1980s, Chinese television offered little consumer information and mainly advertised industrial equipment that had nothing to do with personal consumption. By the late 1980s, television began showing consumer goods, following a sharp increase in the ownership of television sets. In 1985, there were only 16 television sets per 100 households nationwide. By 1993, there were 80 color television sets per 100 urban households and 58 black-and-white television sets per 100 rural households (State Statistics Bureau 1994). By the time we began our research on children's food, sophisticated commercials for new food products were appearing on Chinese television every day.

Chapter 5

1. Studies of transnational processes have also long existed in anthropology, as seen in the earlier concerns of diffusionist and acculturation theorists. Also see the work of Godfrey Wilson and others working out of the Rhodes-Livingston Institute and

Manchester University, and the analysis of earlier anthropological studies of transnationalism in Vincent (1990).

2. I refer to consumption as "a use of goods and services in which the object or activity becomes simultaneously a practice in the world and a form in which we construct our understandings of ourselves in the world" (Miller 1995:30).

3. Following Appadurai's model (1996), localization is the result of the "work of the imagination." According to this model, social groups need to create specificity from a more universal set of abstract ideas or concrete things. In other words, localization is the translation of the social meanings of abstract ideas or concrete things from a general gloss to particular ideas, ideas that make sense in a social group's specific context.

4. This is not to say that all Chinese children share a fixed standard of childhood, nor that their intentions or goals in employing such standards are universal. Instead, I am asserting that eating at fast-food restaurants has become a habitualized aspect of Chinese childhood experience.

5. Raymond 1996.

6. My two fieldwork visits in 1994 and 1995 both took place during the summer when school had let out, so non-weekend observations of customers with children are probably much higher than during the school year.

7. Raymond 1996.

8. Prior to 1994, the official Chinese work week was Monday through Saturday. In 1994, the work week was changed to six days one week, and five days the next. In 1995, the Chinese government officially changed to a five-day work week, Monday to Friday. The day that I am describing is an alternating five-day work week Saturday.

9. "Hostessing" is a fast-food industry euphemism for staff encouragement of customers to eat quickly and not linger at tables. In this case, the staff member directly asked the person to leave his seat (Liang Hui 1992).

10. The first franchise was sold by Colonel Sanders in 1952, and Kentucky Fried Chicken became incorporated in 1955. In 1969, Kentucky Fried Chicken went public, listing on the New York Stock Exchange. Kentucky Fried Chicken was acquired by RJR Nabisco in 1982 and then acquired by PepsiCo in 1986.

11. The relevance of Ferguson's discussion of the state in this case is especially clear, where the state is seen not as a single, unified entity, but as a "relay or point of coordination and multiplication of power relations" (1990:272).

12. "Colonel Sanders' Legacy." Public relations announcement, Kentucky Fried Chicken Corporation. Kentucky Fried Chicken contributed US$630,000 of the initial $1.04 million dollar investment (60 percent), with the Beijing Travel and Tourism Corporation contributing 28 percent and the Beijing Corporation of Animal Products Processing Industry contributing 12 percent.

13. *South China Morning Post*, June 22, 1989.

14. President Clinton's major critique of Bush's foreign policy was his soft line with the Chinese government after the Tiananmen Massacre. In 1993, Kentucky Fried Chicken waited until President Clinton announced his decision to extend the Most Favored Nation Treaty to China before announcing their plans to invest an additional US$200 million in the People's Republic of China. This is an example of what Sassen describes as state complicity in the creation of a transnational arena, an arena that challenges traditional ideas of state sovereignty.

15. The two entrepreneurs cited are Ronghuaji manager Li Yucai and assistant manager Li Yaozhen (*Liberation Daily* 1990).

16. *Hong Kong Standard*, April 16, 1984.

17. McCracken (1988) asserts that the "great transformation" of the West involved not just an "industrial revolution," but also a "consumer revolution" that has shifted Western ideas about the relationship between the individual and society. McCracken's arguments are congruent with Harvey, Miller, Appadurai, and Strathern's discussion of postmodernity and the shift of emphasis from production to consumption.

18. Susan Lawrence, personal communication.

19. In addition to one-time "sponsorship fees" (costing as much as US$3,600), annual tuition fees and room and board could be as much as $1,550; considering that the average annual Beijing household income is between $1,800 and $3,600, it is obvious that these private schools are only for the well-to-do elite and upper middle class of China (Crowell and Hsieh 1995). Public schools also have large fees; for example, in Guangdong's Jiaoling county, many chil-

dren could attend the top local high school only after paying a sponsorship fee of 8,000 yuan (approximately US$964).

20. This competition for attention is similar to the role of "drawing attention to" in Stafford's analysis of Angang education/socialization (1995:11–12).

21. This argument is similar to Barth's (1987) discussion of personal uses of communal ritual symbols.

22. Although these are adolescents, they serve as "models" whom younger children aspire to emulate. However, further research is needed to better understand the dynamics between Beijing "youth" (*qingnian*) and "childhood" (*tongnian*).

Chapter 6

1. I first conducted research in Dachuan in the summer of 1989; the village also was the site of my eight months of fieldwork in 1992. I have since revisited the village every summer. I studied children's consumption of food during my three most recent trips. Dachuan in fact has three geographically separate settlements — the village proper and two outlying hamlets. This chapter is concerned with the village proper. In the outlying hamlets of Dachuan, children have had serious health problems because they and their parents lacked clean water to drink. As late as 1997, they had to fetch drinking water from a river that had been badly polluted by a chemical fertilizer factory located upstream. People in the two outlying hamlets of Dachuan were also much poorer than those living in the village proper, partly because of shortages of land and partly because of the combined effects of poor health and low literacy.

2. According to Wang Shoukui and Yuan Xiaoling in their article (1997:6) for *China Health and Nutrition* (*Zhongguo baojian yingyang*), more than 3,000 companies in China produced and marketed "health-enriching foods and tonics" (*baojian shipin*) prior to 1997, and government agencies had not subjected the medical claims of these products to any testing. Only in mid-1997 were manufacturers required to have their products examined by the National Food Hygiene Inspection Institute. The laboratory results showed that only 59 "health-enriching" foods and tonics could be licensed. The banning of unlicensed health foods dealt a blow to the unqualified companies, but they were allowed to con-

tinue production so long as they dropped the medical claims of their products.

3. For anthropological studies of economic reforms and their effects at the village level, see Huang Shu-min 1989; Judd 1994; Potter and Potter 1990; Ruf 1994; Siu 1989; Yan 1992.

4. On China's birth-control policy, see, e.g., Banister 1987; Croll et al. 1987; Greenhalgh 1993:219–50; Li Chengrui 1987; M. Wolf 1985; Pasternak 1986.

5. This figure was reported in Gao Wei 1997.

6. This 24-hour dietary survey points to the persistence of a simple, nonfat, and starch-based diet. The consumption of potatoes and cereal grains by these children was supplemented by a small amount of vegetables and fruits. For nationwide information on rural children's diets, see Georgia Guldan's Chapter 1 of this book.

7. The local parents viewed calcium supplements as "medicine," and this view can be found in other Chinese villages (see Huang Shu-min et al. 1998:371).

8. What puzzled medical authorities in China was that many of the children surveyed had taken calcium supplements according to suggestions by doctors. For a long time, the consensus in the Chinese medical community was that the problem was one of calcium absorption and therefore drastically increasing the use of vitamin D should improve the absorption of calcium from the intestines. The result was vitamin D poisoning, which caused vomiting, headache, drowsiness, loss of appetite, diarrhea, and hardening of soft tissues. Only in 1989 did a newspaper run by the Ministry of Health draw attention to another possible cause of the calcium-deficiency mystery. It reported that China's most popular calcium supplements — calcium gluconate (a calcium salt) and calcium lactate (a calcium replacer) — contained only 9 percent and 12 percent of calcium respectively. For 40 years, pharmaceutical factories had mistakenly labeled the amount of calcium per tablet. The actual quantity of calcium per tablet was only about one-tenth of the amount on the label (see *China Health and Nutrition* 1997a:52–53; 1997b:52–53). The report led not only to a change in the labels of content and quantity but also to the production of concentrated calcium supplements.

9. One such company is Shanghai Squibb, a Sino-US joint ven-

ture. In 1996, this company turned out 900 million vitamin tablets, held 20 percent of China's vitamin market, and occupied 80 percent of the country's multivitamin sales (Sun Hong 1996).

10. Initially a matter of advocacy, preventive eugenics was written into the Law of Maternal and Infant Health Care. This law, passed in 1994, makes a premarital medical examination intended to identify three categories of diseases — serious hereditary diseases, legal contagious diseases, and acute mental disorders — compulsory for all (Li Bin 1995:13–16). If the genetic or somatic problem is serious enough, long-term contraception or tubal ligation will be used to enforce childlessness; otherwise, the couple will not be allowed to marry. Even if a couple make it through the premarital checkup without problems, prenatal testing is compulsory, with termination of pregnancy if the fetus is found to have a serious disease. This law tacitly admits that it will take time for the premarital medical examination to be adopted through the country.

11. The formation of the special task forces was aimed in particular to prevent unauthorized births, or what the local government called "black babies" (*hei haizi*). That is to say, village women have found different ways to disguise their pregnancies and hide their unregistered newborns. The common practice involved sending female babies to relatives living in other villages; these girls would not be brought back until a few months after a brother of theirs had been born. If the girls were discovered, the parents' standard excuse was they were temporarily staying with their relatives while their mothers were busy working at home. Due to the lack of communication between the birth-control officials in different villages, it was hard to check whether or not these girls' births were authorized. It was even harder for an official to find out if girls were authorized if they had been sent from a village in one township to a village in another township. This loophole was gradually fixed when village files were consolidated at the township level so that fertility information could be shared by birth-control officials working in different townships of Yongjing.

12. In terms of fertility aspirations, the most popular deities in Dachuan are the Three Heavenly Mothers. Their identical, one-meter-high painted clay statues are adorned with silk gowns. Behind the deity statues is a group of smaller statues painted and

dressed like little boys. Swinging beneath two ropes are embroidered hangings made by local women, with pictures and patterns symbolizing birth and happiness. One of the common hangings takes the shape of a lotus, out of which emerges a little child; it symbolizes the embroiderer's ability to bear many sons. Other embroidered hangings depict stylized flowers, plants, insects, and animals, the basic designs of which can be still seen on village children's aprons, collars, shoes, and hats. The temple's embroidered hangings are supposedly blessed by the Three Heavenly Mothers, and they can be acquired by offering money and incense. After they are brought home, hangings are usually kept in a young couple's quilts or stitched to their pillows. These lucky talismans, it is said, will help the couple to give birth to a boy in timely fashion.

13. The wish to enable children, both boys and girls alike, to pass safely through the precarious phases of infancy and early childhood calls for continued visits to the temples.

14. On the relationship of food cures and traditional Chinese medicine, see, e.g., H. Lu 1986, 1994; Stafford 1995:79–111; Anderson 1988:229–43.

15. This figure was cited in New China News Agency 1997.

Chapter 7

1. I want to thank Karen Turner, Jun Jing, and Georgia Guldan for their careful reading of and editorial comments on this chapter.

2. The advertisement of infant formula outside the hospital may well have an effect on new mothers' decisions to use these products (Xun et al. 1995).

3. Chinese researchers also identify these practices as factors influencing the decline in breastfeeding in urban China. See, e.g., Wu Kangmin et al. 1995; Xun et al. 1995; Liu Liming 1993.

4. For an expanded discussion of these contexts, see my dissertation (Gottschang 1998).

5. Funding for my dissertation research was provided by the Committee on Scholarly Communications with China from 1994 to 1996. I want to thank Director Ge Keyou and Dr. Chang Ying at the Academy of Preventive Medicine, Institute of Nutrition and Food Hygiene, for their assistance during my research.

6. Despite several attempts to contact Western companies selling infant formula products in China, none responded to my inquiries about the extent of their sales and marketing in China.

7. All women I observed during my fieldwork received nutritional pamphlets published by Western formula companies.

8. Most women receive vitamin supplements during their prenatal care, but these are distributed by physicians.

9. She used her English in addition to her Chinese name on her name card, and asked me to call her "Candy."

10. The anxiety about the quality of food products is real in China, where fake goods are sold using similar packaging to the original product or where the quality is diminished due to the use of inferior ingredients or unsanitary processing (Chen Ya 1996).

11. Nurse Bai's lecture-discussions followed the UNICEF training materials very closely; I taped several of her classes and compared them to the information provided in the training manuals.

12. Ke (1993) however notes that the advertisements for foreign infant formula may act as an important influence on Chinese women's decisions not to breastfeed.

13. WHO International Code of Marketing Breast Milk Substitutes, adopted in 1981, restricts the promotion of breast milk substitutes in hospitals and requires that all products state that breastfeeding is the best method of infant feeding.

14. "Doing the month" (*zuo yue zi*) is a traditional Chinese practice to protect and restore women's health immediately after the birth. For an in-depth description of these practices, see Pillsbury 1982.

Chapter 8

1. Interview with Cheng Xinhua, an executive of public relations at the headquarters of the Wahaha Group, June 5, 1996.

2. Interview with Zong Qinghou, general manager of the Wahaha Group, June 5, 1996.

3. I thank Jun Jing for letting me quote from the interview he conducted with Xue Meng's father on Jan. 25, 1997.

4. There are no official statistics for factories producing broadly defined children's foods.

Chapter 9

1. In 1995, by contrast, Hong Kong parents gave junior high school students an average of US$107 per month in spending money (*South China Morning Post International Weekly*, Dec. 2, 1995).

2. Research by James McNeal and colleagues in Beijing, cited in *Asiaweek*, Dec. 1, 1995.

3. In 1977 there was only one "outsider" (non-lineage person) in Sik Gong Wai, Ha Tsuen Village, New Territories. Twenty years later, during the winter of 1997, at least twenty houses were inhabited by outsiders, primarily recent immigrants from China (source: household censuses conducted by Rubie S. Watson). Sik Gong Wai was an active center of childhood foraging in 1977–78 when Rubie and I lived in Ha Tsuen (see R. Watson 1985).

4. Based on interviews with Daniel Ng in Hong Kong and Cambridge, Massachusetts, Jan. 14, 1993, June 21, 1993, Dec. 30, 1993, June 16, 1994, and Jan. 19, 1998.

5. I am grateful to my colleague David Schak (the father of two hungry consumers) for coaching on this point.

6. In the 1960s and 1970s, dogs were kept for two reasons: (1) as breeding stock for specialty restaurants, and (2) as ferocious, sometimes dangerous, watchdogs. See J. Watson (1975:14–15) for more on village watchdogs.

7. *South China Morning Post*, March 23, 1996, p. B5.

8. *New York Times*, Jan. 1, 1995, pp. 29, 38.

9. *South China Morning Post International Weekly*, April 27, 1996.

10. *AFP*, May 27, 1998, Clarinet.China:30247.

11. Jun Jing reminds us that there are still parts of the Chinese countryside where hunger has not disappeared, including his own field site in Gansu province (Jing 1997).

12. On the cabbage saga, see *Beijing Review*, Jan. 18, 1993, p. 8; or speak to anyone who lived in Beijing during the 1950s and 1960s. By 1998 China's cabbage production had fallen by one-fifth, compared to records set during earlier decades. Other, more desirable vegetables are now cultivated on fields previously reserved for cabbage (see "Beijing's Wealth Threatens Demise of Cabbage," *AFP*, Nov. 7, 1998, Clarinet.China:35263).

Appendix

1. Peng referred to the ice cream bar solely by its brand name. Many of the snack foods Peng recorded were written in this way; Peng explained what they were to me when we went over the food diary.

Works Cited

ACC Sub-Committee on Nutrition. 1997. "Update on the Nutrition Situation: Summary of Results for the Third Report on the World Nutrition Situation." *SCN News*, no. 14, 9.

Advertiser News Services. 1977. "Beijing Officials See Burgers as Gold." *Honolulu Advertiser*, Sept. 10, A2.

Althusser, Louis. 1971. *Ideology and Ideological State Apparatuses*. New York: Monthly Review.

Anagnost, Ann. 1987. "Politics and Magic in Contemporary China. *Modern China* 11, no. 2:147–76.

———. 1995. "A Surfeit of Bodies: Population and the Rationality of the State in Post-Mao China." In F. Ginsburg and R. Rapp, eds., *Conceiving the New World Order: The Global Politics of Reproduction*, 22–41. Berkeley: University of California Press.

Anderson, Eugene N. 1980. " 'Heating and Cooling' Foods in Hong Kong and Taiwan." *Social Science Information* 19, no. 2:237–68.

———. 1988. *The Food of China*. New Haven: Yale University Press.

Appadurai, Arjun. 1995. "The Production of Locality." In Richard Fardon, ed., *Counterworks: Managing the Diversity of Knowledge*, 204–225. London: Routledge.

———. 1996. *Modernity at Large: Cultural Dimensions of Globalism*. Minneapolis: University of Minnesota Press.

Apple, R. D. 1994. "The Medicalization of Infant Feeding in the United States and New Zealand: Two Countries, One Experience." *Journal of Human Lactation* 10, no. 1:31–37.

Aries, Philippe. 1962. *Centuries of Childhood: A Social History of Family Life*. New York: Vintage Books.

Baker, Greg. 1998. "China." *Life* 21, no. 8 (July):36.

Baker, R. 1987. "Little Emperors Born of a One-Child Policy." *Far Eastern Economic Review* 137, no. 28 (July 16):43–44.

Baker, Victoria J. 1994. "The Problem of Socialization of Only Children in Urban China" (Zhongguo chengshi dusheng ziniu de shehuihua wenti). *Research on Contemporary Youth* (Dangdai qingnian yanjiu) 45, no. 7:45–47.

————. 1995. " 'Little Emperors' and 'Little Empresses' — Chinese Teachers' Views on Only-Child Socialization" ('Xiao huangdi' yu 'xiao huanghou' — zhongguo jiaoshi dui dusheng zinu shehuihuade kanfa). In David Y. H. Wu, ed., *Chinese Child Socialization* (Huaren ertong shehuihua), 130–40. Shanghai: Shanghai Science and Technology Publishing House.

Banister, Judith. 1987. *China's Changing Population*. Stanford: Stanford University Press.

Barnet, Richard, and John Cavanagh. 1994. *Global Dreams: Imperial Corporations and the New World Order*. New York: Simon and Schuster.

Barth, Fredrik. 1987. *Cosmologies in the Making: A Generative Approach to Cultural Variation in Inner New Guinea*. Cambridge: Cambridge University Press.

Beardsworth, Alan, and Teresa Keil. 1997. *Sociology on the Menu: An Invitation to the Study of Food and Society*. London: Routledge.

Becker, Jasper. 1996. *Hungry Ghosts: China's Secret Famine*. London: John Murray.

Beijing Bulletin (Beijing tongxun). 1994a. "The Fad of Standard Fast Food in Beijing and Its Origin" (Jingcheng zhengshi kuaican re qi laili). Feb.:15–16.

————. 1994b. "The Battle of Fast Food in Beijing: Chicken of Eight Allied Forces" (Jingcheng kuaican zhan: Baguo lianjun ji). Feb.:17.

Beijing Review. 1994. "Better Life, but Why Poor Health?" Feb. 28–March 6:7.

Birch, L. L. 1980. "Effects of Peer Models: Food Choices and Eating Behaviors on Preschooler's Food Preferences." *Child Development* 51:489–96.

Bourdieu, Pierre. 1977. *Outline of a Theory of Practice*. New York: Cambridge University Press.

———. 1984. *Distinction: A Social Critique of the Judgement of Taste.* Cambridge, Mass.: Harvard University Press.

———. 1990. "Social Space and Symbolic Power." In *In Other Words: Essays Towards a Reflexive Sociology,* 123–39. Stanford: Stanford University Press.

Brown, Lester. 1995. "China's Food Problem: The Massive Imports Begin." *World Watch* 8:38.

Buck, John. 1930. *Chinese Farm Economy: A Study of 2,866 Farms in Seventeen Localities and Seven Provinces in China.* Chicago: University of Chicago Press.

Cai Limin. 1992. "Borrowing Spirit Money at Shangfang Mountain" (Shangfang shan jie yinzhai). *Chinese Folk Culture* (Zhongguo minjian wenhua) 6:239–56. Shanghai: Shanghai Folklore Association.

Campbell, Colin. 1987. *The Romantic Ethic and the Spirit of Modern Consumerism.* Oxford and New York: Basil Blackwell.

———. 1992. "The Desire for the New: Its Nature and Social Location as Presented in Theories of Fashion and Modern Consumerism." In Roger Silverstone and Eric Hirsch, eds., *Consuming Technologies: Media and Information in Domestic Spaces,* 48–64. New York: Routledge.

Campbell, T. C., J. S. Chen, T. Brun, B. Parpia, Qu Yinsheng, C. M. Chen, and C. Geissler. 1992. "China: From Diseases of Poverty to Diseases of Affluence. Policy Implications of the Epidemiological Transition." *Ecology of Food and Nutrition* 27:133–44.

Cao Lianchen. 1993. "Only Children and Family's Cultural Consumption" (Dusheng ziniu yu jiating wenhua xiaofei). *Research on Mass Culture* (Qunzhong wenhua yanjiu) 5:47–48.

Chadwick, James. 1996. Interview by Michael Laris. November.

Chan, Anita. 1985. *Children of Mao: Personality Development and Political Activism in the Red Guard Generation.* Seattle: University of Washington Press.

Chang, K. C., ed. 1977. *Food in Chinese Culture: Anthropological and Historical Perspectives.* New Haven: Yale University Press.

Chen Chunming. 1997. "Food and Nutrition Policies in China: Using Nutrition Surveillance Data." Paper presented at the 16th International Congress of Nutrition, July 27–Aug. 1, 1997, Montreal, Canada.

Chen Junshi et al. 1990. *Diet, Life-style, and Mortality in China: A Study of 65 Counties*. Oxford: Oxford University Press.

———. 1996. "Major Issues in Maternal and Child Nutrition and the National Plans of Action." *Proceedings of the Tenth International Symposium on Maternal and Infant Nutrition*. Guangzhou: Heinz Institute of Nutritional Sciences.

Chen Pei'ai. 1997. *A History of Chinese and Foreign Commercial Advertisements* (Zhongwai guanggao shi). Beijing: Wujia Press.

Chen Qiuping. 1996. "Health Food Cries for Quality Control." *Beijing Review* 39, no. 25 (June 17):6.

Chen Shujun, ed. 1988. *Chinese Poems and Essays on Fine Food* (Zhongguo meishi shiwen). Guangzhou: Guangdong Higher Education Press.

Chen, Xingyin, Yuerong Sun, and Kenneth Rubin. 1992. "Social Reputation and Peer Relationships in Chinese and Canadian Children: A Cross-cultural Study." *Child Development* 63:1336–43.

Chen Ya. 1996. "Breastfeeding Promotion in China." *Women of China* 9:15 –16.

Chin, Ann-ping. 1988. *Children of China: Voices from Recent Years*. New York: Knoft.

China Daily. 1998. "Future Cola Takes on Giants." July 27, Business Weekly, 8.

China Health and Nutrition. 1997a. "The Problem of Calcium Deficiency Needs Societal Attention." 3:52–53.

———. 1997b. "Calcium Deficiency Is a Worldwide Problem." 4:52–53.

Chinese Academy of Agricultural Sciences. 1994. *Strategies for China's Intermediate and Long-term Development of Food Products* (Zhongguo zhong chang qi shiwu fazhan zhanlue). Beijing: Chinese Academy of Agricultural Sciences Publishing House.

Chinese Nutrition Society Standing Committee. 1990. "Dietary Guidelines for China" (Woguo shanshi zhinan). *Acta Nutrimenta Sinica* (Yingyang xuebao) 12: 10–12.

———. 1997. "Dietary Guidelines for the Chinese People — Balanced Diet, Rational Nutrition, Better Health" (Zhongguo jumin shanshi zhinan — pingheng shanshi, heli yingyang, cujin jiankang). Pamphlet.

Chu, N. F., E. B. Rimm, D. J. Wang, H. S. Liou, and S. M. Shieh. 1998. "Clustering of Cardiovascular Disease Risk Factors among Obese Schoolchildren: The Taipei Children Heart Survey." *American Journal of Clinical Nutrition* 67:1141–46.

"Colonel Sanders' Legacy." 1987. Public Relations Announcement. Kentucky Fried Chicken Corporation. Nov. 12.

Croll, Elizabeth. 1983. *The Family Rice Bowl: Food and Domestic Economy in China*. London: Zed Press.

———. 1986. *Food Supply in China and the Nutritional Status of Children*. Geneva: United Nations Research Institute for Social Development.

Croll, Elizabeth, Delia Davin, and Penny Kane. 1987. *China's One Child Family Policy*. New York and London: Macmillan.

Crowell, Todd, and David Hsieh. 1995. "Little Emperors: Is China's One-Child Policy Creating a Society of Brats?" *Asiaweek* 21, no. 48 (Dec. 1):44–50.

Cui Lili. 1994. "Student Nutrition: A Matter of Concern." *Beijing Review* 37, no. 26 (June 27–July 3):30.

———. 1995. "Third National Nutrition Survey." *Beijing Review* 38, no. 5:31.

Dai Qing and Xue Weijia, eds. 1996. *Whose Yangtze Is It Anyway?* (Shuide changjiang). Hong Kong: Oxford University Press.

Davis, Deborah. 1991. *Long Lives: Chinese Elderly and the Communist Revolution*. 2nd edition. Stanford: Stanford University Press.

Davis, Fred. 1979. *Yearning for Yesterday: A Sociology of Nostalgia*. New York: Free Press.

Demos, John, and V. Demos. 1969. "Adolescence in Historical Perspective." *Journal of Marriage and the Family* 31:632–38.

Dettwyler, Katherine. 1989. "Styles of Infant Feeding: Parent/ Caretaker Control of Food Consumption in Young Children." *American Anthropologist* 91:696–702.

Diamond, Norma. 1969. *K'un Shen: A Taiwan Village*. New York: Holt, Rinehart and Winston.

Ding Xufang, Shou Jieqing, and Wang Guoliang. 1994. "An Inquiry and Analysis of Mental Health among Only Children in Privileged Communities" (Gao cenci shequ dusheng ziniu xinli weisheng de diaocha yu fenxi). *The Sea of Scholarship* (Xuehai) 64, no. 2:50–53.

Douglas, Mary. 1975. *Implicit Meanings*. Boston: Routledge and Kegan Paul.

Douglas, Mary, and Baron Isherwood. 1979. *The World of Goods: Towards an Anthropology of Consumption*. New York: W. W. Norton.

Draper, A. 1994. "Energy Density of Weaning Foods." In A. F. Walker and B. A. Rolls, eds., *Infant Nutrition*, 209–23. London: Chapman and Hall.

Duggan, Patrice. 1990. "Feeding China's Little Emperors." *Forbes* (Aug. 6): 84–85.

Durkheim, Emile. 1951. *Suicide: A Study in Sociology*. New York: Free Press.

Ebrey, Patricia, ed. 1981. *Chinese Civilization and Society: A Sourcebook*. New York: Free Press.

Eckholm, Erik. 1998a. "Relocations for China Dam Are Found to Lag." *New York Times*, March 12, A8.

———. 1998b. "Homes for Elderly Replacing Family Care as China Grays." *New York Times*, May 20, A1, A12.

Escobar, Arturo. 1995. *Encountering Development: The Making and Unmaking of the Third World*. Princeton: Princeton University Press.

Eurofood. 1996. "Potential for Growth in Chinese Baby Food Sector." May 22, p. 3.

Evans, Mark. 1993. "Finger Lickin' Chinese Chicken." *South China Morning Post*, July 26, B3.

Falbo, Tony, et al. 1989. "Physical Achievement and Personality Characteristics of Chinese Children." *Journal of Biosocial Science* 21: 483–95.

Falbo, Toni, Dudley L. Poston, Jr., and Xiao-tian Feng. 1996. "The Academic, Personality, and Physical Outcomes of Chinese Only Children: A Review." In Sing Lau, ed., *Growing Up the Chinese Way*, 265–86. Hong Kong: Chinese University Press.

Fan Cunren, Wan Chuanwen, Lin Guobin, and Jin Qicheng. 1994. "Personality and Moral Character: A Comparative Study of Only Children and Children with Siblings in Primary Schools of Xian" (Xian xiaoxue sheng zhong dusheng zinu yu feidusheng ziniu gexing pinzhi de bijiao yanjiu). *The Science of Psychology* (Xinli kexue) 17:7–74.

Featherstone, Mike. 1990. "Global Culture: An Introduction." In *Global Culture: Nationalism, Globalization, and Modernity*, 1–14. London: Sage.

Feeny, Griffith. 1989. "Recent Fertility Dynamics in China." *Population and Development Review* 15, no. 2:297–322.

Fei, Xiaotong (Fei, Hsiao-t'ung). 1939. *Peasant Life in China: A Field Study of Country Life in the Yangtze Valley*. London: Routledge and Kegan Paul.

Ferguson, James. 1990. *The Anti-Politics Machine*. New York: Cambridge University Press.

Forbes. 1986. "Playing the China Cards: U.S. Products Advertised on Chinese Television." April 7, p. 107.

———. 1993. "Ads for the Sets of China." April 26, p. 12.

Foucault, Michel. 1980. *Power/Knowledge: Selected Interviews and Other Writings, 1972–1977*. New York: Pantheon Books.

———. 1994. *The Birth of the Clinic: An Archeology of Medical Perception*. New York: Random House.

Frank, Andre G. 1969. "The Development of Underdevelopment." In Andre G. Frank, ed., *Latin America: Underdevelopment or Revolution*, 3–17. New York: Monthly Review Press.

Freire, Paulo. 1996. *Pedagogy of the Oppressed*. London: Penguin.

Friedman, Jonathan. 1989. "The Consumption of Modernity." *Culture and History* 4:117–30.

Gamble, Sidney. 1954. *Ting Hsien: A North China Rural Community*. Stanford: Stanford University Press.

Gamble, Sidney, and John Burgess. 1921. *Peking: A Social Survey*. Beijing: Social Research Institute.

Gao Wei. 1997. "Global Show in Beijing to Highlight Food Industry." *China Daily* web-page news, July 25.

Gao Yuan. 1987. *Born Red: A Chronicle of the Cultural Revolution*. Stanford: Stanford University Press.

Gates, Hill. 1993. "Cultural Support for Birth Limitation among Urban Capital-owning Women." In Deborah Davis and Stevan Harrell, eds., *Chinese Families in the Post-Mao Era*, 251–76. Berkeley: University of California Press.

Ge Keyou, ed. 1996. *The Dietary and Nutritional Status of Chinese Population (1992 National Nutrition Survey)*. Beijing: People's Medical Publishing House.

Ge Keyou, Ma Guansheng, Zhai Fengying, Yan Huaicheng, and

Wang Qing. 1996. "Dietary Nutrient Intakes of Chinese Students" (Woguo zhongxiao xuesheng de shanshi yingyang zhuangkuang). *Acta Nutrimenta Sinica* (Yingyang xuebao) 18, no. 2:129–33.

Gillette, Maris. 1997. "Engaging Modernity: Consumption Practices Among Urban Muslims in Northwest China." Ph.D. dissertation, Harvard University.

———. 1999. "What's in a Dress? Brides in the Xi'an Hui Quarter." In Deborah Davis, ed., *The Consumer Revolution in Urban China*. Berkeley: University of California Press.

———. 2000. *Between Mecca and Beijing: Modernization and Consumption Among Urban Chinese Muslims*. Stanford: Stanford University Press.

———. N.d. "Recalling 19th-Century Violence: Social Memory Among Urban Chinese Muslims." Unpublished manuscript.

Gladney, Dru. 1990. "The Ethnogenesis of the Uighur." *Central Asian Survey* 9, no. 1:1–28.

———. 1991. *Muslim Chinese: Ethnic Nationalism in the People's Republic*. Cambridge, Mass.: Council on East Asian Studies, Harvard University.

———. 1998. "Clashed Civilizations? Muslim and Chinese Identities in the PRC." In Dru Gladney, ed., *Making Majorities: Constituting the Nation in Japan, Korea, China, Malaysia, Fiji, Turkey and the United States*, 106–31. Stanford: Stanford University Press.

Good, Byron J. 1994. *Medicine, Rationality and Experience: An Anthropological Perspective*. Cambridge: Cambridge University Press.

Goody, Jack. 1982. *Cooking, Cuisine, and Class: A Study in Comparative Sociology*. Cambridge: Cambridge University Press.

Gordon, Debra, and Margaret Lock. 1988. *Biomedicine Examined*. Dordrecht: Kluwer Academic Publishers.

Gottschang, Suzanne K. 1991. "Insufficient Milk: Woman, Nature and Culture." Master's thesis, Anthropology Department, University of California, Los Angeles.

———. 1998. "The Becoming Mother: Urban Chinese Women's Transitions to Motherhood." Ph.D. dissertation, University of Pittsburgh.

Greenhalgh, Susan. 1990. "The Evolution of the One-Child Policy in Shaanxi." *China Quarterly* 122 (June):191–229.

———. 1993. "The Peasantization of the One-Child Policy in Shaanxi." In Deborah Davis and Steven Harrell, eds., *Chinese Families in the Post-Mao Era*, 219–50. Berkeley: University of California Press.

Guldan, G. S., H. C. Fan, and Z. Z. Ni. 1998. "Can 'Scientific Infant Feeding' Close the Rural-Urban Infant Growth-faltering Gap in Sichuan, China?" *Australian Journal of Nutrition and Dietetics* 55, no. 1 (supplement):36–37.

Guldan, G. S., M. Y. Zhang, G. Zeng, J. R. Hong, and Y. Yang. 1995. "Breastfeeding Practices in Chengdu, Sichuan, China." *Journal of Human Lactation* 11, no. 1:11–15.

Guldan, G. S., M. Y. Zhang, Y. P. Zhang, J. R. Hong, H. X. Zhang, S. Y. Fu, and N. S. Fu. 1993. "Weaning Practices and Growth in Rural Sichuan Infants: a Positive Deviance Study." *The Journal of Tropical Pediatrics* 39, no. 3:168–75.

Guldan, G. S., Y. P. Zhang, Z. Q. Li, Y. H. Hou, F. Long, L. Y. Pu, and J. S. Huang. 1991. "Designing Appropriate Nutrition Education for the Chinese: The Urban and Rural Nutrition Situation in Sichuan." *The Journal of Tropical Pediatrics* 37:159–66.

Guo Ziheng, ed. 1991. *Superior Childbearing, Superior Childrearing, and Eight Million Peasants* (Yousheng youyu yu bayi nongmin). Beijing: China Population Press.

Gupta, Akhil. 1992. "Song of the Nonaligned World: Transnational Identities and the Reinscription of Space in Late Capitalism." *Cultural Anthropology* 7, no. 1:63–79.

Gussler, Judith, and Linda Briesemeister. 1980. "The Insufficient Milk Syndrome: A Biocultural Explanation." *Medical Anthropology* 4:145–74.

Hang Zhi. 1991. "What Is Revealed by the Emergence of a Popular Culture" (Dazhong wenhua de liuxing toulu le shenmo). In Hang Zhi's *A Single Reed* (Yi wei ji). Beijing: Sanlian Press.

Hannerz, Ulf. 1992. *Cultural Complexity: Studies in the Social Organization of Meaning*. New York: Columbia University Press.

———. 1996. *Transnational Connections: Culture, People, Places*. London: Routledge.

Hanson, Eric O. 1980. *Catholic Politics in China and Korea*. Maryknoll: Orbis Books.

Harrell, Stevan. 1988. "Joint Ethnographic Fieldwork in Southern Sichuan." *China Exchange News* 16:3.

———. 1990. "Ethnicity, Local Interests, and the State: Yi Communities in Southwest China." *Comparative Studies in Society and History* 32, no. 3:515–48.

Harrell, Stevan, ed. 1995. *Cultural Encounters on China's Ethnic Frontiers*. Seattle: University of Washington Press.

Harvey, David. 1989. *The Condition of Postmodernity: An Inquiry into the Origins of Cultural Change*. Cambridge, Mass.: Blackwell.

Haviland, William A. 1994. *Anthropology*. New York: Harcourt Brace College Publishers.

He Qinglian. 1988. *Population: China's Sword of Damocles* (Renkou zhongguo de xuanjian). Chengdu: Sichuan People's Publishing House.

Hendry, Joy. 1993. *Wrapping Culture*. Oxford: Clarendon Press.

Hobson, Katherine. 1997. "McDonald's Wins 'McLibel' Case: But the Judge Upholds Allegations of Low Wages, Targeting Children in Ads and Cruelty to Animals." *Honolulu Star-Bulletin*, June 19, B1.

Hong Kong Standard. 1984. "Beijing Duck Making Way For Hamburgers and Fries." April 19, 19.

Hsiao, W. C. L., and Y. L. Liu. 1996. "Economic Reform and Health: Lessons from China." *New England Journal of Medicine* 335, no. 6:430–32.

Hsiung Ping-chen. 1995. "To Nurse the Young: Breastfeeding and Infant Feeding in Late Imperial China." *Journal of Family History* 20, no. 3:217–38.

———. 1996. "Treatment of Children in Traditional China." *Berliner China-Hefte* 10:73–79.

Hu Chunxue. 1993. *An Essential Reading in Childbearing and Childrearing (Sheng er yu nu bidu)*. Beijing: People's Liberation Army Doctors Press.

Hua Xiaoyu. 1990. "Beijing's Kentucky Fever." *China's Foreign Trade* (Nov.):34–35.

Huang Fei. 1997. "Coca Cola Floods Seven Armies of Chinese Goods" (Kekou kele shuiyan guohuo qijun). *China Management Newspaper* (Zhongguo jingying bao), July 22, p. 1.

Huang Ping. 1995. "The Influence of Consumerism among Urban

Residents in Contemporary China" (Xiaofei zhuyi zai dangdai Zhongguo chengshi jumin zhong de yingxiang). In *Papers of the 1994 Academic Conference on Chinese Culture and Market Economy* (Jiusi Zhongguo shichang jingji yu wenhua xueshu yantaohui lunwen ji). Beijing: Chinese Economy Press.

Huang Shau-yen. 1994. "Traditional Therapeutic Diets in China" (Zhongguo chuantong shiliao). In *Papers of the Fourth Academic Conference on Chinese Dietary Culture* (Disanjie Zhongguo yinshi wenhua xueshu yantaohui lunwen ji). Taipei: Foundation of Chinese Dietary Culture.

Huang Shu-min. 1989. *The Spiral Road: Change in a Chinese Village through the Eyes of a Communist Party Leader*. Boulder: Westview Press.

Huang, Shu-min, Kimberley C. Falk, and Su-min Chen. 1996. "Nutritional Well-Being of Preschool Children in a North China Village." *Modern China* 22, no. 4:355–81.

Hull, Valerie J., Shyam Thapa, and Gulardi Wiknjosastro. 1989. "Breast-Feeding and Health Professionals: A Study in Hospitals in Indonesia." *Social Science and Medicine* 20, no.4:355–64.

Huntington, Samuel P. 1973. "Transnational Organizations in World Politics." *World Politics* 25:333–68.

———. 1993. "The Clash of Civilizations?" *Foreign Affairs* 72, no. 3:22–50.

Ikels, Charlotte. 1993. "Settling Accounts: The Intergenerational Contract in an Age of Reform." In Deborah Davis and Stevan Harrell, eds., *Chinese Families in the Post-Mao Era*, 307–33. Berkeley: University of California Press.

———. 1996. *The Return of the God of Wealth: The Transition to a Market Economy in Urban China*. Stanford: Stanford University Press.

Information Office of the State Council. 1996. "The Situation of Children in China." *Beijing Review* 39, no. 17 (April 22–28):20–30.

Jamison, D. T. 1986. "Child Malnutrition and School Performance in China." *Journal of Development Economics* 20:299–309.

Jelliffe, Derrick, and E. F. Patrice Jelliffe. 1981. *Human Milk in the Modern World*. Oxford: Oxford University Press.

Jin Binggao. 1984. "Discussion of the Production and Effect of the Marxist Definition of Nationality" (Shilun makesizhuyi minzu dingyi de chansheng jiqi yingxiang). *Central Minorities Institute Newsletter* (Zhongyang minzu xueyuan xuebao) 3:64–67.

Jing, Jun. 1996. *The Temple of Memories: History, Power, and Morality in a Chinese Village*. Stanford: Stanford University Press.

———. 1997. "Rural Resettlement: Past Lessons for the Three Gorges Project." *China Journal* 38:65–92.

Johnston, Francis. 1987. *Nutritional Anthropology*. New York: Alan R. Bliss, Inc.

Jowett, John. 1989. "Mao's Man-Made Famine." *Geographical Magazine* (April):16–19.

Judd, Ellen. 1994. *Gender and Power in Rural North China*. Stanford: Stanford University Press.

Kan Xuegui. 1996. "Food Hygiene Law Linked to International Standards." *Beijing Review* 39, no. 13:20.

Kane, Penny. 1988. *Famine in China, 1959–61: Demographic and Social Implications*. New York: St. Martin's Press.

Kaufman, Joan. 1983. *A Billion and Counting: Family Planning Campaigns and Policies in the People's Republic of China*. San Francisco: San Francisco Press.

Ke Fangfang. 1993. "An Investigation of Breastfeeding Practices in Rural Areas" (Nongcun muru weiyang zhuangkuang diaocha)." *Health Care of Chinese Women and Children* (Zhongguo fuyou baojian) 3, no. 2:54–58.

Kennedy, Eileen, and Jeanne Goldberg. 1995. "What Are American Children Eating? Implications for Public Policy." *Nutrition Reviews* 53, no. 5 (May): 111–26.

Kessen, William, ed. 1975. *Childhood in China*. New Haven: Yale University Press.

Kett, Joseph F. 1977. *Rites of Passage: Adolescence in America, 1790 to the Present*. New York: Basic Books.

Kleinman, Arthur. 1980. *Patients and Healers in the Context of Culture*. Berkeley: University of California Press.

Kong Wenqing, Zhu Qing, and Zhong Jiangguang. 1996. "Three Little Girls Die Tragically in Wahaha Poisoning Incident" (Wahaha zhongdu shijian san younu buxin shenwang). *Beijing Youth Newspaper* (Beijing qingnian bao), June 5, p. 1.

Kopytoff, Igor. 1988. "The Cultural Biography of Things: Commoditization as Process." In Arjun Appadurai, ed., *The Social Life of Things*, 64–94. Cambridge: Cambridge University Press.

Kristof, Nicholas D. 1993. "China's Crackdown on Births: A Stunning, and Harsh, Success." *New York Times*, April 25, A1 and A12.

Laderman, Carol. 1983. *Wives and Midwives: Childbearing and Nutrition in Rural Malaysia*. Berkeley: University of California Press.

Lam, Y. L. 1993. "Family Backgrounds and Experience, Personality Development and School Performance: A Causal Analysis of Grade One Chinese Children." *Education* 113, no. 1:133–44.

Lambek, Michael. 1995. "Choking on the Qur'an: and Other Consuming Parables from the Western Indian Ocean." In Wendy James, ed., *The Pursuit of Certainty*, 258–81. London: Routledge.

Lawrence, Susan. 1994. "Chinese Chicken: Dancing for Fast-Food Dollars." *U.S. News and World Report*, July 18, p. 46.

Lawson, J. S., and V. Lin. 1994. "Health Status Differentials in the People's Republic of China." *American Journal of Public Health* 84, no. 5:737–41.

Lee, Martyn J. 1993. *Consumer Culture Reborn: The Cultural Politics of Consumption*. New York: Routledge.

Lee, W. T. K., S. F. Leung, and D. M. Y. Leung. 1994. "The Current Dietary Practice of Hong Kong Adolescents." *Asia Pacific Journal of Clinical Nutrition* 3:83–87.

Leicester, John. 1997. "Gallup Poll in China: Coke, Men's Hairdos and TVs." Associated Press, Oct. 26.

Leung, S. S. F. 1994. *Growth Standards for Hong Kong: A Territory-Wide Survey in 1993*. Hong Kong: Chinese University of Hong Kong.

Leung, S. S. F., J. T. F. Lau, L. Y. Tse, and S. J. Oppenheimer. 1996. "Weight-for-Age and Weight-for-Height References for Hong Kong Children from Birth to 18 Years." *Journal of Paediatrics and Child Health* 32:103–9.

Leung, S. S. F., M. Y. Ng, B. Y. Tan, C. W. K. Lam, S. F. Wang, Y. C. Xu, and W. P. Tsang. 1994. "Serum Cholesterol and Dietary Fat of Two Populations of Southern Chinese." *Asia Pacific Journal of Clinical Nutrition* 3:127–30.

Levenstein, Harvey. 1993. *Paradox of Plenty: A Social History of Eating in Modern America*. Oxford: Oxford University Press.

Li Bin. 1995. "Law Protects Mothers and Infants." *Beijing Review* 38, no. 10:13–16.

Li, Chengrui. 1987. *The Population Atlas of China*. Oxford: Oxford University Press.

Li Jinghan. 1933. *Dingxian: A Social Survey* (Dingxian shehui gaikuang diaocha). Beiping: China Mass Education Society.

Liang Hui. 1992. "Ronghua Chicken: Don't Come Back If You Are Unsatisfied" (Ronghuaji: bu manyi ni xiaci bie lai). *China Industrial and Commercial News* (Zhonghua gongshang shibao), Nov. 11, p. 1.

Liang Ying, ed. 1996. *Can China Feed Herself?* (Zhongguo neng yang huo ziji ma?). Beijing: Economic Science Publishing House.

Liberation Daily (Jiefang ribao). 1990. "Ronghua Chicken and Kentucky Fried Chicken" (Ronghuaji yu kendiji), Aug. 16, p. 1.

Lin Naisang. 1989. *China's Culture of Food* (Zhongguo yinshi wenhua). Shanghai: Shanghai People's Publishing House.

Lin, Yao-Hua. 1947. *The Golden Wing: A Sociological Study of Chinese Familism*. London: Routledge and Kegan Paul.

Lipman, Jonathan. 1987. "Hui-Hui: An Ethnohistory of the Chinese-Speaking Muslims." *Journal of South Asian and Middle Eastern Studies* 11, nos. 1 and 2 (combined):112–30.

———. 1997. *Familiar Strangers: A History of Muslims in Northwest China*. Seattle: University of Washington Press.

Liu Liming. 1993. "Sources of Information for Compiling Material on Breastfeeding and Health Education" (Tan muru weiyang jiankang jiaoyu cailiao de xinxi xingcheng). *Health Care of Chinese Women and Children* (Zhongguo fuyou baojian) 8, no. 1:35–36.

Liu Yongcong. 1997. *Childcare in Traditional China* (Zhongguo gudai de yu er). Beijing: Commercial Press.

Liu Yun. 1996. "Will Chinese or Foreign Soft Drinks Dominate This Summer" (Guoyin yangyin jinxia shui tianxia). *International Food* (Guoji shipin) 4: 6–8.

Liu Zhuoye. 1990. "Heinz-UFE Discovers the Chinese Market." *Beijing Review* 33, no. 46 (Nov. 12–18):36–38.

Liy Yi-chu. 1994. "On the Rise and Nutritional Value of the Chinese Theory about the Common Origination of Food and Medicine" (Lun Zhongguo shiyi tongyuan de chansheng jiqi yingyang jiazhi). In *Papers of the Fourth Academic Conference on Chinese Dietary Culture* (Disanjie Zhongguo yinshi wenhua xueshu yantaohui lunwen ji). Taipei: Foundation of Chinese Dietary Culture.

Lowe, H. Y. (Wu Hsing-yuan). 1984. *The Adventures of Wu: The Life Cycle of a Peking Man*. Princeton: Princeton University Press.

Lu Huiling, Hua Gencai, Li Xianfeng, and Huang Yan. 1993. "Epidemiological Study of Primary Obesity Among Children Aged 7–12 in Putuo District, Shanghai" (Shanghaishi putuoqu 7–12 sui ertong danchunxing feipangzhen liuxingbingxue diaocha). *Chinese School Doctor* (Zhongguo xiaoyi) 7:86–88.

Lu, Henry. 1994. *Chinese Herbal Cures*. New York: Sterling.

———. 1986. *Chinese Systems of Food Cures*. New York: Sterling.

Lu Xun. 1969. "Dawn Blossoms Gathered at Dusk." In *Three Decades of Lu Xun's Works* (Lun Xun sanshinian ji), vol. 16:6. Hong Kong: Xinyi.

Lui, S. S. H., V. Ho, W. T. K. Lee, E. Wong, W. Tang, L. Y. Tse, and J. Lau. 1997. "Factors Affecting the Low Breastfeeding Rates in Hong Kong." Presented at the 16th International Congress of Nutrition, July 27–Aug. 1, 1997, Montreal, Canada.

Lull, James. 1991. *China Turned On: Television, Reform, and Resistance*. London: Routledge.

Luo Zhufeng, ed. 1991. *Religion Under Socialism in China*. Armonk, N.Y.: M. E. Sharpe.

Lupher, Mark. 1995. "Revolutionary Little Devils: The Social Psychology of the Rebel Youth, 1966–1967." In Anne Behnke Kinney, ed., *Chinese Views of Childhood*, 321–44. Honolulu: University of Hawaii Press.

Ma Changshou. 1993. *Records of the Historical Investigation into the Shaanxi Hui Uprising of the Tongzhi Period* (Tongzhi nianjian Shaanxi Huimin qiyi lishi diaocha jilu). Xi'an: Shaanxi People's Publishing House.

Ma Liqing and Wang Xiaofeng. 1993. "Analysis of a Survey of Obese Primary and Secondary Students in Shijiazhuang" (Shijiazhuangshi zhongxiao xuesheng feipang diaocha fenxi). *Chinese School Health* (Zhongguo xuexiao weisheng) 14, no. 3:150.

Ma Tianfang. 1971. *Why Do Muslims Not Eat Pork?* (Huimin wei shenme buchi zhurou?). Booklet printed in Taiwan.

MacInnis, Donald. 1989. *Religion in China Today: Policy and Practice*. Maryknoll, N.Y.: Orbis Books.

Martin, Emily. 1989. *The Woman in the Body: A Cultural Analysis of Reproduction*. Boston: Beacon Press.

Mathewson, Ruth. 1996. "Heavy Going for Children." *South China Morning Post International Weekly*, April 27.

McCracken, Grant. 1988. *Culture and Consumption: New Approaches to the Symbolic Character of Consumer Goods and Activities*. Bloomington: Indiana University Press.

McElroy, Ann, and Patricia K. Townsend. 1989. *Medical Anthropology in Ecological Perspective*. Boulder: Westview.

McKhann, Charles. 1995. "The Naxi and the Nationalities Question." In Stevan Harrell, ed., *Cultural Encounters on China's Ethnic Frontiers*, 39–62. Seattle: University of Washington Press.

McNeal, James U. 1992. *Kids as Customers: A Handbook of Marketing to Children*. New York: Lexington Books.

McNeal, James U., and Chyon-Hwa Yeh. 1997. "Development of Consumer Behavior Patterns Among Chinese Children." *Journal of Consumer Marketing* 14, no. 1:45–59.

McNeal, James U., and Shushan Wu. 1995. "Consumer Choices Are Child's Play in China." *Asian Wall Street Journal Weekly*, Oct. 23, p. 14.

Meng Tianpei and Sidney Gamble. 1926. "Prices, Wages and Standards of Living in Peking, 1900–24." *Chinese Social and Political Science Review* (July)(special supplement).

Meng Yuecheng. 1996. "The Expansion of Scientific Research Investment and the Development of Chinese Children's Food Industry" (Jiada keyan touru fazhan minzu ertong shipin gongye). Hangzhou: Wahaha Scientific Research Center, March 25.

Mennell, Stephen, Anne Murcott, and Anneke H. van Otterloo. 1992. *The Sociology of Food: Eating, Diet and Culture*. London: Sage.

Meredith, William. 1991. "The Schools for Parents in Guangdong Province, People's Republic of China." *The Journal of Contemporary Family Studies* 22, no. 3:379–85.

Miller, Daniel. 1987. *Material Culture and Mass Consumption*. Oxford: Blackwell.

———. 1993. *Unwrapping Christmas*. New York: Oxford University Press.

Miller, Daniel, ed. 1995. *Acknowledging Consumption: A Review of New Studies*. New York: Routledge.

Milwertz, Cecilia N. 1997. *Accepting Population Control: Urban Chinese Women and the One-Child Family Policy*. Surrey: Curzon Press.

Mintz, Sidney. 1986. *Sweetness and Power: The Place of Sugar in Modern History*. New York: Penguin Books.

———. 1993. "The Changing Roles of Food in the Study of Consumption." In John Brewer and Roy Porter, eds., *Consumption and the World of Goods*, 261–73. London: Routledge.

———. 1996. *Tasting Food, Tasting Freedom*. Boston: Beacon Press.

———. 1997. "Afterword: Swallowing Modernity." In James L. Watson, ed., *Golden Arches East: McDonald's in East Asia*, 183–200. Stanford: Stanford University Press.

Moore, Sally Falk. 1987. "Explaining the Present: Theoretical Dilemmas in Processual Ethnography." *American Ethnologist* 14, no. 4:727–36.

———. 1994. "The Ethnography of the Present and the Analysis of Process." In Robert Borofsky, ed., *Assessing Cultural Anthropology*, 362–74. New York: McGraw-Hill.

Morley, David, and Kevin Robins. 1995. *Spaces of Identity: Global Media, Electronic Landscapes, and Cultural Boundaries*. London: Routledge.

Mussen, Paul Henry, John Janeway Conger, and Jerome Kagan. 1974. *Child Development and Personality*, 4th edition. New York: Harper and Row.

New China News Agency (Xinhua). 1997. "Noodle Giant Expands Market." *China Daily*, web-page news, Jan. 22.

Newsweek. 1994. "Where the Admen Are." March 14, p. 39.

Niu Wenxin. 1992. "Focal Points of Beijing: Cock Fight" (Jingcheng re shi: Douji). *China Industrial and Commercial News* (Zhonghua gongshang shibao), Oct. 21, p. 1.

Nye, Joseph S., and Robert O. Keohane. 1972. *Transnational Relations and World Politics*. Cambridge, Mass.: Harvard University Press.

O'Neil, Molly. 1998. "Feeding the Next Generation: Food Industry Caters to Teen-Age Eating Habits." *New York Times*, March 14, 1998, B1.

Ohnuki-Tierney, Emiko. 1993. *Rice as Self: Japanese Identities Through Time*. Princeton: Princeton University Press.

Parish, William L., and Martin King Whyte. 1978. *Village and Family in Contemporary China*. Chicago: University of Chicago Press.

Pasternak, Burton. 1986. *Marriage and Fertility in Tianjin, China: Fifty Years of Transition*. Honolulu: East-West Center.

Piazza, Alan. 1986. *Food and Nutritional Status in the PRC*. Boulder: Westview.

Pillsbury, Barbara. 1975. "Pig and Policy: Maintenance of Boundaries Between Han and Muslim Chinese." In B. Eugene Griessman, ed., *Minorities: A Text with Readings in Intergroup Relations*, 136–45. Hinsdale: Dryden Press.

———. 1982. "Doing the Month": Confinement and Convalescence of Chinese Women after Childbirth." *Social Science and Medicine* 12, no. 1B:11–22.

Pliner, P. 1982. "The Effects of Mere Exposure on Liking for Edible Substances." *Appetite* 3:283–90.

Popkin, Barry M., et al. 1993. "The Nutrition Transition in China: A Cross-Sectional Analysis." *European Journal of Clinical Nutrition* 47:333–46.

Popkin, Barry M., M. E. Yamamoto, and C. C. Griffin. 1986. "Breast-feeding in the Philippines: The Role of the Health Sector." *Journal of Bio-Social Science* supplement 9:98–107.

Potter, Jack M. 1974. "Cantonese Shamanism." In Authur P. Wolf, ed., *Religion and Ritual in Chinese Society*. Stanford: Stanford University Press.

Potter, Sulamith Heins, and Jack M. Potter. 1990. *China's Peasants: The Anthropology of a Revolution*. Cambridge: Cambridge University Press.

Powdermaker, Hortense. 1932. "Feasts in Ireland: The Social Functions of Eating." *American Anthropologist* 34:236–47.

Qian Peijin and Li Jieming. 1991. "Cock Fight in Shanghai" (Douji Shanghai tan). *People's Daily* (Renmin ribao), Sept. 22, p. 1.

Qiu Qi. 1994. "Quick Meals at Home Speed Food Sellers' Growth." *Beijing Weekly,* July 24, p. 8.

Raymond, Linda. 1966. "China Facing the Future: KFC Focuses on 'Little Suns.'" *The Courier-Journal* (Louisville, Ky.) January 21, 1996, Business p. 1E.

Ritzer, G. 1993. *The McDonaldization of Society*. Boston: Pine Forge Books.

Rozin, Paul, April E. Fallon, and Marcia Levin Pelchat. 1986. "Psychological Factors Influencing Food Choice." In Christopher Ritson, Leslie Gofton, and John McKenzie, eds., *The Food Consumer*, 107–126. New York: John Wiley and Sons.

Ruf, Gregory. 1994. "Pillars of the State: Laboring Families, Authority, and Community in Rural Sichuan, 1937–1991." Ph.D. dissertation, Columbia University.

Sassen, Saskia. 1996. *Losing Control? Sovereignty in an Age of Globalism*. New York: Columbia University Press.

Shanghai Educational Television. 1994. *Breastfeeding* (Muru weiyang). Videorecording (45 minutes).

Shen, T. F., and J. P. Habicht. 1991. "Nutrition Surveillance: Source of Information for Action." In *Proceedings of International Symposium on Food Nutrition and Social Economic Development*, 377–87. Beijing: Chinese Science Publisher.

Shen, T. F., J. P. Habicht, and Y. Chang. 1996. "Effect of Economic Reforms on Child Growth in Urban and Rural Areas of China." *New England Journal of Medicine* 335, no. 6:400–406.

Shen Zhiyuan and Le Bingcheng. 1991. "Investigating the Worship of Ge Xian Weng Bodhisattva at Lingfeng Mountain" (Lingfeng shan gexian weng pusa xinyang diaocha). In *Chinese Folk Culture* (Zhongguo minjian wenhua), 3:172–83. Shanghai: Shanghai Folklore Association.

Shi, L. Y. 1993. "Health Care in China: A Rural-Urban Comparison after the Socioeconomic Reforms." *Bulletin of the World Health Organization* 71, no. 6:723–26.

Shirk, Susan L. 1982. *Competitive Comrades: Career Incentives and Student Strategies in China*. Berkeley: University of California Press.

Sidel, Ruth. 1972. *Women and Child Care in China*. New York: Hill and Wang.

Simoons, Frederick J. 1961. *Eat Not This Flesh: Food Avoidances in the Old World*. Westport, Conn.: Greenwood Press.

Siu, Helen. 1989. *Agents and Victims in South China: Accomplices in Rural Revolution*. New Haven: Yale University Press.

Smil, Vaclav. 1985. "Eating Better: Farming Reforms and Food in China." *Current History* 84:248–51.

———. 1995. "Who Will Feed China?" *The China Quarterly* 143 (Sept.):801–813.

South China Morning Post. 1989. "US Restaurant Chain Reopens in Tiananmen." June 22, B4.

Spence, Jonathan. 1992. *Chinese Roundabout: Essays in History and Culture.* New York: W. W. Norton.

Stafford, Charles. 1995. *The Roads of Chinese Childhood.* Cambridge: Cambridge University Press.

Starr, Paul. 1982. *The Social Transformation of American Medicine.* New York: Basic Books.

State Statistics Bureau. 1988. *State Statistical Abstract.* Beijing: China Statistics Press.

———. 1994. *Chinese Statistical Yearbook.* Beijing: China Statistics Press.

Stephens, Sharon, ed. 1995. *Children and the Politics of Culture.* Princeton: Princeton University Press.

Stipp, Horst H. 1988. "Children as Consumers." *American Demographics* 10, no. 2:27–32.

Strathern, Andrew. 1996. *Body Thoughts.* Ann Arbor: University of Michigan Press.

Strathern, Marilyn. 1992. *Reproducing the Future.* New York: Routledge.

———, ed. 1995. *Shifting Contexts: Transformations in Anthropological Knowledge.* New York: Routledge.

Su Songxing. 1994. "Only Children: From a New Situation to Developing a Field of Research" (Dusheng ziniu cong xin guoqing xiang xin kexue de fazhan). *Research on Contemporary Youth* (Dangdai qingnian yanjiu) 1:10–15.

Su Yingxiong, Wu Kaiquan, Wang Zheng, Shi Xingguo, and Piao Yongda. 1991. "Investigation of the Nutritional Status of Primary and Secondary Students in Chengdu" (Chengdushi zhongxuesheng 1991 nian yingyang zhuangkuang diaocha). *Chinese School Health* (Zhongguo xuexiao weisheng) 14, no. 5:263–64.

Sun Hong. 1996. "Vitamin Company to Widen Investment." *China Daily,* web-page news, Nov. 18.

Sun Xun. 1991. "Influence of Obesity on Blood Pressure in Youth" (Ertong shaoniande feipang dui xueya yinxiangde diaocha). *Chinese School Doctor* (Zhongguo xiaoyi) 5, no. 4:62–63.

Taeuber, Irene. 1964. "China's Population: Riddle of the Past, Enigma of the Future." In Albert Feuerwerker, ed., *Modern China*, 16–26. Englewood Cliffs, N.J.: Prentice-Hall.

Tao Menghe. 1928. *Livelihood in Peking: An Analysis of the Budgets of Sixty Families* (Beiping shenghuofei zhi fenxi). Beiping: Social Research Institute.

Taren, D., and J. A. Chen. 1993. "Positive Association Between Extended Breastfeeding and Nutritional Status in Rural Hubei Province, People's Republic of China." *American Journal of Clinical Nutrition* 58:862–67.

Tempest, Rone. 1996. "China Faces New Urban Food Worry: Surplus, Not Shortage." *Los Angeles Times*, May 5, A4.

Thomas, Jane. 1994. "Persistence and Change: Dietary Patterns, Food Ideology and Health." Speech delivered at the Fairbank Center for East Asian Research, Harvard University, Aug. 11.

Thomas, Martha, ed. 1997. "China's Baby-Friendly Hospitals Mean More Breastfeeding." *BFHI News* (Feb.):2.

Tobin, Joseph J., David H. Y. Wu, and Dana H. Davidson. 1989. *Preschool in Three Cultures: Japan, China, and the United States.* New Haven: Yale University Press.

Tuistra, Fons. 1996. "Cola Kings Work Up a Thirst on Grand Battleground." Gemini New Service, Sept. 10.

Turner, Mia. 1996. "Too Stuffed to Jump: Indulgent Parents and Big Macs Are Swelling the Ranks, and Waistlines, of China's Chubby Children." *Time International Magazine* 148(Sept. 16):13.

Ulijaszek, S. J. 1994. "Between-population Variation in Preadolescent Growth." *European Journal of Clinical Nutrition* 48, supplement 1:5–14.

UNICEF Beijing. 1992. "Post-flood Nutrition and Intervention Initiative Report."

United Nations. 1995. *Baby-Friendly Hospital Initiative Newsletter* 5:1.

Vallier, Ivan. 1973. "The Roman Catholic Church: A Transnational Actor." In Joseph Nye and Robert Keohane, eds., *Transnational Relations and World Politics*, 129–52. Cambridge, Mass.: Harvard University Press.

Van Esterik, Penny. 1989. *Beyond the Breast-Bottle Controversy.* New Brunswick, N.J.: Rutgers University Press.

Vincent, Joan. 1990. *Anthropology and Politics: Visions, Traditions, and Trends*. Tempe: University of Arizona Press.

Wahaha Group. 1995. "Using Capital Management Concepts" (Yunyong ziben jingying sixian). Aug.

Wall Street Journal. 1995. "Marketing: China's (Only) Children Get the Royal Treatment." Feb. 8, B1.

———. 1996. "Nestle's China Ice Cream Pact." Aug. 14, A12.

Wallerstein, Immanuel. 1974. "The Rise and Future Demise of the World Capitalist System: Concepts for Comparative Analysis." *Comparative Studies in Society and History* 16:387–415.

Wan, Chuanwen. 1996. "Comparison of Personality Traits of Only and Sibling School Children in Beijing." *Journal of Genetic Psychology* 155:377–88.

Wang Fenglan, Shi Zongnan, and Tong Fang. 1991. "Discussion and Suggestions Concerning the Promotion of Our Country's Breastfeeding Problem" (Guanyu cujin woguo muru weiyang wenti de taolun he jianyi). *Chinese Women and Children's Health* (Zhongguo fuyou bao jian) 6, vol. 2:6–8.

Wang Jiangang. 1989. "Multiple Social Effects of Television Commercials" (Dianshi guanggao de duochong shehui xiaoyi). In *Research in Television News Broadcasting* (Xinwen dianshi guangbo yanjiu) 5:23–34; 6:40–52.

Wang Lin, ed. 1993. *A Manual of Dietary and Hygienic Knowledge* (Yinshi weisheng zhishi shouce). Beijing: China Light Industry Publishing House.

Wang Mingde and Wang Zihui. 1988. *Food in Ancient China* (Zhongguo gudai yinshi). Xian: Shaanxi People's Publishing House.

Wang Renxiang. 1994. *Food and Chinese Culture* (Yinshi yu Zhongguo wenhua). Beijing: Beijing People's Publishing House.

Wang Shaoguang. 1995. "The Politics of Private Time: Changing Leisure Patterns in Urban China." In *Urban Spaces in Contemporary China: The Potential for Autonomy and Community in Post-Mao China*, 149–72. Washington, D.C.: Woodrow Wilson Center Press.

Wang Shoukui and Yuan Xiaoling. 1997. "The Passing of Standards for Health Food Set for May 1." *China Health and Nutrition* (Zhongguo baojian yingyang) (July):6.

Wang Xiangrong. 1993. "The Outline of Chinese Food Structural

Reform and Development for the 1990's." *China Food Newspaper*, June 16, p. 1.

Watson, James L. 1975. *Emigration and the Chinese Lineage: The Mans in Hong Kong and London.* Berkeley: University of California Press.

———. 1987. "From the Common Pot: Feasting with Equals in Chinese Society." *Anthropos* 82:389–401.

———. 1997. "McDonald's in Hong Kong: Consumerism, Dietary Change, and the Rise of a Children's Culture." In James L. Watson, ed., *Golden Arches East: McDonald's in East Asia*, 77–109. Stanford: Stanford University Press.

Watson, James L., ed. 1997. *Golden Arches East: McDonald's in East Asia.* Stanford: Stanford University Press.

Watson, Rubie S. 1985. *Inequality Among Brothers: Class and Kinship in South China.* Cambridge: Cambridge University Press.

———. 1986. "The Named and the Nameless: Gender and Person in Chinese Society." *American Ethnologist* 13:619–31.

Weber, Max. 1968. *Economy and Society.* New York: Bedminster.

Wei Lilin and Wang Shangcheng. 1994. "An Initial Commentary on the Development of the Chinese Fast-Food Industry" (Fazhan zhongshi kuaicanye chuyi). *Beijing Evening News* (Beijing wanbao), March 22, p. 1.

Wen Chihua. 1995. *The Red Mirror: Children of the Cultural Revolution.* Boulder: Westview.

Wen Jinhai. 1992. "From Kentucky Fried Chicken to McDonald's: An Examination of the Fast-Food Fad" (Cong kendeji dao maidanglao: Kuaican re xianxiang toushi). *Xingyang Daily* (Xingyang ribao), Sept. 19, p. 1.

White, Merry. 1994. *The Material Child: Coming of Age in Japan and America.* Berkeley: University of California Press.

Whyte, Martin, and William Parish. 1984. *Urban Life in Contemporary China.* Chicago: University of Chicago Press.

Wolf, Eric R. 1982. *Europe and the People Without History.* Berkeley: University of California Press.

Wolf, Margery. 1972. *Women and the Family in Rural Taiwan.* Stanford: Stanford University Press.

———. 1985. *Revolution Postponed: Women in Contemporary China.* Stanford: Stanford University Press.

World Health Organization, 1998. *Complementary Feeding of Young*

Children in Developing Countries: A Review of Current Scientific Knowledge. Geneva: World Health Organization.

Wu Guanghua, ed. 1993. *Chinese-English Dictionary*, vols. 1 and 2. Shanghai: Shanghai Transportation University Press.

Wu, David Y. H. 1994. "Drowning Your Child with Love: Family Education in Six Chinese Communities." (The 8th Barbara Ward Memorial Lecture.) *The Hong Kong Anthropologist* 2:2–12.

———. 1996. "Parental Control: Psychocultural Interpretations of Chinese Patterns of Socialization." In Sing Lau, ed., *Growing Up the Chinese Way*, 1–28. Hong Kong: Chinese University Press.

Wu Kangmin, Dong Renwei, Xu Weiguang, Xun Yucheng, and Liu Qing. 1995. "An Investigation of the Current Situation of Breastfeeding and Factors of Nutrition in Urban Chengdu" (Chengdu shiqu muru weiyang xianzhuang jiqi yingxiang yinsu diaocha). *Journal of West China University of Medical Sciences* 10, no. 2:174–76.

Wu Ruixian, Yang Fan, and Cai Li. 1990. *Healthy Recipes for Children* (Ertong yaoshan). Beijing: Foreign Languages Press.

Xie Jili. 1992. "New Views on Breastfeeding" (Youguan muru weiyang de xin guandian). *Journal of Nurse Training* (Hushi jinxiu zazhi) 7, no. 1:10–11.

Xinhua. 1997. "A Survey Shows That Hong Kong Children Eat Too Much Junk Food." Feb. 19.

Xue Suzhen. 1995. "Social Trends and the Principal Special Characteristics in Chinese Child Socialization" (Shehui bianqian yu zhongguo ertong shehuihua zhuyao tezheng). In David Y. H. Wu, ed., *Chinese Child Socialization* (Huaren ertong shehuihua), 4–9. Shanghai: Shanghai Science and Technology Publishing House.

Xun Zhongyong, Lu Xiuping, Li Qinghua, Zhou Mei, Wang Yongqin, and Yan Bufan. 1995. "An Investigation of Urban and Rural Breastfeeding Habits" (Chengxiang muru weiyang ji muru xiguan diaocha). *Journal of Weifang Medical College* (Weifang yixueyuan xuebao) 17, no. 3:207–8.

Yan, Yunxiang. 1992. "The Impact of Rural Reform on Economic and Social Stratification in a Chinese Village." *Australian Journal of Chinese Affairs* 27:1–24.

———. 1994. "Dislocation, Reposition, and Restratification: Structural Changes in Chinese Society." In Maurice Brosseau and Lo

Chi Kin, eds., *China Review*, 15. Hong Kong: Chinese University Press.

———. 1995. "The Rise of Fast Food and Its Impact on Local Dietary Culture in Beijing" (Beijing kuaican re jiqi dui chuantong wenhua de yingxiang). In *Papers of the Fourth Academic Conference on Chinese Dietary Culture* (Disijie Zhongguo yinshi wenhua xueshu yantaohui lunwen ji). Taipei: Foundation of Chinese Dietary Culture.

———. 1996. *The Flow of Gifts: Reciprocity and Social Networks in a Chinese Village*. Stanford: Stanford University Press.

———. 1997a. "The Triumph of Conjugality: Structural Transformation of Family Relations in a Chinese Village." *Ethnology* 36:191–212.

———. 1997b. "McDonald's in Beijing: The Localization of Americana." In James L. Watson, ed., *Golden Arches East: McDonald's in East Asia*, 39–76. Stanford: Stanford University Press.

Yang, Bin, Thomas Ollendick, Qi Dong, Yong Xia, and Lei Lin. 1995. "Only Children and Children with Siblings in the People's Republic of China: Levels of Fear, Anxiety, and Depression." *Child Development* 66:1301–11.

Yang, Dali. 1996. *Calamity and Reform in China: State, Rural Society and Institutional Change Since the Great Leap Forward*. Stanford: Stanford University Press.

Yang, Mayfair Mei-hui. 1994. *Gifts, Favors, Banquets: The Art of Social Relationships in China*. Ithaca, N.Y.: Cornell University Press.

Yang, P. Y., S. K. Zhan, J. L. Ling, and C. X. Qiu. 1989. "Breastfeeding of Infants Between 0–6 Months Old in 20 Provinces, Municipalities and Autonomous Regions in the People's Republic of China." *The Journal of Tropical Pediatrics* 35:277–80.

Yang Ximeng and Tao Menghe. 1930. *A Study of the Standard of Living of the Working Families in Shanghai* (Shanghai gongren shenghuo chengdu de yige yanjiu). Beiping: Social Research Institute.

Yang Yashan. 1987. *A History of Chinese Sociology* (Zhongguo shehuixue shi). Jinan: Shandong People's Publishing House.

Ye Guangjun and Feng Ningping. 1996. "The Status and Preventive Strategy of Childhood Obesity in China." Paper presented at the 10th International Symposium on Maternal and Infant Nutrition, Beijing, Nov. 11–12.

———. 1997. "Obesity, a Serious Problem on the Children's Health." *Proceedings of the Tenth International Symposium on Maternal and Infant Nutrition.* Guangzhou: Heinz Institute of Nutritional Sciences.

Yen Lee-Lan, Pan Wen-Han, Chen Chung-Hung, and Lee Yen-Ming. 1994. "The Prevalence of Obesity in the Seventh Graders in Taipei City, 1991: A Comparison of Various Body Screening Indices." *China Health Care Journal* (Zhonghua weizhi) 13, no. 1:11–19.

Yuan Xiaohong. 1997. "Baby-Friendly Action in China: Protection, Promotion, and Support of Breastfeeding." Paper presented at the 1997 Asian Conference of Pediatricians, Hong Kong, June 15–17.

Zha, Jianying. 1995. *China Pop: How Soap Opera, Tabloids, and Best-sellers Are Transforming a Culture.* New York: New Press.

Zhang Xia. 1993. "Too Many Devour Only Fast-food Culture." *China Daily*, April 22, p. 3.

Zhang Zhihua. 1993. "A Discussion of the Positive and Negative Factors in the Education of Only Children" (Guanyu dusheng ziniu ertong jiaoyu de youli he buli yinsu de tantao). *Research on Youth and Adolescence* (Qing shaonian yanjiu) 1 and 2 (combined issue):79–81.

Zhao, Bin. 1996. "The Little Emperor's Small Screen: Parental Control and Children's Television Viewing Time." *Media, Culture, and Society* 18:639–58.

Zhao Feng. 1994. *Do You Love Chinese or Foreign Consumer Goods* (Guohuo yanghuo ni ai shui). Tianjin: Tianjin People's Press.

Zhu Baoxia. 1994. "Breastfeed Babies, Says Conference." *China Daily*, July 30, p. 3.

Zong Qinghou. 1996. "Revitalizing the Greatness of Chinese Nutritional and Health Foods" (Chongzhen Zhongguo ying-yang baojian pin xiongfeng). Speech at the Conference on the Development of China's Children's Foods, Beijing, March 28.

Index

BFHI. *See* Baby-Friendly Hospital Initiative

Biomedicine, 177, 178, 183

Birth control, 13, 147, 235n11

Birth rates, 18, 157

Borden Company, 160

Bourdieu, Pierre, 89, 91

Breastfeeding, 27, 45, 46, 143, 178; benefits of, 166, 167, 169, 176, 183; and complementary feeding, 31–34, 164, 167, 173, 178; decline of, 13, 29–30, 32, 42, 160, 161, 236n3; extended, 33–34; practice of, 3, 170–73, 176; and psychological bonding, 166–67, 169; recommendation of, 30–31; state-sponsored promotion of, 164, 184; training in, 163–70, 181. *See also* Hospitals; Weaning

Breastfeeding (Shanghai Educational Television, 1994), 168

Bush, George, 232n14

Business strategy: and cultural strategy, 188–92; and political strategy, 192–97

Captain Planet (children's TV show), 131

Chadwick, James, 61, 68

Chee, Bernadine W. L., 3, 48–70, 73, 96, 109, 155, 202, 210, 211

Chengdu, 27, 29, 32, 41

Childbearing, 157, 237n14; scientific knowledge of, 12, 13, 14, 15; superior methods of (*yousheng cuoshi*), 143, 146

Child care, 3, 14, 95, 144; and elderly women, 150–51; and grandparents, 95, 110, 137–38, 145; rural, 141, 150; scientific, 13, 101, 146, 175; traditional, 141, 157, 175; variety in, 138–39

Child development, 4, 10, 13, 110

Child growth, 33, 34; in developing countries, 36, 37; differences in, 37, 38–39; and health, 35–43; mainland *vs.* Hong Kong, 27–28, 35, 36, 41, 42; and obesity, 27, 41, 42, 207; urban *vs.* rural, 29, 32, 35, 37, 38–39, 42, 47. *See also* Breastfeeding; Weaning

Childhood (*tongnian*): celebration of, 204–5; diseases of, 142; management of, 13; new concept of, 4, 203, 206; studies of European and North American, 210; and youth (*qingnian*), 233n22

Child rearing, 131; courses in, 225n1; in rural areas, 144; scientific knowledge of, 12, 14, 15, 144–46, 182; superior methods of (*youyu cuoshi*), 143, 144, 146; traditional, 139, 141, 180–82

Children: birthday celebrations for, 6, 105–6, 120, 156, 199, 202, 203, 204; as consumers, 4, 5, 67–68, 103, 199–203; decision-making by, 4, 5, 103, 200–201, 202, 210, 230n1a; dietary patterns of, 29–35, 195; diet of, 4, 7, 37, 141, 151, 234; and family spending, 6–7, 67,

schools, 128–31, 133, 134; and toys, 104, 200, 205–7. *See also* Marketing strategies

Fast-food restaurants, 103, 115, 117–20, 130; in Beijing, 67, 116, 127, 202; children's birthday parties in, 120, 199, 202; Chinese-style, 126–27; in Hong Kong, 201, 202, 203; Korean, 132; and Muslims, 84. *See also specific restaurants*

Fei Xiaotong, 21

Ferguson, James, 232n11

Fertility: declining, 2, 11, 22, 48, 147; goddesses of, 149, 150; and local temples, 148, 149

500 top enterprises (*qiye wubai qian*), 187

Food: and advertising, 67, 96, 104, 153–55; attitudes toward, 159; availability of new, 94; baby, 18, 160, 164, 194, 200; changes in supply of, 28; children's, 7, 9, 10–11, 199, 203, 225n4; children's consumption of, 2, 3, 4, 14, 49–50, 63, 96, 140, 157, 199, 233n1; commoditization of, 200; consumption of, 49–50, 94, 130; convenience, 154, 209; domestication of, 116, 133; and economic reform, 73, 135; festivals, 105, 136, 155; and generational differences, 3, 25–26, 73, 94–97, 106–7, 210–11, 230n1a; hand-made, 85–87; hot *vs.* cold, 98–99, 152; and independent buying power

of young, 4, 5, 6–7, 67, 103, 200–201, 202, 210; inspection of, 233n2; as investigatory tool, 49–50; in moral education, 106; neutral, 84–85; offerings of, at temples, 150; packaging of, 103–4, 130; and peer-group pressure, 3, 52–55, 210; and play, 104; and public health agendas, 140; quality of, 172, 237n10; rationing of, 4, 10, 24, 112; and school education, 3; shortages of, 8; and social values, 20–21; specialized vocabulary for, 7; trendy, 3, 53–55, 69, 109, 156; urban *vs.* rural system of, 28; Western, 79–84, 87, 88, 89, 90, 91, 92, 93, 126; *yin-yang* in, 98, 151–52

Food, factory-processed, 5, 24, 29, 78; and Islamic diet, 71, 72, 74, 80–84, 93; and television, 157, 158; and urban reform, 103, 111; and Western diet, 79–93

Food, snack (*xiaochi*), 69, 73, 95, 227n1; money spent on, 130, 199, 200; in Muslim district, 72, 74, 82, 83, 93; and parents, 52–53, 58, 62, 83, 101, 155; and single children, 57, 66–67; and toys, 205, 207; and the West, 78, 79

Food cycles, 50

Food Hygiene Law, 172

Food industry: and children, 4, 5–6, 194; and food

Religion: and cultural authority, 147–52, 157, 159; and health, 149–52; popular, 139, 140, 141, 157, 159. *See also* Islam

Ritual, 203–5

Ronghuaji (Glorious China Chicken) restaurants, 121–22, 124–28, 131, 133

Sanders, Colonel, 5, 117, 119, 126, 128, 202, 231n10

Sassen, Saskia, 123, 232n14

Schools: and fast-food companies, 128–31, 133, 134; for parents, 225n1; public *vs.* private, 129, 232n19. *See also* Education

Science, 88–89, 91, 92; cultural authority of, 141–46; of infant feeding, 33, 160–84; and infant formula companies, 162, 163; medical authority of, 176, 179, 181; modern, 139, 140, 146, 159; and modernity, 162, 175, 178, 181, 182; and nature, 176–77; nutrition, 100, 101, 102, 160, 170; and promotion of breast milk, 161, 162; state-sponsored promotion of, 141–46, 157, 162; symbolism of, 182

Seastar Overseas Company (*Haixing haiwai gongsi*), 79

Shaanxi province, 78, 84, 90–91, 229n1

Shandong province, 5, 40

Shanghai, 8, 123, 124, 128, 206, 207

Shanghai Squibb, 234n9

Sichuan province, 27, 229n13; children's dietary patterns in, 29–35; creation of jobs in, 187, 196, 197; growth differences in, 36–37. *See also* Three Gorges Dam project

Singapore, 16

Singletons (only children), 3, 48–70; and child socialization, 56, 64, 207; and peer pressure, 52–55; and social pressure, 51–52; spoiled, 1–2, 52, 112, 129; *vs.* retirees, 210–12; vulnerability of, 66–70

Sino-Japanese War, 9, 23, 111

Snacking. *See* Food, snack

Socialist Market Economy. *See* Economic reform

South Korea, 16

Soviet Union, 17, 20, 21, 111

Spring Festival. *See* New Year, lunar

Stafford, Charles, 148, 233n20

Starr, Paul, 140

State Family Planning Commission, 144

Sterilization, forced, 147

Strathern, Andrew, 183

Strathern, Marilyn, 116

Student Nutrition Day, 45

Supermarkets (*chaoji shichang*), 79, 103

Symbolism, 49, 126, 129, 131, 203, 206, 227n3, 233n21

Taco Bell, 124

Taiwan, 16; birthday celebrations in, 204; food companies

186–88, 193–96, 198; and traditional medicine, 189, 191
Wahaha Nutritional Drink (*Wahaha yingyang yinliao*), 185, 188, 189, 194, 209, 229n12
Wall's ice cream, 54, 62, 109, 228n8
Walt Disney products, 130
Watson, James L., 3, 4, 199–212, 230n1
Weaning (*duan nai*), 9, 30, 37, 44, 137, 143; traditional food for, 10, 31–32, 200. *See also* Breastfeeding
Weber, Max, 139
West, the: diet of, 78–93; infant formula from, 179–80, 237nn6,7; medicine from, 95, 100, 102, 137, 139, 157; pregnancy in, 177
Whimsy International, 206
Winter Festival, 105
World Health Organization (WHO), 12, 30, 161, 165, 177, 178, 193; Code of, 176, 237n13
Wu, David, 1, 48, 49, 64
Wu Hsing-yuan (H. Y. Lowe), 9
Wu Shushan, 6, 130

Xi'an, 229n1; Muslim district in, 3, 71–93; Prophet's Birthday celebration in, 230n7
Xiao kang (small prosperity) livelihood, 24–25
Xie Jili, 178
Xue Meng, 191

Yang, Mayfair, 56
Yang Lang, General, 149
Ye Gongshao, 1
Yeh Chyon-Hwa, 67
Yili Fast Food restaurant, 126
Yin-yang, 98, 151–52
Yongjing county, 147
Yoshinoya, 129
Yuan Xiaohong, 164
Yunxiang Yan, 202

Zhang Xiaogang, 17
Zhao Yang, 3, 185–98, 209
Zhao Zhigang, 52
Zhejiang province, 185–86
Zhong Jiangguang, 186
Zong Qinghou, 190, 191
Zhu Qing, 186
Zhu Shoumin, 188

Library of Congress Cataloging-in-Publication Data

Feeding China's little emperors : food, children, and social change /
edited by Jun Jing.
    p.   cm.
  Includes bibliographical references and index.
  ISBN 0-8047-3133-0 (cloth : alk. paper)-- ISBN 0-8047-3134-9
  (pbk.: alk. paper)
  1. Children--China--Nutrition.   2. Nutrition policy--China.
  I. Jing, Jun
TX361.C5 .F44 2000
363.8'083'0951--dc21   99-047015

⊗ This book is printed on archival-quality paper.

Original printing 2000

Last figure below indicates year of this printing:
09 08 07 06 05 04 03 02 01 00

Typeset by BookMatters in 9.5/14 Galliard